D1159823

DATE DUE

9/16/02			

ERASMUS DARWIN AND THE ROMANTIC POETS

ERASMUS DARWIN AND THE ROMANTIC POETS

Desmond King-Hele

St. Martin's Press   New York

ISBN 0–312–25796–1

Library of Congress Cataloging-in-Publication Data
King-Hele, Desmond, 1927–
Erasmus Darwin and the Romantic Poets
Includes index.
1. Darwin, Erasmus. 1731–1802—Influence. 2. English
poetry—18th century—History and criticism. 3. English
poetry—19th century—History and criticism. 4. Romantism—England. 5. Nature in
literature. 6. Science in literature. I. Title.
PR579.D38K5 1985   821′.7′09   85–22200
ISBN 0–312–25796–1

Contents

List of Illustrations

List of Illustrations

1 Introduction

Immature poets imitate; mature poets steal.

T. S. Eliot, *Selected Essays*

The writings of Erasmus Darwin were much admired in the 1790s –
Coleridge called him 'the first *literary* character in Europe, and the most
original-minded Man' – and his work was plundered by a number of
greater English poets who followed in his path, notably Blake,
Wordsworth, Coleridge, Shelley and Keats. My aim in this book is to
trace the effect of Darwin's ideas, images and words on the poets of the
next two generations.

I am all too well aware that the book is an exercise in probability.
Though the flow of ideas makes up the spirit of an age, the ideas
themselves are slippery customers. If two poets write in similar vein, the
later may be indebted to the earlier, or it may be that both were drinking
from the same stream of ideas; or perhaps one or both had the idea
independently. The very process of poetic creation is a fusion of ideas
and images from diverse sources, and if the finished product is well
baked, the original ingredients may be difficult to guess. To try to
minimize the chance of being misled, I have concentrated more on
apparent verbal echoes than on resemblances in ideas. Even a clear echo
may of course be a chance parallel, but the idea of chance itself becomes
very improbable when the apparent echoes are numerous. That is why I
have to give a good number of examples, at some risk of tedium.

I confidently expect readers to be sceptical at first, but I hope the
doubts will tend to evaporate as the many parallels in wording between
Darwin and the later poets are unfolded. If the parallels are deliberate
borrowing, they speak for his influence at once; if they are subconscious,
that reveals influence at a deeper level. If I suspect that the resemblances
are mere coincidences, I say so; whatever my opinion may be, the
evidence is displayed 'for the candid reader to determine', as Darwin put
it.

Literary imitation is the sincerest form of flattery, and also quite
respectable unless the imitator goes so far as to fall into the crevasse of

1

plagiarism. Fortunately, that scarcely ever happens here: the Romantic poets were subconscious borrowers from Darwin and might be surprised at the extent of their debts.

Darwin himself sees Imitation as a central characteristic of the human mind. His theory of 'the Progress of the Mind' is described in Canto III of his poem *The Temple of Nature*. When we have received ideas from the external world via our senses, the characteristic attribute of our mind is its tendency to make us imitate these ideas – in social behaviour, in learning to speak and in the arts of poetry, painting and music. From the ideas imbibed through our senses, he says,

> the fine power of IMITATION springs,
> And apes the outlines of external things;
> With ceaseless action to the world imparts
> All moral virtues, languages, and arts.   (*Tem.Nat.* III 285–8)

'This propensity to imitation', he says in a note, 'not only appears in the actions of children, but in all the customs and fashions of the world; many thousands tread in the beaten paths of others, who precede or accompany them, for one who traverses regions of his own discovery.' Our innate tendency to copy also affects

> The sculptor's statue, and the poet's song,
> The painter's landscape, and the builder's plan,
> And IMITATION marks the mind of Man.   (*Tem.Nat.* III 332–4)

This last line is the banner under which I march briskly through this book, picking on instances where unconscious imitation of Darwin seems highly probable, but also mentioning others where an initially plausible resemblance melts into mere coincidence. My march is dangerous because I am only looking for – and therefore only see – the resemblances to Erasmus Darwin. I have not studied in detail the works of all his contemporaries and predecessors, one of whom might sometimes prove to be a more likely model. Darwin himself is of course indebted to earlier writers; but that is another story, which is not relevant as long as the poets on my list modelled themselves on Darwin rather than on Darwin's model.

So I shall march ahead single-mindedly, not pretending to offer a balanced appreciation of the authors visited, but merely outlining their careers and then looking at the links with Darwin in their poems or their lives. Chapter 2 is a quick review of Darwin's life and work. Chapters 3 and 4 detail his influence on Blake and on Wordsworth. Chapters 5 and 6 are devoted to Coleridge, as a poet and in prose. The march changes to a walkabout in Chapter 7, with visits to Cowper, Crabbe, Campbell, Goethe and other poets of the time, very few of whom ignored Darwin. The 'second generation' of Romantic poets occupy the next three chapters: Chapter 8 is on Shelley, Chapter 9 on Keats, and Chapter 10 ranges over their contemporaries Byron, Clare, Hunt and others. Chapter 11 is a rounding off and retrospect.

Throughout the book the word 'Darwinian' has the first meaning given in the *Oxford English Dictionary* – namely, 'Of or pertaining to Erasmus Darwin (1731–1802), and to his speculations or poetical style'.

2 Erasmus Darwin

A humanist, physician to all men.

J. Keats, *Fall of Hyperion*

Erasmus Darwin (Fig. 1) probably achieved more in a wider variety of intellectual disciplines than anyone since. A physician by profession, he lived from 1731 until 1802. He spent most of his energy trying to relieve human suffering and he gained the highest reputation as a doctor. He had 'a mind of universal sympathy' and a genius for friendship. His remarkable scientific insight into the functioning of nature led him to many discoveries, and he was keen on exploiting advances in science and technology to improve the quality of human life. His great literary talent was more than recognized when his poem *The Botanic Garden* won excessive praise in the 1790s. His command over the whole spectrum of knowledge was much admired: Coleridge thought he had 'a greater range of knowledge than any other man in Europe', as well as being 'the most inventive of philosophical men'.[1]

Darwin's interest and activity knew no bounds, and in this chapter I shall first rush through his life as it happened and then look back at his achievements in four spheres – as a doctor, an inventor and technologist, a man of science and a writer.

A FULL LIFE

Erasmus was born on 12 December 1731 at Elston, five miles south-west of Newark in Nottinghamshire. He was the seventh and youngest child of Robert Darwin (1682–1754), a lawyer who retired early, and his wife Elizabeth (1702–1797), who by all accounts was beautiful, strong-minded and so healthy that she nearly outlived her youngest son. Although Erasmus left Elston to pursue his medical career, his family remained there: the small church has 16 memorials to Darwins, at dates ranging from 1654 to 1947.

In 1741 Erasmus was sent to Chesterfield School, then the leading

4

school in the north of England, with two of his brothers. He seems to have been quite happy there, and in 1750 with his brother John he entered St John's College, Cambridge. The upkeep of two sons at Cambridge was a strain on their father's finances, and they had to live frugally. Medicine was the subject of Erasmus's studies and he attended lecture-courses in London as well as Cambridge. By 1751 he was showing his tendency to roam widely: he wrote a smooth poem of 92 lines for a volume in memory of Frederick Prince of Wales, and another poem in praise of the Gurney system of shorthand which he used for his lecture notes. He left Cambridge in 1754 for a further two years of studies at the Edinburgh Medical School. There he met James Keir (1735–1820), who was to be a lifelong friend.

In 1756 he was qualified as a doctor and keen to apply his knowledge in the real world. His first try was at Nottingham, but the prophet was not to be honoured in his own county. No patients came, so he left.

In November 1756 he arrived at Lichfield, carrying a letter of introduction to Dr Thomas Seward, canon residentiary of the Cathedral and a fellow-member of St John's College. Almost immediately Darwin was allowed to treat a patient who had been given up by other doctors: by luck or skill (or both) Darwin restored him to health. His reputation was made, and he went from strength to strength in his medical career. But it was hard work, and he spent much of his life bumping over the vile roads in his carriage, en route to the rich and distant patients who provided his livelihood.

Darwin was a large and powerful-looking man, about six feet tall and certainly overweight by modern standards. He believed in good eating – 'eat or be eaten' was one of his sayings – and a reserve of fat probably did give his patients a better chance of surviving both the disease and its treatment, which was usually a blend of blood-letting and poisonous drugs. Darwin himself knew that 'all the boasted nostrums only take up time', and were at best non-poisonous placebos. The ingredients of his great reputation were probably (a) allowing patients to recover of their own accord, (b) his kind, conscientious, confident and cheerful manner, which was a tonic in itself, (c) his keen observation of symptoms and their correct interpretation, and (d) his psychological insight, particularly in psychosomatic disease.

He soon began to exercise his scientific insight too, via his experiments with steam engines, which led to his first scientific paper, on 'the ascent of vapour'. This well-argued paper was published in the *Philosophical Transactions* of the Royal Society in 1757. He was elected a Fellow of the Royal Society in 1761, the first of five generations of Darwins who were

Fellows of the Society continuously until 1962 – a unique family achievement.

In December 1757 he took the first step towards becoming a family man by marrying the seventeen-year-old Mary Howard. Soon afterwards they went to live in the pleasant house at the edge of the Cathedral Close which still stands today as 'Darwin House'. Though the marriage seems to have been very happy, Mary's health was precarious, and was not improved by having five children in eight years, of whom three sons survived infancy. The eldest, Charles, grew up to be a brilliant student, but died tragically at the age of nineteen. The second son, Erasmus, became a lawyer, following the example of both his grandfathers. The third son, Robert, became a physician.

In the late 1750s Darwin met two of his lifelong friends. The first was Matthew Boulton (1728–1809), a young buckle-maker in Birmingham, who had his eyes on far horizons. His energy and enterprise were to earn him the title of 'the first manufacturer of England' and 'the father of Birmingham'. The second friend, a much older man, was Benjamin Franklin (1706–1790), who 'snatched the lightning from the heavens' and was soon to 'snatch the sceptre from tyrants'. Darwin's already intense interest in science and technology received a further fillip from Franklin, who may have urged Darwin and Boulton to form in Birmingham a society comparable to the American Philosophical Society founded in Philadelphia by Franklin in the 1740s.

In the early 1760s Darwin was busy with inventions of all kinds. He wanted to work with Boulton in manufacturing a steam-carriage; but Boulton was preoccupied with setting up his new factory at Soho and did not wish to chance his arm on what would have been the first steam car. For his horse-drawn carriages Darwin devised improved methods of steering and springing, to make his journeys more tolerable. Inspired perhaps by Boulton's example, he even became an entrepreneur himself in 1765, as one of four partners in an iron-works, a slitting mill near Alrewas. The other partners were Samuel Garbett the pioneer industrialist, Robert Bage the paper-maker and novelist, and John Barker, a Lichfield merchant who seems to have been the general manager.[2]

Darwin's genius for friendship flowered during the mid 1760s and drew together the members of the 'Lunar Society of Birmingham'. This is really too grandiose a name for what was only a loose association of friends. Yet the Lunar members by their enthusiasm and enterprise did more than any other group to drive forward the Industrial Revolution in Britain and hence the technological world that we see about us today.

Darwin's interest in canals led to the first of his new friends. Darwin was probably involved in the plan for a canal between Lichfield and the river Trent in 1758, for which James Brindley made a survey. In 1765 a far more ambitious canal was in prospect – the Trent-and-Mersey or Grand Trunk Canal, to link Liverpool with Nottingham. Darwin jumped in with his usual enthusiasm and offered his services to the chief promoter of the canal, an enterprising young pottery manufacturer from Burslem, Josiah Wedgwood (1730–1795), who wanted to avoid having his wares continually smashed on the rutted and pot-holed roads. Darwin helped by writing pamphlets in favour of the canal and, even more, by convincing influential patients that they should support the canal project rather than refusing to allow it to cross their land.

Another key figure in the Lunar group who arrived in 1765 was Dr William Small (1734–1775). He had been Thomas Jefferson's teacher and mentor in America, and he returned with Franklin, who advised him to settle in Birmingham. A man of great knowledge and smiling courtesy, Small became the 'favourite friend' of both Boulton and Darwin, and hub of the Lunar circle until his early death.

Darwin's carriage designs brought the next recruit, Richard Lovell Edgeworth in 1766. He was a rich young man with nothing particular to do, and he decided to follow Darwin's example and become an inventor – which he did most successfully. Darwin was impressed by his mechanical and conjuring skills: 'Dear Boulton, I have got with me a mechanical Friend, Mr Edgeworth from Oxfordshire – the greatest Conjuror I ever saw. . . . He has the principles of Nature in his Palm. . . . And can see through two solid Oak Boards without Glasses! wonderful! astonishing! diabolical!!!'[3]

In 1767 a more practical engineer, of surpassing skill, made his first visit to the Midlands – James Watt (1736–1819). He came to see Samuel Garbett, Darwin's business partner, who introduced Watt to Darwin and to Small. Two years earlier Watt had made his invention of the improved steam engine, but he was rather gloomy about its prospects. Darwin, the energetic and optimistic steam-enthusiast, was just the man to motivate him: fortunately, he took to Darwin at once, confiding the secret of his engine on this first visit. Their friendship endured quite unclouded for thirty-five years, and was of great benefit to Watt, who said of Darwin, 'It will be my pride, while I live, that I have enjoyed the friendship of such a man.'[4]

It was in 1767 too that James Keir, Darwin's student friend, came to live nearby, when he retired from the Army to study chemistry. He was to be one of the chief pioneers of the chemical industry with his factory at Tipton, where he made alkali and soap, and much else. 'A very agreeable man', according to Watt, tactful and considerate, he often acted as 'chairman' of the Lunar meetings.

The Lunar group as it existed in 1770 also included John Whitehurst (1713–1788) the Derby watchmaker and geologist; and, at the other extreme, the young Thomas Day (1749–1789), a rich and eccentric friend of Edgeworth. The name 'Lunar' arose because the meetings were usually held on the Sunday nearest the Full Moon, so that the members could have light when riding home.

Another of Darwin's major interests began in 1767, when huge fossil bones were found during the cutting of the Harecastle Tunnel on the Grand Trunk Canal. As a doctor, Darwin was expected to know about bones. To cover his ignorance, he resorted to joking, and told Wedgwood that 'the horn is larger than any modern horn I have measured, and must have been that of a Patagonian ox I believe'.[5]

Joking apart, Darwin was deeply impressed, and within two years he had come to believe in what we now call biological evolution. He could not openly declare this heretical creed when so many of his rich patients were pillars of the Church. Instead he found an indirect way. His family arms were three scallop shells, so he added the motto *E conchis omnia*, or 'everything from shells' – and had it painted on his carriage. But he reckoned without Dr Seward, who was already alert to Darwin's irreligious tendencies and wrote some sarcastic verses accusing him of 'renouncing his Creator':

> Great wizard, he by magic spells
> Can all things raise from cockle shells.[6]

Darwin could not afford to insult the Church: so he had the motto painted out, and kept quiet on the subject for twenty-four years.

Towards the end of the 1760s, Darwin's wife Mary became ill more often, with spasms of violent pain. She died in 1770, at the age of thirty, leaving Darwin with three sons to bring up: Charles, aged eleven; Erasmus, aged ten; and Robert, who was four. Darwin's sister Susannah moved in to look after the children.

Soon after Mary's death, Darwin sat for the portrait by Joseph Wright (Fig. 1), which was said to be an excellent likeness. He was now thirty-eight, and a man who relished the pleasures of the world. An anonymous friend (or enemy?) tells us that he 'resolved to relinquish Bacchus' quite early in life, probably because he noticed signs of gout; 'but his affection for Venus was retained to the last period of his life'. So it is not surprising that he was soon taking pleasure in the company of the eighteen-year-old Mary Parker, who bore him a daughter Susan in 1772 and another daughter Mary in 1774. The girls grew up in his house, in the relaxed fashion of that era, and he was especially kind to them in later years.

In the 1770s Darwin stayed at home less and was at his most sociable. The Lunar circle was thriving, but he also moved in the social-literary circle of Lichfield presided over by Canon Seward, who had edited the plays of Beaumont and Fletcher, and his daughter Anna, who was testing her wings as a poet. The circle included Richard Edgeworth and his unconventional friend Thomas Day, who later wrote *Sandford and Merton*, one of the best-known books of the century. Another member was Brooke Boothby, a country gentleman of literary tastes and a confidant of Rousseau. Samuel Johnson, whose stepson had been engaged to marry Anna's sister, should perhaps also be counted in, though his visits to Lichfield were now quite rare. Darwin did not get on well with him: there was no room at Lichfield for two outspoken sages, and Darwin was at a disadvantage in conversation because he stammered.

Darwin's inventiveness raced on at full throttle in the 1770s. His most famous invention was a speaking-machine, which astonished everyone. No drawings of it have survived, but it was a mechanical device with bellows and leather tongues, reeds and pipes, and it could speak individual words quite distinctly. The construction must have been ingenious, and so was the theory of phonetics on which he based the design: he discussed the theory with Franklin and published it among the notes to his poem *The Temple of Nature*.

More useful, if less spectacular, was a vertical-axis windmill, perfected after some years of experiments, which showed that it was more efficient than an ordinary windmill. For thirteen years Darwin's windmill was in continual use for grinding colours in Wedgwood's factory at Etruria, until displaced by steam. The vertical-axis design has come into favour again following the revival of interest in wind power during the 1970s.

Another impressive invention was Darwin's copying-machine, or 'bigrapher', based on the pantograph principle but cleverly engineered so that there was little restriction in writing with the primary pen, which was faithfully followed by the secondary. There is a letter of Darwin's in the British Library written using the machine:[7] his handwriting is not noticeably cramped, and the copy is so good that I have never been able to decide which of the two versions is the original. Darwin's machine was more faithful than a modern photocopier, which generally uses paper and ink different from the original. This invention also caused quite a stir, and James Watt was needled into devising a method that could be used *after* the letter had been written. He succeeded – 'I have fallen on a way of copying writing chemically, which beats your bigrapher hollow',[8] he wrote to Darwin – and Watt's copier became standard office equipment for a century.

In the mid 1770s Darwin was gripped by a new enthusiasm for botany, and he spent much effort in laying out a botanic garden about a mile west of Lichfield. The verses that he and Anna Seward wrote about it eventually grew into his poem *The Botanic Garden*.

In 1778 Darwin suffered another personal tragedy. His nineteen-year-old son Charles, whose exceptional talent was attested by all who knew him, was studying at the Edinburgh Medical School. He cut his finger while dissecting; the wound turned septic and he died. Darwin, who travelled to Edinburgh in time to see his son die, lost his *joie de vivre* for several years.

While in Edinburgh Darwin made a new friend, James Hutton (1726–1797), now recognized as the founder of modern geology. They wrote each other geological letters – the one that has survived is quite jokey – and this correspondence helped Darwin to crystallize his own views on the history and structure of the Earth and its strata.

A year or two before Charles's death, Darwin had fallen deeply in love with Mrs Elizabeth Pole, the beautiful wife of Colonel Pole of Radburn Hall in Derbyshire. The Colonel was a leading landowner and a military hero who had fought in eleven battles and was left for dead on the field in three of them. At the battle of Minden a musket ball entered his left eye and passed through his head. Clearly he was not a man to be trifled with, and Darwin had to confine his wooing of Elizabeth to distant sighs and passionate verses, like these addressed to the river Derwent:

> And tell her, Derwent, as you murmur by,
> How in these wilds with hopeless Love I burn,
> Teach your soft gales and echoing caves to sigh,
> And mix my briny sorrows in your Urn.

With his depression at the death of Charles and his frustrated love, 1779 and 1780 were sad years, though he went on inventing and gardening.

Then, in November 1780, Colonel Pole conveniently died. Darwin was not his doctor, so he was under no suspicion. Elizabeth, beautiful, wealthy and witty, was soon pursued by the gilded youth of Derbyshire, 'young fox-hunting squires' and 'dashing militaries', as Anna Seward puts it. Darwin was fat, lame and nearly fifty. Everyone thought she was 'playing with the old dog'.

But everyone was wrong. Elizabeth married Darwin in March 1781, and they enjoyed twenty-one years of a very happy married life. They lived first at Radburn Hall, which was and still is a splendid mansion deep in the countryside, though only four miles west of Derby.

Darwin's second marriage brought a great change in his life. No longer was he 'the life and soul of the party' and the energizer of the Lunar Society. Radburn Hall is more than thirty miles from Birmingham, so he now rarely appeared at Lunar meetings. Instead he became domesticated and scholarly, and it was at Radburn Hall that he began his six years of work in making two translations of Linnaeus's *A System of Vegetables*, published in 1785, and *The Families of Plants*, published in 1787. They run to 2000 pages of detailed plant description, and it was after this marathon effort that he relaxed into light verse in *The Loves of the Plants*. The translations were published as the work of 'A Botanical Society at Lichfield', but the society consisted only of Darwin, Brooke Boothby and a proctor in the Cathedral Court, William Jackson.[9] There is every reason to believe that Darwin did most of the work, but was shy of publishing in his own name.

Radburn Hall may have been a good place for translating Linnaeus, but it was too isolated for conducting a medical practice, and soon Darwin was looking for somewhere to live in Derby. He took a town-house (now demolished) in Full Street, with a large garden sloping down to the river Derwent: the family lived there from 1783 until 1802.

It was a large house, but the family more than filled it. In the ten years after their marriage, Darwin and Elizabeth had seven children, of whom only one died as a child, and to these were added three children from Elizabeth's previous marriage, and Susan and Mary Parker. By all accounts it was a happy family, thanks chiefly to Elizabeth, even if rather chaotic at times. Darwin's eldest surviving son, Erasmus, became a solicitor in Derby. His third son, Robert, moved away to begin practice as a doctor at Shrewsbury in 1786.

The most frequent visitors at Full Street in the 1780s were the Wedgwoods, for Josiah Wedgwood became Darwin's closest friend, and Josiah's eldest daughter Susannah often stayed with the Darwins.

Darwin kept up his friendships with Boulton and Watt, and went on two journeys to London with Watt in 1785. He would call on his old Birmingham friends when visiting the Quaker armament manufacturer Samuel Galton (1753–1832), whose wife was a most grateful, frequent – and lucrative – patient of Darwin's. The wealthy Galton was often host to the Lunar Society in the 1780s, when the meetings tended to centre on the work of Joseph Priestley (1733–1804), who had settled in Birmingham a few months before Darwin's second marriage. If there was a chance of Darwin's departure being 'the kiss of death' for the Society, the arrival of 'the father of pneumatic chemistry' at the height of his powers was certainly 'the kiss of life'. The Society, and Priestley's researches, flourished through the 1780s.

Darwin missed the Lunar Society, and it was not long before he set up the Derby Philosophical Society. He wrote to Boulton on 4 March 1783: 'We have established an infant philosophical Society at Derby, but do not presume to compare it to you well-grown gigantic philosophers at Birmingham.'[10] The Derby Philosophical Society was very much under Darwin's control, and he seems to have modelled it on Franklin's American Philosophical Society: he emphasized the importance of building up a library of scientific books, and the new books were circulated to members on loan for two weeks. The Society thrived during the 1780s and lasted for 70 years. The founder-members of the Society included two other Derby doctors, Dr John Beridge and Dr John Pigot, and also William Strutt, son of the pioneer textile manufacturer Jedediah Strutt.

By this time Darwin's fame as a doctor had become legendary, and some of the legends are difficult to swallow. For example, Anna Seward says, 'It is well known that Dr Darwin's influence and example have sobered the county of Derby', and Maria Edgeworth caps this with her report that he 'persuaded most of the gentry in his own and neighbouring counties to become water-drinkers'.[11] Over-indulgence in alcohol was a frequent problem with Darwin's wealthier patients, and his firm methods emerge in a very long letter to the fifth Duke of Devonshire in 1783. The Duke, he says, might restore his health 'by obstinately persevering in drinking' only 'about half' of his accustomed amount. Bad news for the Duke! But even worse is to come: 'I express myself strongly upon this head, as I know in this kind of disease Health is not to be bought at any other price.'[12] If that is how he treated a Duke, perhaps the lesser gentry were frightened into submission?

It was in the 1780s that Darwin was most deeply involved in what we should now call scientific research. In 1785 he gave the first complete explanation of artesian wells – after having bored one in his own garden. In 1787 he propounded the principle of adiabatic expansion of air (as it is now called), and used it to explain how clouds usually form – a fundamental discovery, especially in the British climate. These papers were published in the *Philosophical Transactions* of the Royal Society.

At the beginning of 1789, Darwin was fifty-seven and could have been described as assiduous in botany, fertile in mechanical invention, famous as a doctor, and of high repute in physical science.

His image changed abruptly in April 1789, with the publication of *The Loves of the Plants*, the second and lighter part of *The Botanic Garden*. This frolic over the sex lives of plants was followed three years later by the more serious first part of the poem. Mistitled *The Economy of Vegetation*, this was really a selective encyclopedia of versified science.

The outcome was astonishing. On the strength of these 2200 glittering couplets, backed by scientific notes running to 100,000 words, Darwin became the most famous English poet of the 1790s, thought by many to be the equal of Milton or Shakespeare. He himself remained unimpressed. At the height of his fame, in October 1792, he wrote to an old friend, Richard Dixon: 'I sold a work called "The Botanic Garden" for 900£ to Johnson the bookseller near St Paul's, it is a poem; perhaps you may borrow it from some circulating library.'[13]

In 1794 he published his treatise on animal life, *Zoonomia*, with a long chapter expounding his theory of what we now call biological evolution. The second part, a medical case-book giving treatments for all diseases, came out in 1796. *Zoonomia*, which runs to 1400 pages and weighs 4 kg, raised Darwin to a new pinnacle of medical fame: the book was hailed by Dr Thomas Beddoes as 'perhaps the most original work ever composed by mortal man', which would 'place the Author among the greatest of mankind, the founders of sciences'.[14] But there were also ominous rumblings among the reviews about the evolutionary aspects: the *British Critic* complained that Darwin discards 'all the authority of revelation' in favour of 'the sports of his own imagination'.[15] Being championed by the energetic Dr Beddoes also proved damaging to Darwin, because Beddoes was regarded as a dangerous radical. Beddoes was linked with Darwin through their extensive correspondence on medical matters, and his reputation rubbed off on Darwin.

These years inevitably brought changes in the lives of his children. He had long been dissatisfied with conventional education, and as usual he took practical action: in 1794 he set up his daughters Susan and Mary Parker in a school at Ashbourne, and wrote for their guidance a book on *Female Education in Boarding Schools* (1797). Education for girls, he says, 'should unite health and agility of body with cheerfulness and activity of mind': some hours each day should be devoted to bodily exercise, and scientific subjects like botany, chemistry and mineralogy should figure in the curriculum. The idea of educating girls to be feather-brained weaklings was abhorrent to him. Susan and Mary Parker made a great success of the school for more than thirty years.

Darwin's son Robert was thriving as a doctor at Shrewsbury, and in 1796 he married Susannah Wedgwood, Josiah's eldest daughter. Their two sons were to be named after Robert's elder brothers, Charles and Erasmus.

A reaction against Darwin's excessive fame was inevitable, and, after some pinpricks earlier, 1798 saw three lethal attacks. The weightiest was a 560-page book, *Observations on the Zoonomia of Erasmus Darwin*, by Thomas Brown. The existence of the book was a tribute to Darwin's fame, but Brown criticized his medical and philosophical ideas severely and at great length. The second attack was from rural Somerset, where Wordsworth and Coleridge with their *Lyrical Ballads* ushered in a new era of poetry and condemned the 'gaudiness' of Darwin's verse. The third attack was political, and consisted of a parody, 'The Loves of the Triangles', written largely by George Canning, a Government minister: he ridiculed Darwin's style, his belief that humans have evolved from lower animals, and other ideas subversive of the established order. The parody permanently punctured Darwin's inflated reputation as a poet, and even his authority in medical matters was somewhat undermined.

But his best books were still to come. *Phytologia*, published in 1800, was an excellent 600-page survey of plant life and agriculture, with many impressive new insights. Darwin specified the processes of photosynthesis much more fully than anyone before, and he was the first to recognize the essential roles of nitrogen and phosphorus in plant nutirition.

In March 1802 Darwin and his family moved out of Derby to a country house four miles to the north, Breadsall Priory. He was seventy, and seemed in good health, but he died of a heart attack a few weeks later, on 18 April 1802.

His last and best poem *The Temple of Nature* was published in 1803. He traces the evolution of life from microscopic specks in primeval seas through fishes, amphibia and reptiles to land animals and finally 'the human animal'. Then he explains how society has arisen and developed. In his naturalistic history of life he calmly assumed an evolutionary scenario that was a century too early to be accepted. The reviewers condemned Darwin for leaving out God, whom they deemed the chief character in the drama, and *The Temple of Nature* had nothing like the success of *The Botanic Garden*.

FULL IN ACHIEVEMENT

Looked at in retrospect, Darwin's achievements divide into four broad areas – medicine, technology, science and literature.

His career as a physician was most honourable and successful. As one historian of biology remarked, 'within the narrow resources of 18th-century medicine, he was supreme'.[16] But he did not much enlarge those narrow resources. He worked as a physician largely within the conventional framework, and his innovations did not really break the mould, except perhaps in his eager support of the 'pneumatic medicine' of Beddoes, and possibly in some of his electrical treatments.

His income as a physician depended on making relatively long journeys to rich patients and charging for the time and trouble. For local patients, he usually gave free treatment. Anna Seward, whose biography is often quite waspish, is categorical about this:

> While resident in Lichfield, to the priests and lay-vicars of its cathedral, and their families, he always cheerfully gave his advice, but never took fees from any of them. Diligently also did he attend to the health of the poor in that city, and afterwards at Derby, and supplied their necessities by food, and all sort of charitable assistance.[17]

There is much to admire in Darwin's medical practice. His care and concern emerge clearly from his many letters to patients. He always tries to explain his intentions and give reasons for the treatment he is suggesting. He never fobs off his patients with jargon or pretend-knowledge, though it would have been easy for him to take a 'superior' attitude. His 'legendary reputation' probably depended on his great powers of observation, his kindness to patients, his grasp of human psychology, his awareness of psychosomatic factors, and his recognition that few of the medicines really helped to combat the disease. He did much to relieve suffering through kindness, commonsense and prescriptions of opium. His gentle treatment of mental illness was in salutary contrast to the brutal methods usually favoured.

Yet the advances he made in medicine were limited, and he seemed to be unlucky in missing discoveries nearby. For example, he derived a fair amount of his income from smallpox inoculation, and probably knew as many milkmaids as Jenner; but he never hit upon vaccination. Once he knew about it, however, he soon saw the possibilities and wrote to Jenner in 1802 that vaccination 'may in time eradicate the smallpox from all civilized countries' – as happened 177 years later – and suggested 'that the christening and vaccination of children may always be performed on the same day'.[18] From his experience with smallpox inoculation Darwin remarked how 'one grain of variolous matter, inserted by inoculation' would in two weeks 'produce ten thousand times the quantity of a similar material thrown out on the skin in pustules'.[19] But he did not go on to propound the germ theory of disease.

Darwin's conservatism in medicine contrasts with the mixture of vivid imagination and scientific insight that he displayed in other spheres of thought. He was cautious in medicine because it was his livelihood: avoiding damage to his career was a matter of much concern to him until he was well into his fifties.

Darwin apparently did go beyond the conventional in his electrical treatments, which were credited with effecting many cures. Electricity was his standard treatment for paralysis, for example when Josiah Wedgwood's daughter Mary Anne became partially paralysed in 1779: 'Dr Darwin . . . ordered our little girl to be electrified two or three times a day'[20] – and apparently with good effect. Another patient, suffering from jaundice, was given 'half a score smart electric shocks . . . through the liver and along the course of the common gall-duct',[21] again with success. From the reactions of paralytic limbs to electricity, Darwin concluded that nerve impulses were electrical, but he never pursued this insight.

Darwin often applied his mechanical inventiveness for the benefit of his patients. He was continually designing electrical machines, possibly for medical use but more probably because of their intrinsic fascination. Other 'marvels of medical technology' that he invented range from an inhaling machine to a 'rotative couch', or medical centrifuge, as it would now be called.

Even as an inventor, Darwin did not give himself free rein. He was chary of publicity: 'I do not court this kind of Reputation, as I believe it might injure me',[22] he wrote to the Society of Arts in 1769 when giving details of his carriage designs; and he allowed the credit for his new designs to go to Edgeworth, who duly received the Society's Gold Medal. Thus Darwin often did not pursue his ideas to fruition, and achieved much less than he was capable of doing as an inventor.

Even so, the inventions that he brought to finished products are varied and impressive. His improved method of steering carriages was by a system of cranks which ensured that both the steerable wheels turned about the same centre, rather than remaining parallel, so that the carriage did not scuff and drag on turning. Further he specified that the centre of rotation for the front wheels should lie on the line of the back axle. He had several such carriages constructed, and tested them out over 30,000 miles or more on his medical rounds in the early 1760s. Until recently, modern cars had the Darwinian method of steering, usually called Ackermann steering, after Rudolph Ackermann, who reinvented it some thirty years later.

Three other 'finished products' were the speaking-machine, the vertical-axis windmill and the copying-machine, which I have already mentioned. Another was his improved drill plough for sowing seed more uniformly: this is described fully in *Phytologia*, with twelve detailed drawings and fifteen pages of instructions on its use. Another was his 'electrical doubler', well known in its day, which apparently consisted of a rotating plate of glass between two metal plates: it must have made the sparks fly in no uncertain manner.

In the 1780s Darwin devoted much effort to making improved oil-lamps, as shown by a long series of letters to Wedgwood,[23] who was to have manufactured them but never did so. Darwin also devised a ferry boat, drawn by chains, to cross the river Derwent from the end of his garden to the orchard on the opposite bank, about 100 yards away. Another aqueous invention that he perfected was an elaborate 'water-machine' using a small head of water to raise water to a greater height. There is a drawing of the machine in *Phytologia*.

Three sketches in his manuscript 'Commonplace Book' record inventions that were 200 years ahead of their time. The first is an 'artificial bird' with flapping wings powered by a bottle of compressed air, like the control surfaces of some modern guided missiles. The second is a sketch of what appears to be a rocket motor with hydrogen and oxygen as propellants. This dates from 1779, only a few years after the discovery of oxygen. Darwin had specified the propellants for the Space Shuttle's main engine, and it was done by prescience, not by luck. The third sketch is of a multi-mirror telescope (1779): the first such design came into operation at Mount Hopkins, Arizona, in 1979; and many more are planned.

There are dozens of other inventions in his Commonplace Book that never came to fruition in his own day, as far as is known, and I can only mention a few of these. The most massive was a canal lift, with a huge water-filled box to take the barge, suspended by chains and balanced by another box, so that no resistance 'is to be overcome but the vis inertiae and friction, as the water box is always the same weight, whether the boat is in it or not'.[24] Arkwright's mill, near Matlock, seized Darwin's interest, and he has many pages of sketches for improvements in spinning-machines. Other severely utilitarian designs include a water-closet of improved design; a multi-bladed steam turbine (rather like the later Parsons turbine); lever-type weighing machines; water turbines; sewing machines; a continuous-flow rotary pump; a surveying machine;

and automated ventilators for greenhouses. In more playful mood he dabbled with perpetual-motion machines; designed a machine for moving chess-men; and devised a 'factitious spider' that moved under the influence of rotating magnets.

Darwin's personal inventions are impressive, but his social contribution to technology, via the Lunar Society, was of more lasting importance. For he seems to have been the chief energizer of the Lunar group. He set the jovial tone of the meetings, knowing that dullness never sparks advances, and that lively speculation tempered by informed criticism was the key to the technological revolution he so clearly recognized and fostered. He was the eternal optimist, confident that he could design a machine to meet almost any demand, and this is probably how his speaking-machine originated: he said it could be done; they said, 'Well, get on with it', and he did. His positive attitude to all such problems was a real inspiration to Watt, who often took a gloomy view. Darwin's enthusiasm may sometimes have lured Boulton into innovative ventures beyond his means; but when this happened, the Lunar group, especially Thomas Day, helped Boulton with loans – which he was often reluctant to repay.

Technology took a great leap forward in the late eighteenth century, with the Boulton and Watt steam engine as one of its main driving forces; and no single group was more influential than the Lunar Society in promoting these advances. Wedgwood too was subjected to a stream of ideas for improvement from Darwin, on the chemical composition of his ceramics, on the use of vertical-axis windmills and on extending his operations to metal-plus-ceramic rather than ceramic alone, as in the oil-lamps. All in all, the Lunar group was a remarkable self-activating machine for technological advance; but without Darwin I suspect that the vital spark would often have been missing. Certainly the Society changed its nature after Darwin's removal to Derby in 1781. The emphasis on technology faded, and was gradually replaced by enthusiasm for the work of Joseph Priestley, one of the greatest of experimental chemists, whose eleven years at Birmingham were the happiest and most productive of his life.

However, it may have been Darwin who raised the subject which occupied Priestley, Watt and others in the early 1780s – the nature of water. Up till 1780 it was generally thought that water was an element, but on 6 January 1781 Darwin wrote to Watt apologizing for his absence from a Lunar meeting and offering to divulge a 'secret', namely 'that water is composed of aqueous gas, which is displaced from its earth by oil of vitriol'.[25] This obscure remark could be read as implying that water is not an element and that hydrogen is one of its components. However that may be, the Lunaticks were intrigued, and Priestley began his long series of experiments on sparking hydrogen with oxygen (to use the modern terms), which eventually led to the recognition of water as H_2O, after a long controversy involving Watt, Cavendish and Lavoisier as well as Priestley.[26]

Darwin's separation from the Lunar group produced a divergence of views on chemistry and provoked his most important service to the subject. He discarded the 'phlogiston' theory and adopted the 'French heresy' of Lavoisier, in which 'dephlogisticated air' was called *oxygen* and phlogiston was declared unreal. The 'French heresy' was bitterly opposed by Priestley and by Darwin's old friends Keir and Watt, who all knew more about chemistry than he did. To desert his friends was hard for Darwin, but he carried it off with good humour and gentle raillery: for example, he congratulated Keir on having 'strangled the new nomenclature in its cradle'. Darwin's decision, which might have been merely a private matter, was of great influence because he proclaimed his views in *The Botanic Garden*, the most popular poem of its day, which the literary world took as its guide to science. According to the *Oxford English Dictionary* the first positive published occurrences of the words *oxygen*, *hydrogen* and *azote* are in *The Botanic Garden*: the words may have appeared earlier in lesser-known books, but Darwin's initiative did more than anything else to establish and popularize the 'new chemistry' in Britain.

Darwin also took great interest in mineralogy and geology, and in the 1760s he went on expeditions to the caves of the Peak District with John Whitehurst, collecting specimens and forming his own views on geological history. These views matured in the course of his correspondence with James Hutton in the 1780s. Geology is dominant among the Notes to *The Botanic Garden*, and Darwin steers a middle course between the extremes of vulcanism and sedimentary theory. He recognizes the role of volcanic lava and states that 'the central parts of the Earth consist of a fluid lava', explaining the behaviour of the compass by proposing 'that part of this fluid is iron'. These ideas (which appealed to Blake) are in agreement with modern views, and so are his ideas that limestone, coal and petroleum are formed from organic material deposited as sediments. Darwin also wrote about the hot springs at Matlock and Buxton, rightly concluding that their warmth derived from heat deep in the Earth and not from chemical reactions, as was generally believed.

Darwin's most important work in physical science was on the

behaviour of gases. He specified what is known as the 'ideal gas law', connecting pressure, volume and temperature, in a letter in 1763, some thirty years before its official discovery. He continued working on the subject and, in a classic paper in the *Philosophical Transactions* of the Royal Society in 1788, he showed by many experiments that whenever air is allowed to expand into a region of lower pressure without addition of heat, its temperature falls. This was the first clear statement of the principle of adiabatic expansion, as it is called: a familiar example is air let out of an inflated tyre – the air feels colder as it escapes.

Darwin applied this principle to explain the main mode of formation of clouds. When 'a stratum of air' rises and is 'released from a part of the superincumbent pressure', it cools so that the vapour in it 'becomes condensed and is precipitated in showers'.[27]

This was one of several discoveries in meteorology: Darwin was very keen on observing and predicting the weather, which controlled his comfort and progress on his medical rounds. He had the idea of weather maps, suggesting that the 'weather tables in distant parts of Europe' should be 'collected and compared'. He seized on the importance of what are now called warm and cold fronts, where wind direction and temperature change abruptly. He made this discovery with the help of a wind vane that came through the roof of his house to the ceiling of his study, so that he could continuously monitor the changes in wind; and in 1777 he proposed an automated instrument for recording the passage of fronts (to use the modern wording). Though fronts now often dominate the weather maps, their importance was not recognized until the 1920s, so this is another prescient insight.

Darwin also offered a model of the whole atmosphere, with three layers. The first corresponds to our 'troposphere' and the second to our 'stratosphere'; in the third layer, above 40 miles, he believes, 'the common air ends, and is surrounded by an atmosphere of inflammable gas [hydrogen] tenfold rarer than itself. In this region I believe fireballs sometimes to pass, and at other times the northern lights to exist.' The existence of an outermost atmosphere of hydrogen, though at a greater height than Darwin specified, was established in the 1960s; fireballs do usually flare up at heights near 60 miles; and the aurora borealis does extend from heights of about 60 miles upwards. So Darwin was right with all three of his ideas, and he also mentions and correctly explains the night airglow, seen so clearly by astronauts and usually said to have been discovered in 1909.

Darwin goes even further away from the Earth in *The Botanic Garden* when he tells us how the Universe began:

'Let there be light!' proclaim'd the Almighty Lord,
Astonish'd Chaos heard the potent word; –
Through all his realms the kindling Ether runs,
And the mass starts into a million suns.
Earths round each sun with quick explosions burst,
And second planets issue from the first;
Bend, as they journey with projectile force,
In bright ellipses their reluctant course.   (*Ec.Veg.* I 103–10)*

This pen-picture was much admired at the time: by Horace Walpole as 'the most sublime passage in any author, or in any of the few languages with which I am acquainted'; and, quite independently, by Anna Seward as 'of excellence yet unequalled in its kind, and never to be excelled in the grandeur of its conceptions'.[28] The lines also seem quite impressive to modern astronomers, because of the resemblances to the fashionable 'big-bang theory' of creation, especially when Darwin answers objectors by saying that the expanding mass would not have fallen back under 'the known laws of gravitation' if 'the whole of Chaos, like grains of gunpowder, was exploded at the same time'.

In keeping with this fission theory, Darwin sees the Earth as a child of the Sun:

The whirling Sun this ponderous planet hurl'd,
And gave the astonish'd void another world.

Darwin thought the Moon was torn out of the Earth, leaving the Pacific Ocean as the scar. He addresses the Gnomes of Earth who witnessed this violent event:

Gnomes! how you shriek'd! when through the troubled air
Roar'd the fierce din of elemental war;
When rose the continents, and sunk the main,
And Earth's huge sphere exploding burst in twain.
Gnomes! how you gazed! when from her wounded side
Where now the South-Sea heaves its waste of tide,
Rose on swift wheels the Moon's refulgent car,
Circling the solar orb, a sister-star.   (*Ec.Veg.* II 73–80)

---

* In quotations from *The Botanic Garden*, I give the canto and line numbers in either *The Economy of Vegetation* (*Ec.Veg.*), which is Part I, or *The Loves of the Plants* (*Lov.Pl.*), which is Part II.

This theory of the Moon's origin was put on a sound mathematical basis in the 1880s by Erasmus's great-grandson Sir George Darwin, who is often known as the 'father of geophysics'; and it has many advocates today. These cosmological ideas, explosive, disturbing, and compellingly presented, impressed Blake and several other of the Romantic poets, as we shall see.

Equally impressive were Darwin's prophecies of technological advances, such as the use of steam engines for cars and winged aircraft:

> Soon shall thy arm, Unconquer'd Steam! afar
> Drag the slow barge, or drive the rapid car;
> Or on wide-waving wings expanded bear
> The flying-chariot through the fields of air.   (*Ec.Veg.* I 289–92)

It is in biology, however, that Darwin is best known as a scientist, for his ideas on biological evolution (as we now call it) recorded in *Zoonomia* (1794). He had been convinced of the truth of evolution for more than twenty years and he argues confidently. He first points out the great changes produced in animals naturally, 'as in the production of the butterfly with painted wings from the crawling caterpillar; or of the respiring frog from the subnatant tadpole'; and also 'by artificial or accidental cultivation, as in horses, which we have exercised for the different purposes of strength or swiftness, in carrying burthens or running races' (*Zoonomia* i 504). He notes that monstrosities, or mutations as we should now say, are often inherited: 'Many of these enormities of shape are propagated, and continued as a new variety at least, if not as a new species of animal' (i 505). These examples, and many others that he gives, show that variations can and do occur, and may be inherited.

What then are the controlling forces? If air and water are available, 'the three great objects of desire, which have changed the forms of many animals by their exertions to gratify them, are those of lust, hunger and security'. Apropos 'those of lust', Darwin explains how the males of many species, such as boars, stags, cocks and quails, have developed 'weapons to combat each other' for the purpose of 'exclusive possession of the females':

> The final cause of this contest amongst the males seems to be, that the strongest and most active animal should propagate the species, which should thence become improved.   (i 507)

The spur of hunger, Darwin tells us, 'has diversified the forms of all species of animals'. Each has adapted to its means of acquiring food – the hard noses of swine, the rough tongues of cattle, the varied beaks of birds, etc. His third criterion, the need of animals for security, 'seems much to have diversified the forms of their bodies and colour of them', with some animals acquiring swiftness of foot, or wings, to escape; others hard shells, protective camouflage and so on.

Such changes, of which some (as with pigeons and dogs) have come within a few hundred years, give him a confident belief in evolution:

> Would it be too bold to imagine, that in the great length of time since the earth began to exist, perhaps millions of ages before the commencement of the history of mankind, would it be too bold to imagine, that all warm-blooded animals have arisen from one living filament . . . . (i 509)

This rhetorical sentence goes on for several lines more, but there is no question mark at the end. Darwin correctly assigns a time scale of several hundred million years, as against the 5800 years allowed by contemporary Biblical interpreters, and the 40 million years allowed by Charles Darwin. Erasmus also stresses, later in his rhetorical sentence, that evolution proceeds 'by its own inherent activity', and the gradual realization that this meant 'without divine intervention' brought down on Darwin's head the wrath of the godly, who were numerous and powerful – and included Coleridge, who was eloquent in his denunciations of Darwin's evolutionary scheme.

Darwin's account of evolution was incomplete, and did not have enough facts to convince sceptics; but he went a long way towards defining the theory later associated with his grandson Charles, and he was generally in accord with modern thinking. He was very conscious of the struggle for existence and painted a lurid picture of its operation throughout the natural world in his last poem *The Temple of Nature*. He also saw beyond its apparent cruelty. First, it was a necessary part of the process for *improving* species. Second, it was not only the survival of the fittest but also, by and large, the survival of the happiest, because the survivors are generally healthier and happier than the victims. He saw each organic being as possessed of a quota of happiness, whence his concept of 'organic happiness' and the idea that evolution tends to enhance organic happiness.

After evolution, the most all-embracing of biological processes is probably photosynthesis, without which life on Earth would not have developed. Darwin made an important contribution here too. Photosynthesis may be summarized as

$$\text{carbon dioxide} + \text{water} + \text{light energy} \rightarrow \text{oxygen} + \text{sugar},$$

and although Darwin did not write this neat equation he specified all its features in *Phytologia* (1800), as the following quotations show:

> This carbonic gas [carbon dioxide] is the principal food of plants. . . . Next to carbonic acid the aqueous acid, if it may be so called, or water, seems to afford the principal food of vegetables. . . . When vegetable leaves are exposed to the sun's light, they seem to give up oxygen gas. . . . The wonderful effect of vegetable digestion in producing sugar may be deduced from the great product of the sugar cane. (*Phytologia*, pp. 188–93)

This goes much further than any previous description of photosynthesis.

Darwin's recognition of the essential plant nutrients is in some ways even more impressive, because the processes were not elucidated until fifty years after his death. He first fixes on 'the azote, or nitrogen', which 'seems much to contribute to the food or sustenance of vegetables', and specifies its absorption via trapping in the soil or through the formation of ammonia ('volatile alkali'). He also points to the role of nitrates in plant nutrition. His second necessary element is carbon, an obvious choice in view of the carbon dioxide uptake. His third essential nutrient is phosphorus, and he goes on to advocate a search for calcium phosphate in Britain. Darwin was the first to suggest that nitrogen and phosphate are essential for plant growth.[29]

There are many other good ideas in *Phytologia*. Darwin goes some way towards defining the carbon and nitrogen cycles in nature. He explains how to bore artesian wells with the best chances of success. He has ingenious suggestions for pesticides, including the biological control of aphids by the syrphid fly. His ideas for timber production by the afforestation of 'unfertile mountains' with 'pines, Scotch fir' were adopted in Britain 100 years later. He was the first to bring out clearly the individuality of buds, and he noted how such 'linear or paternal' generation gave no scope for variation, while 'sexual, or amatorial, generation' provided the variation on which evolution could work. 'Sexual reproduction is the chef d'oeuvre, the master-piece of nature' (p. 103).

Phytologia ends with a wider perspective on animal and vegetable nature – and some minerals too – in his philosophy of organic happiness. Strata such as limestone and coal, being the remains of animal or vegetable life, can be regarded as 'monuments of the past felicity of organized nature' (p. 560).

We have now reached the fourth and final facet of Darwin's genius, his way with words. The obituarist in the *Monthly Magazine* was no admirer – as shown by his rude remark that Darwin's stomach 'possessed a strong power of digestion' – but even he admitted that 'no man . . . had a more imperial command of words'.[30] The words that fell into line under Darwin's command numbered about two million, divided among seven books, all (apart from the first two) very different from each other and strongly original.

The first two books, the translations from Linnaeus, are so deadly dull that I doubt whether anyone has read them straight through. Of course they are not intended as light reading: they are reference books, being catalogues of plant characters extending to 2000 pages. They remind us of Samuel Johnson's 'maker of dictionaries, a harmless drudge'; and there was much drudgery in Darwin's work. But it had its creative aspects too, because he took great pains to find the best possible English words for the Latin of Linnaeus, and he consulted many experts in botany and English usage, from Sir Joseph Banks to Samuel Johnson. Darwin feelingly referred to 'the general difficulty of the undertaking, in which almost a new language was to be formed'. This is true, and was recognized at the time: the books won glowing reviews, and brought many new words into the English language. Darwin retained the habit of coining new words: there are more than 30 in *The Botanic Garden*. The alleged author of the translations, 'A Botanical Society at Lichfield', was another 'coinage', and Anna Seward was much amused at the bafflement of 'scientific travellers' who visited Lichfield in search of the Society.

To relieve the tedium of the translation, Darwin had the idea of popularizing the subject by a frivolous 'translation' into verse. *The Loves of the Plants* was the result, and he finished the first draft by 1784. He saw how it could serve as the second and lighter part of a long poem begun in the late 1770s, about his botanic garden at Lichfield. Between 1784 and 1788 *The Loves of the Plants* went ahead as planned and was published anonymously in April 1789. The first edition had four cantos of about 400 lines each. By then Part I of the poem had grown beyond recognition into a wide-ranging review of all science, but particularly Earth science, with notes so extensive that they formed a selective scientific encyclopaedia. Part I kept its original title, *The Economy of Vegetation*, which had always been clumsy and was now also misleading. It had four cantos of about 500 lines each, devoted to Fire, Earth, Water and Air respectively, with numerous footnotes and lengthy 'Additional Notes'. Though dated 1791, Part I did not appear until about June 1792, and by then *The Loves of the Plants* was in its (somewhat longer) third edition. So the first edition of the complete *Botanic Garden* consisted of the first edition of *The Economy of Vegetation* and the third edition of *The Loves of the Plants*. These are the editions that I have used in my quotations.

In 1789 *The Loves of the Plants* seems to have delighted everyone, young and old, male and female. Horace Walpole, not usually easy to please, wrote that 'the author is a great poet. . . . I send you the most delicious poem upon earth . . . all is the most lovely poetry. . . . *The Botanic Garden*, the *Arabian Nights* and King's Chapel are above all rules.' Edgeworth wrote:

> I have felt such continued, such increasing admiration in reading the Loves of the Plants, that I dare not express any of my Enthusiasm, lest you should suspect me of that tendency to Exaggeration, which you used to charge me with.

Anna Seward accepted the sexiness of the poem because 'the sexual nature of plants' has been proved, and she called it 'a brilliant little world of Genius and its creations'.[31]

When *The Economy of Vegetation* was published in 1792, it was acclaimed as stronger and better than *The Loves of the Plants*. Darwin's command of cosmic imagery seemed to challenge and outdo Milton, as shown by the comments already quoted on his verses about the creation of the Universe out of Chaos. William Cowper wrote a seven-page review full of praise; the great engineer Thomas Telford called it 'a very wonderful and masterly performance'; the *Monthly Review* thought it better than its predecessor, with 'splendid' verse; the *Critical Review* called it 'truly elegant and philosophical' and said its merits 'occur in every page and might give occasion for undistinguishing panegyric';[32] and so on. For about five years Darwin became the most highly regarded poet of the day, and made a deep impression on Blake, Wordsworth and Coleridge, as well as older poets like Cowper and Crabbe, as we shall see in later chapters.

Darwin's prestige was enhanced by his apparent mastery of all knowledge, and was further boosted, or so it seemed at the time, by the publication of *Zoonomia; or the Laws of Organic Life*. Volume 1 (1794) consists of 582 quarto pages of general essays; Volume 2 (1796) has 772 pages on the treatment of particular diseases, which are listed under Genera, Classes and Species. It was an impressive performance, and most of the reviewers were too awe-struck to be critical. The *Monthly Magazine* called it 'one of the most important productions of the age', while the *European Magazine* quoted the opinion that *Zoonomia* 'bids fair to do for Medicine what Sir Isaac Newton's *Principia* has done for Natural Philosophy'.[33]

These judgments are too kind, but there is much of interest in Volume 1, in addition to the chapter on evolution already discussed. Darwin gives a clear description of the oxygenation of blood. His treatments of mental illness and alcohol addiction, his recognition of psychosomatic effects and his zeal for microscopy – all these deserve praise.

But for Wordsworth and Coleridge it was the general essays that proved most compelling, particularly the chapters on Sleep and Dreams and on Reverie: these led to Wordsworth's idea of poetical reverie and Coleridge's concept of dramatic illusion.

The treatments of individual diseases in Volume 2 are generally unimpressive. There is far too much baring of the lancet and trying every medicine in the pharmacopoeia. The diseases are split into four classes – diseases of Irritation, Sensation, Volition and Association. Irritation 'is excited by external bodies'; Sensation 'is excited by pleasure or pain'; Volition 'by desire or aversion'; and Association covers indirect effects. This may seem as clear as mud, but Darwin seems to have had no difficulties. For example, drunkenness is a disease of Irritation, being caused by an external stimulus. The most unsatisfactory category is Sensation, which includes almost everything from smallpox to sneezing. 'Association' has some validity in covering side-effects. 'Volition' is the most satisfactory of the four, corresponding roughly to what would now be called mental illness. Darwin has a wide-ranging menu of diseases of volition, including superstition, fear of hell, and credulity – a most deplorable endemic disease among 'the bulk of mankind', making them 'the dupes of priests and politicians'.

After *Zoonomia* came the very different *Plan for the Conduct of Female Education in Boarding Schools* (1797). Though written slightly tongue-in-cheek, to avoid offending parents of potential pupils, Darwin's plan was a bold step along the road to sexual equality. That girls should be taught science and modern languages, and be given adequate physical exercise, may seem obvious now, but it was radical then. This is the shortest and most readable of Darwin's books, and it has earned a distinctive place in the history of girl's education in England.[34]

Darwin spent the next three years writing *Phytologia*, published in 1800 and already sufficiently sampled in my discussion of photosynthesis and plant nutrition. It earned several golden opinions, and Sir Humphry Davy included Darwin among 'the most enlightened philosophers who have studied the physiology of vegetation'.[35]

Darwin's second long poem, *The Temple of Nature*, published in 1803, is in my view his finest achievement as a writer. While *The Botanic Garden* can be stigmatized as a rag-bag of scientific ideas tipped over a salacious catalogue of the reproductive anatomy of plants, *The Temple of Nature* has a coherent theme of great profundity and insight. That theme is the history of life on Earth, and Darwin presents it as an evolutionary biologist, almost as if he knew what the modern world-view would be.

Darwin's own title for the poem was *The Origin of Society*, and this nicely shows the affinity with his grandson's *The Origin of Species* and also Erasmus's wider view. He explains not only how animals originated and evolved, but also how the human animals created society. (It is not surprising that Darwin's publisher Joseph Johnson changed the title at the last moment, for he had been imprisoned in 1798 for selling an irreligious pamphlet. It is only the title-page that is changed, and 'Origin of Society' remains as the 'running head' on each right-hand page.)

The Temple of Nature is in four cantos totalling 1928 lines: the rhyming couplets are as pithy as in *The Botanic Garden*, though less showy. Darwin's aim 'is simply to amuse' by showing us the pageant of life in the order in which, as he believes, it unfolded. This pageant of nature's progress is presented by 'the Hierophant', who is also called Urania and the Priestess of Nature (and is really Darwin in disguise).

Canto I of *The Temple of Nature* is devoted to 'Production of Life'. A few quick couplets take up through the formation of the Earth. At first there was only lifeless ocean. Then,

> Nurs'd by warm sun-beams in primeval caves,
> Organic Life began beneath the waves. . . .
> Hence without parent by spontaneous birth
> Rise the first specks of animated earth   (I 233–4, 247–8)

Darwin's ideas on the origin of life are close to the orthodox modern view that life arose spontaneously via organic molecules in the oceans or atmosphere acted on by solar ultra-violet radiation, lightning or other energy sources. Darwin needs only three couplets to summarize the subsequent course of evolution:

> First forms minute, unseen by spheric glass,
> Move on the mud, or pierce the watery mass;
> These, as successive generations bloom,
> New powers acquire, and larger limbs assume;
> Whence countless groups of vegetation spring;
> And breathing realms of fin, and feet, and wing. (I 297–302)

There were 'vast shoals' of tiny sea creatures with shells, he says, and when they died, they formed the strata of coral, chalk and limestone. Then, 'after islands or continents were raised above the primeval ocean, great numbers of the most simple animals would attempt to seek food at the edges or shores of the new land' and 'might thence gradually become amphibious' (I 327, note). Or, turned into verse,

> Cold gills aquatic form respiring lungs,
> And sounds aerial flow from slimy tongues. (I 333–4)

The change from water to air is seen today, he says, in creatures having both gills and lungs, and in the birth of the human infant.

Canto II, 'Reproduction of Life', goes over some of the same ground (or water) from a different viewpoint. In the beginning, Darwin believed, reproduction was asexual:

> The Reproductions of the living Ens
> From sires to sons, unknown to sex, commence. . . .
> Unknown to sex the pregnant oyster swells,
> And coral-insects build their radiate shells. . . .
> Birth after birth the line unchanging runs,
> And fathers live transmitted in their sons;
> Each passing year beholds the unvarying kinds,
> The same their manners, and the same their minds.
> (II 63–4, 89–90, 107–10)

This sameness is relieved by sex, which Darwin very much approves of, because it improves the species and enhances organic happiness. He brings on an amusing pageant of all life's creatures following Love's flower-decked car: the whole procession, from the 'love-lorn' tigress to 'the enamour'd Flowers',

> hail the Deities of Sexual Love.   (II 410)

To balance the physical bias of this Canto, we have Canto III,
'Progress of the Mind'. Urania tells the listening nymphs that most
animals have weapons or armour, but humans rely on hand, eye and
brain. Forms learnt by touch in infancy are confirmed by eye:

> Symbol of solid forms is colour'd light,
> And the mute language of the touch is sight.   (III 143–4)

This leads to Darwin's theory of ideal beauty from 'the nice curves which
swell the female breast', and his philosophy of art and science based on
'the fine power of Imitation', which we have already met in Chapter 1.
After a long tribute to Reason, basis of 'all human science worth the
name', Darwin compares our wisdom with the instinctive 'wisdom' of
the wasp, bee or spider, thus linking 'the reasoning reptile to mankind'.
This teaches us to have concern for other creatures, and even more for
other humans. 'The seraph, Sympathy', he says, 'charms the world with
universal love', and the Temple of Nature has this motto inscribed above
it:

> In Life's disastrous scenes to others do,
> What you would wish by others done to you.   (III 487–8)

This precept, 'if sincerely obeyed by all nations, would a thousand-fold
multiply the present happiness of mankind', Darwin remarks in a note.
    In Canto IV of the poem, 'Of Good and Evil', Darwin versifies his
theories of evolution and organic happiness, starting with the wide web
of slaughter that indelibly marks the struggle for existence:

> The wolf, escorted by his milk-drawn dam,
> Unknown to mercy, tears the guiltless lamb;
> The towering eagle, darting from above,
> Unfeeling rends the inoffensive dove;
> The lamb and dove on living nature feed,
> Crop the young herb, or crush the embryon seed.   (IV 17–22)

The owl kills small creatures, which themselves prey on others; insects
lay eggs in larger animals. Even the plants are at war:

> Yes! smiling Flora drives her armed car

Through the thick ranks of vegetable war;
Herb, shrub, and tree, with strong emotions rise
For light and air, and battle in the skies;
Whose roots diverging with opposing toil
Contend below for moisture and for soil.   (IV 41–6)

In the oceans too 'the grim monarch of insatiate Death' reigns supreme.
So, Darwin concludes,

Air, earth, and ocean, to astonish'd day
One scene of blood, one mighty tomb display!
From Hunger's arm the shafts of Death are hurl'd,
And one great Slaughter-house the warring world!   (IV 63–6)

Human ills are plentiful too – slavery, war, disease, pestilence, hunger
and 'the curst spells of Superstition'. Is there nothing but woe then? On
the contrary, Darwin/Urania tells us, good and evil are nicely balanced.
Humans enjoy the pleasure of consciousness, the delights of natural
scenery, the warmth of sunshine, the fragrance of flowers, the taste of
fruits, the charms of music, painting and all the imaginative arts; and
above all they may 'drink the raptures of delirious love'. There are also
the satisfactions of philanthropy, the triumphs of science and the
heroism of those who fight tyrannic governments.

Finally Darwin brings on his philosophy of organic happiness. He
explains the problems of overpopulation, by acorns, aphides and every
other life-form, which 'would each o'erpeople ocean, air and earth'.
Similarly,

human progenies, if unrestrain'd,
By climate friended and by food sustain'd,   (IV 369–70)

would spread uncontrollably;

But war, and pestilence, disease, and dearth,
Sweep the superfluous myriads from the earth.   (IV 373–4)

For Darwin, 'every pore of Nature teems with life' and every speck of life
adds just a little to the total of organic happiness. 'Alchemic powers'
ensure that a new life burgeons

when a Monarch or a mushroom dies,   (IV 383) as the 'restless atoms pass from life to life'; and so man

> Should eye with tenderness all living forms,
> His brother-emmets and his sister-worms. (IV 427–8)

The mountains of limestone, being the remains of creatures that once enjoyed life,

> Are mighty Monuments of past Delight. (IV 450)

Not everyone will applaud Darwin's triumphant conclusion:

> Shout round the globe, how Reproduction strives
> With vanquish'd Death – and Happiness survives. (IV 451–2)

But it is an effective finale to this evolutionary poem so far ahead of its time.

The Temple of Nature was not well received in 1803, because Darwin, by his naturalistic approach to the origin and development of life, had usurped the role reserved for God. The reviewer in the *British Critic* found the poem so shocking that he could not bear it: 'We are full of horror, and will write no more'.[36] So *The Temple of Nature*, although a much better poem than *The Botanic Garden*, had relatively little influence. I have given it a good airing in this chapter because it is not often mentioned in later chapters.

NOTES

1. *Collected Letters of S. T. Coleridge*, ed. F. L. Griggs, i 177. The fullest biography of Erasmus Darwin is D. King-Hele, *Doctor of Revolution* (Faber, 1977).
2. For details of this enterprise, see *Letters of Erasmus Darwin*, pp. 18–27.
3. *Ibid.*, p. 40.
4. J. Muirhead, *James Watt* ii 279.
5. *Letters of Erasmus Darwin*, p. 43.
6. From MS at William Salt Library, Stafford. See also *Gent.Mag.*, *54*, 87 (1784).
7. British Library, Add. MS 42071, ff. 48–52.
8. J. Muirhead, *James Watt* ii 115.
9. See *Letters of Erasmus Darwin*, p. 110, for details of Jackson.
10. *Ibid.*, p. 128.
11. A. Seward, *Memoirs of the Life of Dr Darwin*, p. 5; R. L. and Maria Edgeworth, *Memoirs* ii 82.

12. *Letters of Erasmus Darwin*, p. 131.
13. *Ibid.*, p. 225.
14. J. E. Stock, *Memoirs of the Life of Thomas Beddoes* (Murray, 1811) pp. 131, 133.
15. *British Critic*, *5*, 113–22 (1795).
16. H. Williams, *Great Biologists* (Bell, 1961) p. 80.
17. A. Seward, *Memoirs of the Life of Dr Darwin*, pp. 5–6.
18. *Letters of Erasmus Darwin*, p. 336.
19. *Temple of Nature*, Note VIII.
20. *Letters of Josiah Wedgwood* ii 541.
21. E. Darwin, *Zoonomia* i 352.
22. *Letters of Erasmus Darwin*, p. 54.
23. *Ibid.*, pp. 146–71.
24. Commonplace Book (at the Darwin Museum, Down House, Downe, Kent), p. 59.
25. *Letters of Erasmus Darwin*, p. 104.
26. See D. King-Hele, *Doctor of Revolution*, pp. 141–3.
27. *Philosophical Transactions*, *78*, 43–52 (1788).
28. H. Walpole, *Letters* (OUP, 1905) xv 110; A. Seward, *Memoirs of the 'Life of Dr Darwin*, p. 193.
29. See Sir John Russell, *History of Agricultural Science in Great Britain* (Allen and Unwin, 1966) p. 63.
30. *Monthly Magazine*, *13*, 459, 462 (June 1802).
31. H. Walpole, *Letters* (1905) xiv 124, 125, 126, 141; Edgeworth, *Memoirs* ii 131 (with corrections from the MS, in Camb. Univ. Lib.); A. Seward, *Memoirs of the Life of Dr Darwin*, pp. 283, 376.
32. See *Analytical Review*, *15*, 287–93 (1793); L. T. C. Rolt, *Thomas Telford* (Longman, 1958) p. 29; *Monthly Review*, *11*, 182–7 (1793); *Critical Review*, *6*, 162–71 (1792).
33. *Monthly Magazine*, *2*, 485 (1796); *European Magazine*, *27*, 77 (1795).
34. See, for example, D. Gardiner, *English Girlhood at School* (OUP, 1929) pp. 347–56; and B. Simon, *Studies in the History of Education* (Lawrence and Wishart, 1960) pp. 50–6.
35. H. Davy, *Agricultural Chemistry* (Longman, 1813) p. 9.
36. *British Critic*, *23*, 174 (1804).

REFERENCES

Collected Letters of S. T. Coleridge, ed. E. L. Griggs, 6 vols (OUP, 1956–71).
R. L. and Maria Edgeworth, *Memorirs of R. L. Edgeworth*, 2 vols (Hunter, 1820; Irish Univ. Pr., Shannon, Ireland, 1969).
D. King-Hele, *Doctor of Revolution; The Life and Genius of Erasmus Darwin* (Faber, 1977).
Letters of Erasmus Darwin, ed. D. King-Hele (CUP, 1981).
Letters of Josiah Wedgwood, ed. K. E. Farrer (1903) (Morten, Manchester, 1974).
J. Muirhead, *The Origin and Progress of the Mechanical Inventions of James Watt*, 3 vols (Murray, 1854).

Anna Seward, *Memoirs of the Life of Dr Darwin* (Johnson, 1804).

The place of publication is London, unless otherwise stated.

Erasmus Darwin's works, in the editions quoted here:
[E. Darwin] *The Loves of the Plants* (1789), 3rd edn (Johnson, 1791). (This is Part II of *The Botanic Garden.*)
[E. Darwin] *The Economy of Vegetation*, 1st edn (Johnson, 1791). (This is Part I of *The Botanic Garden*; dated 1791, but published 1792.)
E. Darwin, *Zoonomia*, Vol. I (1794), (Johnson, 1796); Vol. II (Johnson, 1796).
E. Darwin, *A Plan for the Conduct of Female Education in Boarding Schools* (Johnson, 1797).
E. Darwin, *Phytologia* (Johnson, 1800).
E. Darwin, *The Temple of Nature* (Johnson, 1803).
(For a fuller bibliography, see *Doctor of Revolution*, pp. 339–40.)

Styles of numeration:
volume and pages in multi-volume books: *Zoonomia* ii 359–65.
volume and pages in periodicals: *British Critic*, 5, 113–22 (1795).
canto and line numbers in poems: *Temple of Nature* iv 41–6.

3 Blake

> While the Lilly white shall in Love delight.
> W. Blake, *Songs of Experience*

It may seem bad luck that I have to begin my chronicle of imitation with William Blake, who is generally regarded as one of the most original of English poets. But he comes first chronologically, having been born in 1757, thirteen years before Wordsworth, so I cannot postpone him till the end. Blake was already thirty-two years old when *The Loves of the Plants* appeared; his opinions were formed, and differed in many ways from Darwin's. So the idea that Darwin influenced Blake is not inherently plausible: the cards are stacked against me.

William Blake (Fig. 2) was born in London and spent his whole life there, apart from three years with William Hayley at Felpham in Sussex. He was apprenticed to an engraver and earned his living largely by that craft. The finest artist among the English poets and the finest poet among the English artists, Blake despised convention and believed passionately in liberty of expression. He was a man of visions, and they animated his art. His poems were fusions of art and verse, being issued as illuminated manuscripts, beginning with *Songs of Innocence* and *The Book of Thel* (both 1789) and proceeding through the early 1790s to *Songs of Experience* (1794). The heavier symbolic prophetic works came later, and include *Vala, or the Four Zoas*, begun about 1795, *Milton* (1804–8) and *Jerusalem* (1804–20). Blake died in 1827.

THE BOOK OF THEL

Blake's first book of verse, *Songs of Innocence*, is far removed from Darwin in style and content; but we run full-tilt into Darwin with *The Book of Thel*, engraved later in 1789. Blake's title-page, shown as Fig. 6, is virtually a cartoon-version of *The Loves of the Plants*, which was published in April 1789. As David Erdman has noted,[1] Blake's title-page shows Thel as shepherdess watching not sheep but the extraordinary spectacle of two huge blossoms of a pasqueflower (*Anemone pulsatilla*), with a gowned maiden stepping out of one flower and a naked youth leaping out of the other to seize her with amorous intent. Blake's drawing is the pictorial expression of the personified pistils and stamens of Darwin's poem. In his note on Anemone, Darwin quotes Pliny as saying that the flower 'never opens its petals, but when the wind blows, whence its name'. So Darwin calls up 'propitious Zephyr' to get the action going:

> So shines the Nymph in beauty's blushing pride,
> When Zephyr wafts her deep calash aside,
> Tears with rude kiss her bosom's gauzy veil,
> And flings the fluttering kerchief to the gale.
>
> (*Lov.Pl.* I 339–42)*

After this erotic start, Darwin brings on a 'glittering throng' of 'beaux and belles'. Blake's single pair of lovers is more effective pictorially: his Nymph is already without a calash, and her ardent beau is all set to tear 'her bosom's gauzy veil'.

'Pictorially and metaphorically', Erdman points out, *The Book of Thel* 'is a curious counterpart' of *The Loves of the Plants*: 'some of Blake's flowers and their human forms seem to derive from Darwin's text, notes and illustrations. . . . Darwin's emphasis on sexual encounter and aggressive masculinity seems particularly relevant.'[1] To this I would add another similarity: the exceedingly delicate touch that marks both poems. Darwin portrays a world of pistils, stamens, petals, pollen, insects, dewdrops – all liable to be blown away by a breeze. Blake's touch is equally delicate. Like Darwin's poem, Blake's is full of sexual nuances, which I shall not pursue because they lead into a quagmire of ifs and buts, whereas my aim is to display clear parallels, not to become bogged down in arguable interpretation.

Shorn of all symbolism, the story of Blake's poem is easily told. For 125 lines the enigmatic Thel, initially a shepherdess (but also called a virgin and 'a shining woman'), holds conversations with a lily, a cloud, a worm and the matron Clay.

The first and most obvious parallel is that Blake personifies flowers; what is more, the lily is among the first group of flowers mentioned by Darwin –

> With secret sighs the Virgin Lily droops.   (*Lov.Pl.* I 15)

---

* All references to *The Loves of the Plants* give canto and line numbers in the *third* edition (dated 1791), to conform with later chapters.

This line may have given Blake the idea for his lily, the 'little virgin of the peaceful valley' who 'bow'd her modest head' (Plate 2, lines 3, 17).

The second parallel springs from Blake's similar cast of characters – blossoms, leaves, butterflies, blades of grass, the 'weak worm', drops of dew – and their similar treatment. Blake has chosen to operate in the botanical world of the gentle, the weak and the delicate, as defined by Darwin:

> Say on each leaf how tiny Graces dwell;
> How laugh the Pleasures in a blossom's bell;
> How insect-Loves arise on cob-web wings,
> Aim their light shafts, and point their little stings.
>
> (*Lov.Pl.* I 35–8)

The 'bright form' of Blake's Cloud emerges

> Hovering and glittering on the air,

and tells Thel he will

> Unseen descending, weigh my light wings upon balmy flowers,
> And court the fair-eyed dew to take me to her shining tent.
>
> (Plate 3, lines 6, 12–13)

This is in the same spirit and often in the same words as Darwin's Canto I, where his little creatures are continually hovering and glittering, flying as clouds, or seeking dew: for example, there are 'hovering Sylphs' in line 1 and 'glittering nations, tenants of the air' in line 143; mistletoe 'seeks amid the clouds her soaring loves' in line 264; in line 363, *Dypsacus*, growing 'where no soft shower descends, no dew distills', pleads to the Naiads for dew; and Anemone herself, with 'pearly dew' dropping from her eyelids, asks the 'gentle Air' to breathe its 'balmy influence' (lines 320–4).

The third area of resemblance is pictorial: there are five fine drawings of plants given as full-page Plates in the first edition of *The Loves of the Plants*, and Blake seems to have found inspiration in nearly all of them, either for *Thel* or later poems. The first of Darwin's Plates is of *Meadia* (Fig. 7), which Erdman[1] sees as the source of the long stamens and the blossoms in Blake's Plate 5 (Fig. 8). Erdman also comments that on the title-page 'we might take Thel herself for Darwin's "sad Anemone" pining for the wind's "cherub lips", since the two small figures beside her are performing Darwin's script'.[1]

Another of Darwin's Plates, shown here as Fig. 9, is *Dionaea
muscipula*, the Venus flytrap, with its eyelid-like traps carrying hundreds
of sharp pointed spines like eyelashes. The lines immediately after the
Plate (in the the first edition) describe the aggressive stamens of holly:

> Each grasps a thousand arrows in his hand;
> A thousand steely points on every scale.   (*Lov.Pl.* I 162–3)

The eyelid-traps fringed with eyelash spines seem to have joined forces
with the 'thousand arrows' to inspire Blake's marvellous summary of
male visual aggression,

> Why are Eyelids stor'd with arrows ready drawn,
> Where a thousand fighting men in ambush lie?
>   (*Thel*, Plate 6, lines 13–14)

Some facets of Blake's narrative also have parallels in Darwin.
Towards the end of Plate 2 (lines 13–15) Blake abruptly terminates
Thel's conversation with the Lilly and brings on glittering rain-drops:

> 'Queen of the vales', the Lilly answer'd, 'ask the tender cloud,
> And it shall tell thee why it glitters in the morning sky,
> Any why it scatters its bright beauty thro' the humid air.'

There is a similar flip-over from lily to pearly rain-drops in the last two
couplets of Darwin's first Canto:

> Swift bees returning seek their waxen cells,
> And Sylphs cling quivering in the lily's bells.
> Through the still air descend the genial showers,
> And pearly rain-drops deck the laughing flowers.
>   (*Lov.Pl.* I 481–4)

In another curious episode, where Thel watches matron Clay as 'she
bow'd over the weeping infant' (Fig. 8), Erdman sees a parallel with
Darwin's picture of Tulipa, who in autumn 'folds her infant closer in her
arms' (I 206) within the bulb buried in mother Earth.

Many of the numerous verbal resemblances between *The Book of Thel*
and *The Loves of the Plants* arise because the subject matter and tone are
so similar that Blake inevitably uses many of the same adjectives as
Darwin – faint, gentle, bright, glittering, dewy. For example, 'dew(y)'

appears four times in the 125 lines of *Thel* and eight times in Darwin's Canto I; and 'flowers' appears six times in *Thel*, while Darwin mentions twenty-five flowers by name in his first 125 lines. Blake's 'Queen of the vales' may derive from Darwin's 'Queen of the dewy vale', and his 'gilded butterfly' from Darwin's 'catch in silken nets the gilded fly';[2] other resemblances exist, but none that I would judge to be significant.

So Darwin's poem, published in April, had within a few months flowered more gloriously than he knew – or could have imagined – by inspiring *The Book of Thel*, the first and most charming of the illuminated symbolic poems of William Blake, 'the most perfect poem among the symbolic books', as Mona Wilson called it.[3]

ENGRAVING FOR DARWIN

Already familiar with *The Loves of the Plants*, Blake very soon came to know *The Economy of Vegetation*. For in 1790 his friend Joseph Johnson the radical publisher commissioned him to make engravings for the poem. Since Blake admired *The Loves of the Plants*, the work would have been willingly undertaken, and not a tedious chore as has sometimes been suggested. The engravings were superb and certainly helped towards the great success of *The Economy of Vegetation*. Thus it was that Blake at the height of his powers as a poet but unknown except to his friends, helped Darwin to become the most famous poet of the decade.

Darwin and Blake probably never met, and there is no evidence that Darwin knew of Blake's poems. But they were linked through two mutual friends, Joseph Johnson the publisher and Henry Fuseli the painter. Johnson was the most discerning and influential publisher of the 1790s: he befriended Blake and Mary Wollstonecraft, and he fully appreciated Blake's talents, telling Darwin in July 1791 that Blake was 'capable of doing anything well'.[4] Darwin liked to make his own judgments, rather than take other people's: but he respected Johnson's opinions, and in face of this sweeping commendation he agreed that publication of *The Economy of Vegetation* should be delayed so that Blake could obtain access to the Portland Vase (or possibly a Wedgwood copy). The four fine engravings of the Vase in the published poem made the delay well worth while for Darwin. The engravings were also fruitful for Blake, John Beer suggests,[5] as models for Plates in his *America*, particularly Plate 14, which has a woman with a snake between her legs, as in the Vase.

Henry Fuseli[6] first came to England in 1763, when he met Johnson. He returned in 1779 and soon became Blake's most highly regarded friend,

> The only Man that e'er I knew
> Who did not make me almost spew.[7]

Darwin probably met Fuseli in London in 1781, the year of his famous picture 'The Nightmare', and it was Fuseli who in 1784 recommended Johnson to Darwin as a possible publisher of *The Loves of the Plants*, for which Fuseli offered to provide illustrations.[8] In the event, four of the Plates in *The Botanic Garden* originated with Fuseli, although they are not in all editions. One was 'The Nightmare', discussed in Chapter 6; the other three were specially provided by Fuseli. One of these, the frontispiece 'Flora and the Elements', was engraved by Anker Smith. The other two were engraved by Blake, and both were significant in his development, as John Beer has shown.[9] One, 'The Fertilization of Egypt' (or 'Waters of the Nile') shows a back view of the dog-headed priest (Anubis) raising his hands in prayer to the dog-star shining above. Below the priest there looms 'an aged figure with vast beard and outstretched arms',[10] an image later much favoured by Blake as a symbol of a tyrannic ruler of Earth or Heaven. Blake's second engraving of a Fuseli original is the powerful 'Tornado', which appeared only in the third edition. This serpent-laden figure is drawn from Darwin's text, but it took on a deeper significance for Blake, for whom 'the serpent-coils around a figure are a permanent image for the ambiguity of energy and its relation to the human "selfhood"'.[9] In both these Fuseli–Blake illustrations the subjects were probably agreed between them beforehand and chosen for their imaginative appeal.

So it was not just by good luck that Darwin had Blake as his illustrator. Darwin was an intensely visual poet – the main complaint against *The Botanic Garden* (after the initial acclaim had subsided) was that it merely painted glittering pictures. Darwin himself admitted this when he called *The Loves of the Plants* 'diverse little pictures suspended over the chimney of a Lady's dressing-room, connected only by a slight festoon of ribbons'. Few poets have been more visual than Darwin. But of course Blake is among those few, for in his poems art and words are most happily married. Blake liked Darwin's word-pictures, as *The Book of Thel* shows: so it was appropriate that he should have been engraver-in-chief for *The Economy of Vegetation*.

Blake would have approved of Darwin's theory of painting, as A. S. Roe has pointed out.[11] In a note on the halo, Darwin says it has become a part of the symbolic language of painting, and it is much to be wished that this kind of hieroglyphic character was more frequent in that art; as it is much wanted to render historic pictures both more intelligible, and more sublime; and why should not painting as well as poetry express itself in metaphor, or in indistinct allegory? (*Ec.Veg.* I 358 note)

Blake expressed similar sentiments in his 'Descriptive Catalogue' of 1809:

shall Painting be confined to the sordid drudgery of fac-simile representations of merely mortal and perishing substances, and not be as poetry and music are, elevated into its own proper sphere of invention and visionary conception? No, it shall not be so! Painting, as well as poetry and music, exists and exults in immortal thoughts. (*Complete Writings*, p. 576)

THE FRENCH AND AMERICAN REVOLUTIONS

Blake and Darwin were also in full agreement over the American and French Revolutions, and Darwin's celebration of the success of the French Revolution in *The Economy of Vegetation* would have pleased Blake. He is very likely to have seen Darwin's lines in proof in 1790, because they are next to the description of the Portland Vase and Johnson would probably have drawn his attention to them.

Darwin brings in the French Revolution through a chained Giant, the warrior Liberty:

Long had the Giant-form on GALLIA'S plains
Inglorious slept, unconscious of his chains;
Round his large limbs were wound a thousand strings
By the weak hands of Confessors and Kings;
O'er his closed eyes a triple veil was bound,
And steely rivets lock'd him to the ground;
While stern Bastile with iron cage inthralls
His folded limbs, and hems in marble walls. (*Ec.Veg.* II 377–84)

In a footnote Darwin has an account of prisoners 'fastened by their necks to the walls of their cells' and skeletons found 'with irons still

fastened to their decayed bones', quoted from the *Letters from France* by
Helen Maria Williams.

Blake's poem *The French Revolution* was produced in proof by
Johnson in 1791, but not published (probably because of the danger of
prosecution). Blake imagines the Governor of 'the Bastile' restlessly
dragging his 'strong limbs' from tower to tower. In the tower called
Horror was a man

> Chain'd hand and foot, round his neck an iron band, bound to the
> impregnable wall.

In the tower named Darkness was a man

> Pinion'd down to the stone floor, his strong bones scarce cover'd
> with sinews; the iron rings
> Were forg'd smaller as the flesh decay'd, a mask of iron on his face
> hid the lineaments . . .   (lines 28, 30–1)

The resemblances are quite close, and Blake may have been remembering Darwin's picture – or possibly the *Letters from France*.

David Worrall[12] has suggested that Darwin's geology also finds its
way into *The French Revolution*. Darwin believed that volcanoes are fed
by a 'central fire', and the Additional Note VI to *The Economy of
Vegetation*, entitled 'Central Fires', gives good reasons in support of the
idea that 'the centre of the earth consists of a large mass of burning lava'
(where the word *burning* of course means *burning hot*, not 'combining
with oxygen'). Darwin believed 'the central parts of the earth to consist
of a fluid mass', and thought 'part of this fluid is iron', thus explaining
the Earth's magnetism. This is not only in conformity with modern views
but also made a lasting appeal to Blake, whose later prophetic poems
often feature lava and sometimes molten iron too. In *The French
Revolution* the 'central fire' imagery appears at the crucial point where
the King of France pronounces on 'the day of havoc': 'the King glow'd
. . . his heart flam'd, and utter'd a with'ring heat'; after speaking,

> He ceas'd, silent pond'ring; his brows folded heavy, his forehead
> was in affliction,
> Like the central fire.   (lines 79–80)

Fiery imagery continues in Blake's prophetic poem *America* (1793).
Plate 1 of this poem shows a man chained to the ground like Darwin's
'warrior Liberty', but it is Plate 3 that brings back the fires:

The Guardian Prince of Albion burns in his nightly tent:
Sullen fires across the Atlantic glow to America's shore,
Piercing the souls of warlike men who rise in silent night.
Washington, Franklin, Paine and Warren, Gates, Hancock and
    Green
Meet on the coast glowing with blood from Albion's fiery Prince.
                                 (lines 1–5)

The flame-imagery, the over-lurid tone, the blood and the slightly incongruous proper names are all rather reminiscent of Darwin's lines about the 'Tyrant Power' despatching from England 'to the West' a flight of Vampire birds that 'champ'd their beaks for blood', but were 'stabbed' by 'immortal Franklin'; meanwhile in America

The patriot-flame with quick contagion ran,
Hill lighted hill, and man electrised man.   (*Ec.Veg.* II 367–8)

Blake calls the Prince 'a dragon form, clashing his scales' who terrorizes with 'his glowing eyes'. This creature, drawn at the top of Plate 4 of *America*, resembles Darwin's 'sleepless dragon':

Bright beam'd his scales, his eyeballs blazed with ire.[13]

S. Foster Damon[14] has pointed out another probable echo of Darwin in *America*, when Blake tells us about the era 'when the moon shot forth' one 'dread night':

Then burst the center from its orb, and found a place beneath;
And Earth conglob'd, in narrow room, roll'd round its sulphur Sun.
                       (Plate b, lines 6–7)

The parallel with Darwin is again in Canto II of *The Economy of Vegetation*, when he describes how

Earth's huge sphere exploding burst in twain

and gave birth to

            the Moon's refulgent car,
Circling the solar orb, a sister-star . . .
And roll'd round Earth her airless realms of frost.
                       (II 76, 79–80, 82)

'Sulphur' and 'Earth's firm centre' appear a few lines earlier (69–70), though there are other possible sources for the sulphur.[15]

Darwin's cosmogony is again evident in Plate 5 of *America*, where Blake refers to the 'terror like a comet', 'the planets three' and the Sun being 'rent'. Worrall has carefully analysed this, 'the most striking passage in *America*', and its links with Darwin.[16]

THE *MARRIAGE* AND THE *VISIONS*

The Marriage of Heaven and Hell (1790–3) is not really a poem (apart from some 'free verse' at the start), but more a statement of principles, including the 'Proverbs of Hell' – 'The road of excess leads to the palace of wisdom', etc. These Proverbs finish in Plate 10, where the Devil is seen completing his reading of a long scroll. On his left is a keen disciple with a similar profile (possibly Blake himself?), and on his right a slower pupil. The plant by the pupil's side sports one of the eyelid-traps of *Dionaea muscipula*, the Venus flytrap. The wing-like plant behind the disciple's shoulder is more obscure; but Erdman notes Geoffrey Keynes's suggestion that it is based on *Gloriosa superba*, the Plate adjacent to *Dionaea* in *The Loves of the Plants* (3rd edition). Erdman himself suggests that 'the tendril flower that rises from the wing derives from yet another Darwin plate, that of the vallisneria spiralis'.[17] The resemblance to the distinctive Venus flytrap is unarguable, but the other two identifications seem to me rather dubious. Blake is constantly drawing spiral tendrils like those of vallisneria, based presumably on reality rather than on Darwin's poem.

No such doubts arise with *Visions of the Daughters of Albion* (1793), which Worrall calls 'the most remarkable example of Blake's Darwinizing'.[18] In Canto IV of *The Loves of the Plants* Darwin mentions flowers which are seen to emit sparks of light in the evening after a sunny day, and in his Note he states: 'The light was most brilliant on Marigolds, of an orange or flame colour' (*Lov.Pl.*, p. 183). Blake must have been impressed by the idea, for the crucial Plate iii of the *Visions*, shown here as Fig. 10, has a marigold with rays of light radiating from it, as well as a Loves-of-the-Plants human form leaping from the flower – a baby human form arising to be embraced by Oothoon:

> And thus she spoke to the bright Marygold of Leutha's vale:
> 'Art thou a flower? art thou a nymph? I see thee now a flower,
> Now a nymph! I dare not pluck thee from thy dewy bed!'
>
> (Plate 1, lines 5–7).

Sparks were also seen in sunflowers, and Oothoon becomes sunflower-like in line 13: 'I turn my face to where my whole soul seeks'. What she seeks is beauty, and 'If in the morning sun I find it, there my eyes are fix'd/In happy copulation.'[19] She offers to spread 'silken nets' to catch 'girls of mild silver, or of furious gold' and intends to 'view their wanton play/In lovely copulation' (Plate 7, lines 23–5). This is very like Darwin's viewing of the amorous antics of the plants; and Blake probably drew on Darwin's picture of the promiscuous lovers on Tahiti, where Venus spreads a 'silken net' to catch the 'smiling youths' and 'blushing maids'.[20]

SONGS OF EXPERIENCE

The five poems of Blake that I have so far looked at are rather esoteric, or so some may say: they ask instead about the *Songs of Innocence and Experience*. At first sight, the simple format of these songs seems to set Blake at a distance from Darwin. Stylistically, that is so. But *The Botanic Garden* apparently made a deep impression on Blake, and some of the *Songs* have strong links with Darwin.

The *Songs of Innocence* were probably completed quite early in 1789, before *The Loves of the Plants* was published. Though Fuseli and Johnson saw the draft manuscript of Darwin's poem in 1784, Blake is unlikely to have seen it before publication. I have found no clear signs of Darwin's influence in the *Songs of Innocence*, so I shall confine my comments to the *Songs of Experience*, written between 1789 and 1793, and engraved in 1794.

In these poems Blake quite often 'used flowers as sexual symbols', thus neatly reversing Darwin's technique of humanizing the sexual activities of flowers, as D. G. Gillham pointed out.[21] 'My Pretty Rose Tree' and 'The Lilly' are examples. One of the best poems in this vein is 'The Sick Rose', which has a design quite like the title-page of *Thel*. The rose is being eaten by an 'invisible worm' that

> Has found out thy bed
> Of crimson joy:
> And his dark secret love
> Does thy life destroy.

The idea of a worm devouring a bud, though commonplace in itself, has a special importance in *The Botanic Garden*, because it sabotages the sexual self-expression of the flowers: Blake might have taken his cue from lines like

Guard from rapacious worms its tender shoots.[22]

The 'dark secret love' of the insect for the rose might also have originated
in Darwin's poem, where 'illicit loves' produce a 'vegetable mule'
between Clove and Dianthus, and the even more 'unallow'd desires' of
the Nightingale for the rose create the fanciful 'half-rose, half-bird, a
beauteous Monster' with 'vocal rose-buds' and 'crimson petals'.[23] All
Blake's words are used – indeed overused – in *The Loves of the Plants*: for
example, Darwin has 'mossy beds' (I 27), a floral lover clad in a 'crimson
vest' (I 43), 'tiptoe Joys' (II 318) and Tremella singing of her 'secret love'
(I 430). All this *proves* nothing; you could dismiss the parallels as mere
chance and argue that Darwin had no influence. Or, if you know of
Blake's probable use of Darwin's Anemone, Venus flytrap and Meadia
in *Thel* and of Marigold in the *Visions*, you could go to the other extreme
and argue that 'The Sick Rose' would not exist in its present form if
Blake had not been familiar with *The Botanic Garden*.

The rampant worm in 'The Sick Rose' is a reminder that insects and
their kin abound in *The Loves of the Plants*: indeed they often rival the
flowers. Darwin addresses butterflies, beetles, moths, glow-worms,
spiders, snails and bee-nymphs in lines 22–30 of Canto I; and in lines
36–8 (already quoted on p. 37) he speaks of 'insect-Loves' with 'cob-
web wings'. Like Blake he cherishes all living things. Blake's charming
poem 'The Fly', springing from his belief that 'every thing that lives is
holy, life delights in life', is in full accord with Darwin's plea to 'eye with
tenderness all living forms'.[24]

Knowing the link between Darwin, sunflowers and Oothoon, we
ought not to pass by Blake's eight-line poem about the Sunflower, which
begins:

> Ah, Sun-flower, weary of time,
> Who countest the steps of the Sun.

Possible parallels with Darwin are in his account of the plants of the
Horologe, or Watch of Flora, which

> trace with mimic art the march of Time . . .
> And count the quick vibrations of his wing,
>
> (*Lov.Pl.* II 170, 172)

and in his description of the sunflower itself:

With zealous step he climbs the upland lawn . . .
And watches, as it moves, the orb of day.   (*Lov.Pl.* I 227, 230)

This gives us every significant word in Blake's lines, except *weary*; but the resemblances could still be mere chance.

In the second verse of 'Ah! Sun-flower' we meet a 'pale virgin shrouded in snow'. A 'stock image' of little significance? Possibly. But snow-bound virgins are among Darwin's favourite people, and in Canto I of *The Loves of the Plants* he takes 16 lines to tell us how the fair Tremella perished in the snow. Five lines are enough to give the bare bones (or is it the bare flesh?) of the story:

> As the bleak blast unfurls her fluttering vest,
> Cold beats the snow upon her shuddering breast . . .
> Congealing snows her lingering feet surround . . .
> Veil her pale bosom, glaze her lifted hands,
> And shrined in ice the beauteous statue stands.
>
> (I 447–8, 455, 461–2)

A 'pale virgin shrouded in snow', indeed: but who can tell whether Blake had in mind this shocking picture from his favourite Canto of *The Loves of the Plants*?

Another shocking picture in *The Loves of the Plants* was that of the Upas tree, 'a poison-tree in the island of Java'. The story originated in the *London Magazine* in 1783, but it was Darwin who gave the fable wide currency by seeming to accept the exaggerated tale of the tree's poisonous properties.[25] He calls it the 'Hydra-Tree of death' and says 'animals of all kinds' are 'destroyed by the effluvia' (*Lov.Pl.* III 219–50 and note). Blake's poem 'A Poison Tree' is firmly linked with Darwin's 'poison-tree': Blake's tree bore poisoned apples, which his foe stole, and Blake's illustration shows a dark and wide-spreading tree with 'my foe outstretched beneath'. Darwin's tree probably also served as the model for Blake's tree of Mystery bearing 'the fruit of deceit', in 'The Human Abstract', as Geoffrey Grigson noted.[25] This link becomes clearer in Blake's later poems, where we shall meet the Upas tree again.

From 'The Human Abstract' it is only a short step to a poem with one very similar line and a similar design – 'The Tyger', most famous of the *Songs of Experience*. Fire is the ruling motif of 'The Tyger', so there are bound to be parallels with Canto I of *The Economy of Vegetation*, which is all about Fire. For example, all Blake's ironmongery – hammer, chain, furnace and anvil – can be found in *The Economy of Vegetation*, and in similar contexts too.[26] But I shall disregard this blacksmith's gear and shall look instead at the essence of the poem. Blake's first line and second verse are:

> Tyger! Tyger! burning bright . . .
> In what distant deeps or skies
> Burnt the fire of thine eyes?
> On what wings dare he aspire?
> What the hand dare seize the fire?

Three possible parallels with Darwin suggest themselves here, the first being the fierce-eyed monsters in *The Economy of Vegetation*:

> With Tyger-paw He prints the brineless strand . . .
> Rolls his fierce eye-balls, clasps his iron claws . . .
> Bright beam'd his scales, his eye-balls blazed with ire,
> And his wide nostrils breath'd inchanted fire.
>
> (IV 434, 437; I 343–4)

The second parallel concerns Blake's word-sequence 'deeps . . . on . . . wings . . . aspire . . . fire', which may be found (in the correct order too) in *The Loves of the Plants*, when Darwin

> Calls up with magic voice the shapes that sleep
> In earth's dark bosom, or unfathom'd deep;
> That shrined in air on viewless wings aspire,
> Or blazing bathe in elemental fire.　　　　(II 297–300)

There is another 'aspire/fire' rhyme in Canto I (lines 281–2); and two more in *The Economy of Vegetation* (I 225–6 and I 255–6). The third parallel is in the form of an answer by Darwin to Blake's rhetorical question, 'What the hand dare seize the fire?' For, when Shadrec, Meshec and Abednego enter the fiery furnace,

> Fierce flames innocuous, as they step, retire;
> And calm they move amid a world of fire!　　(*Lov.Pl.* IV 69–70)

Are these similarities fortuitous or significant? The latter seems rather more likely to me. But it is for you to judge, and your verdict will depend on whether or not you believe that Darwin's poem was by now part of Blake's mental furniture.

There are further possible links with Darwin in the fifth verse of 'The Tyger':

When the stars threw down their spears,
And water'd heaven with their tears,
Did he smile his work to see?
Did he who made the Lamb make thee?

In the first line Blake may be thinking of meteors, otherwise known as 'falling stars' or 'shooting stars', *their spears* being their straight-line tracks. If so, the relevant parallel in Darwin is 'showers of stars rush headlong from the sky',[27] and Blake's second line might have been suggested by Darwin's *showers*, or by the many tears shed over heaven by Darwin's nymphs and Goddesses. But Blake may also be referring to the aurora, or 'northern lights', often described in ancient times as 'burning spears' in the sky. The linking of these ancient descriptions with the aurora was not well known, and the most likely source for Blake's knowledge of it is Darwin's account of the aurora in the long Additional Note I to *The Economy of Vegetation*, where he writes:

The antiquity of the appearance of the northern lights has been doubted. . . . There is however reason to believe them of remote antiquity though inaccurately described; thus the following curious passage from the Book of Maccabees (B.II. c.v) is such a description of them, as might probably be given by an ignorant and alarmed people. 'Through all the city, for the space of almost forty days, there were seen horsemen running in the air, in cloth of gold and armed with lances, like a band of soldiers; and troops of horsemen in array encountering and running one against another, with shaking of shields and multitude of pikes, and drawing of swords, and casting of darts, and glittering of golden ornaments and harness'.

If the meteor/aurora interpretation is valid, Darwin's influence can scarcely be doubted. There may be a deeper interpretation – the rebel angels laying down their arms after revolting[28] – and, if so, Darwin is contributing only verbal echoes rather than the core of the image.

Blake's final question – 'did he who made the Lamb make thee?' – posed 'the problem of evil' so worrying to those who believed in a benevolent God. The problem faced Darwin daily from the start of his medical career: did He who made the flowers make smallpox? Darwin had to find an answer, for his own peace of mind; and eventually he did so. He published his conclusion in his own 'Songs of Experience', or thoughts on a lifetime of medical experience, *Zoonomia*, which also came out in 1794. Darwin believed the Tyger and the Lamb had developed by different evolutionary routes from a single ancestral 'living filament':

> When we revolve in our minds the great similarity of structure which obtains in all the warm-blooded animals, as well quadrupeds, birds, and amphibious animals, as in mankind: from the mouse and bat to the elephant and whale; one is led to conclude that they have alike been produced from a similar living filament. In some this filament in its advance to maturity has acquired hands and fingers, with a fine sense of touch, as in mankind. In others it has acquired claws or talons, as in tygers and eagles. In others, toes with an intervening web, or membrane, as in seals and geese. In others it has acquired cloven hoofs, as in cows and swine; and whole hoofs in others, as in the horse . . .   (*Zoonomia* i 506)

Blake would not have relished the answer that the Tyger and Lamb were distant cousins, and there is no sign that he took notice of Darwin's correct and well-timed answer to his agonized query.

URIZEN, AHANIA AND LOS

Blake did take notice of Darwin in *The Book of Urizen* (1794), a myth of the creation of the world, with much cataclysmic imagery –

> The roaring fires ran o'er the heavens
> In whirlwinds and cataracts of blood . . .
> (Plate 5, lines 12–13)

Though Blake turned to *Paradise Lost* for some features of his cataclysmic style – the piling of excess on excess – he may also have been led on by Darwin's arresting picture of Earth's creation:

> When high in ether, with explosion dire,
> From the deep craters of his realms of fire,
> The whirling Sun this ponderous planet hurl'd,
> And gave the astonish'd void another world.
> When from its vaporous air, condensed by cold,
> Descending torrents into oceans roll'd.   (*Ec.Veg.* II 13–18)

Blake produces the Earth more mysteriously, from a 'void immense', but then becomes quite scientific, creating its oceans from vapour-laden winds –

> condensing in torrents
> They fall and fall.   (Plate 4, lines 20–1)

This is an obvious paraphrase of Darwin's last couplet, with *descend* changed to *fall*.

A verbal echo of this kind is a useful pointer to Blake's exploitation of Darwin's cosmogony. As R. E. Simmons suggested, Blake is probably describing 'the origin of the Earth as a chunk of matter thrown off by the Sun'[29] when he tells us that

> Los wept . . . for in anguish
> Urizen was torn from his side.   (Plate 6, lines 2–4)

Subsequently, Urizen is

> By earthquakes riven, belching sullen fires,

while around him

> the eternal Prophet howl'd,
> Beating still on his rivets of iron,   (Plate 10, lines 4, 7–8)

like Darwin's 'Giant-form' chained down by 'steely rivets'. There are many such resemblances, dubious individually but quite impressive en masse.

Blake's use of Darwin's cosmogony and geophysics has been discussed in detail by David Worrall, who concludes that Darwin 'supplies Blake with images of solar and telluric earthquake and volcanic action clear and powerful enough to match his concept of "Prophetic wrath", and he uses them widely in his books of creation, *The Book of Urizen* and *The Book of Los*'.[30] Worrall's discussion is carried further by Nelson Hilton, who comments that in *The Book of Urizen* 'Darwin's cosmological dynamic seems to inform both Urizen . . . and Los'.[31] It is neither appropriate nor practicable for me to go over the detailed arguments of Worrall and Hilton; but the tenor of both their essays is that Blake thoroughly absorbed Darwin's ideas on Earth-creation and archeo-geology, and then incorporated those ideas, in a far-ranging and complex manner, in his own prophetic vision.

D. C. Leonard[32] has suggested that Blake may also be indebted to
Darwin for some of the 'biogenetics' in *The Book of Urizen*. Particularly
relevant are Darwin's lines on the birth of the crocodile:

> So from his shell on Delta's shower-less isle
> Bursts into life the Monster of the Nile;
> First in translucent lymph with cobweb threads
> The Brain's fine floating tissue swells, and spreads;
> Nerve after nerve the glistening spine descends . . .
>
> (*Ec.Veg.* IV 423–7)

Blake has a monster, born apparently in Egypt, with 'a vast Spine
writh'd in torment' and 'nerves of joy' (Plate 10); he refers to a 'spider's
web' and says 'the Web is a Female in embrio' (Plate 25). To me these
parallels are not in themselves convincing, but, knowing that Blake relies
on Darwin's cosmogony, we might well expect some unconscious
memory of Darwin's embryology to filter through.

Darwin's evolutionary ideas may have been discussed in Johnson's
circle in 1793 while *Zoonomia* was in proof and, if so, could be the source
of Blake's rather surprising lines,

> Many forms of fish, bird and beast
> Brought forth an Infant form
> Where was a worm before.   (*Urizen*, Plate 19, 34–6)

The Book of Ahania (1795) carries on *The Book of Urizen*, and tells
how Fuzon, embodiment of passion, rebels against Urizen. The first line
of *Ahania* introduces Fuzon flying 'on a chariot iron-wing'd'; this may
possibly derive from Darwin's 'flying-chariot' borne 'on wide-waving
wings', which has the words 'with iron-lips' immediately below it
(*Ec.Veg.* I 291–2 and note to 281). Be that as it may, Darwin's Upas Tree
is surely reincarnated in Blake's 'accursed Tree of Mystery': as Geoffrey
Grigson remarked, 'one cannot doubt that Blake's tree has grown out of
Darwin's'.[25] The gist of Darwin's long note on Upas is as follows:

> There is a poison-tree in the island of Java, which is said by its
> effluvia to have depopulated the country for 12 or 14 miles round
> the place of its growth [where] the face of the earth is quite barren,
> and rocky, intermixed only with the skeletons of men and animals;
> affording a scene of melancholy beyond what poets have described,
> or painters delineated.   (*Lov.Pl.* III 238 note)

Darwin's verses about the tree, which run to 36 lines, dwell on its 'fell poison' and its multiplicative growth:

> from one root, the envenom'd soil below,
> A thousand vegetative serpents grow. (*Lov.Pl.* III 239–40)

In Blake's poem Fuzon wounds Urizen, but is himself killed; and Urizen carries away his corpse. Then Urizen sits on a 'barren rock', and the Tree starts growing around him:

> the horrid plant bending its boughs
> Grew to roots when it felt the earth,
> And again sprung to many a tree . . .
> Enrooting itself all around,
> An endless labyrinth of woe!
> (Plate 3, lines 65–7; Plate 4, lines 3–4)

When Fuzon's corpse was nailed 'on the topmost stem' of the Tree, 'Effluvia vapor'd above' and 'hover'd thick'

> Till petrific pain scurf'd o'er the Lakes
> As the bones of Man, solid and dark. . . .
> Perching around the hurtling bones,
> Disease on disease, shape on shape
> Winged screaming in blood and torment.
> (Plate 4, lines 20–1, 24–6)

So Blake follows closely in Darwin's footsteps, with the excessive growth of the tree-roots, the 'poisonous effluvia' of the Tree, the barren rocky earth, a bonanza of bones – and 'a scene of melancholy beyond what poets have described' (until Blake showed how to do it).

The Book of Los (1795) is a related creation myth, more humanistic in imagery, and Worrall[30] has pointed out several parallels. Some of these are cosmological, as in *Urizen*; and some are biological, as for example when Blake fixes on the lungs as the crucial step in life: 'The Lungs heave incessant . . . the Lungs heave on the wave . . . in a stifling black fluid, he woke' (Plate 4, lines 54, 60, 62). This seems to hark back to Darwin's note about the human embryo, which lives unbreathing in a dark fluid for months, and then 'must learn to breathe almost within a minute after its birth, or it dies'. Oxygen (air's pure essence) is vital, Darwin says, to all things living

From the crown'd forehead to the prostrate weed,

and the birth trauma of the embryo is captured in the line

The embryon panting in the arms of Death.[33]

Blake then sees the Lungs sprouting 'intricate pipes' that draw in 'the spawn of the waters' and branch out into an 'immense Fibrous Form' (Plate 4, lines 69–70; Plate 5, line 1). Darwin stresses the intricate structure and immense surface area of the lungs (*Ec. Veg.* Add. Note XXXVII); he instructs oxygen (two lines before saving the embryo) to 'unfold the bursting spawn' (*Ec.Veg.* I 408); and he describes many 'itinerant vegetables' that spread over the sea, such as *Fucus natans*, which 'floats on the sea, in very extensive masses' (*Lov.Pl.* IV 368 note). So it seems that Blake's rather peculiar biology in *The Book of Los* may have roots in Darwin.

Blake should have been particularly impressed by Darwin's account of the functioning of the lungs in *Zoonomia* (i 476), for this is one of the first descriptions in English of the oxygenation of blood in the lungs, written at a time when the leading chemists in England, such as Priestley and Keir, did not accept the oxygen theory or nomenclature.[34]

THE FOUR ZOAS

Vala, or the Four Zoas was the first of Blake's long prophetic books: he worked on it for many years, beginning in 1795. Links with Darwin still exist, but some underlying differences also emerge.

Three possible links lurk in the title. One of the four Zoas, Vala or Luvah, represents the element Fire. So it may be, as Erdman has noted,[35] that both *Vala* and *Luvah* are puns on *lava*; and we have already seen how Blake latched on to Darwin's idea of molten lava in the Earth's central fires. Second, each of the Zoas represents one of the four elements, Earth, Air, Fire and Water,[36] like each of the cantos in Darwin's *Economy of Vegetation*. Third, the word *Zoa* (*Zöa*) might have originated directly (though not quite correctly) from the Greek Zôa, 'living things'; but Darwin's recently published *Zöonomia* (for that is how the title was often printed in 1794) seems just as likely a source.

Zoonomia may also have influenced the poem itself, as Hilton has shown.[37] In the chapter 'Of generation' in *Zoonomia*, Darwin not only explained biological evolution (which Blake did not accept) but also

uoted with approval the idea of Hume that generation deserves to
tand above reason, because

> reason can only make a machine . . . but the power of generation
> makes the maker of the machine. . . . The world itself might have
> been generated rather than created. . . . What a magnificent idea of
> the infinite power of THE GREAT ARCHITECT! THE CAUSE OF
> CAUSES! PARENT OF PARENTS! ENS ENTIUM!   (*Zoonomia* i 513)

This idea was attractive to Blake and may have influenced the start of his
Four Zoas:

> Begin with Tharmas, Parent power, dark'ning in the West.
> 'Lost! Lost! Lost! are my Emanations! Enion, O Enion . . .'[38]

The 'Parent power' could derive from Darwin, especially as Blake's two
previous lines have *Generation* and *Regeneration*; but the derivation of
Enion, O Enion' from 'Ens Entium' is, I think, more ingenious than
convincing.
    Another important concept in *The Four Zoas* is the 'Mundane Shell',
and this may have owed its origin to Darwin's picture of 'the Egg of
Night', which floated in Chaos and broke open to disclose 'the cradle of
the world' (*Ec.Veg.* I 413). Also Darwin's belief that plants and the
meanest insects enjoy life is fully endorsed by Blake –

> The roots shoot thick thro' the solid rocks, bursting their way
> They cry out in joys of existence.[39]

Many readers are repelled from *The Four Zoas* by the prevalence of
'howlings, dismay and sharp blightings', but at the very end of the poem
Blake returns to the delicate-nature style of *Thel*:

> The Sun arises from his dewy bed, and the fresh airs
> Play in his smiling beams giving the seeds of life to grow,
> And the fresh Earth beams forth ten thousand thousand springs of
>   life.[40]

These lines sum up the theme of Canto IV of *The Economy of Vegetation*;
and the very last line of Blake's poem,

> The dark Religions are departed and sweet Science reigns,

might serve as a motto for the whole of Darwin's poem. With this line in mind, Hilton suggests that 'Darwin is the English poet contemporary with Blake who most shares Blake's breadth of vision and his aim of ushering in the reign of "sweet science".[37]

These resemblances are worth mentioning not because they imply any direct 'influence' of Darwin, but because they are symptoms of Blake's Darwinization. As Hilton remarks,

> Darwin had done – successfully, in the popular eye – what Blake wanted to do. With a somewhat analogous scope of vision and a somewhat analogous sense of the epistemic break reflected by the 'scientific method', Darwin created a system all the more troubling to Blake's imagination.[37]

Recognizing their differences, Blake tried to keep Darwin at arm's length, as it were, but never quite succeeded.

The real difference between them is best illustrated by their attitudes to technology. Here is Darwin telling us how Venus admired the production of iron by Vulcan:

> With radiant eye She view'd the boiling ore,
> Heard undismay'd the breathing bellows roar,
> Admired their sinewy arms, and shoulders bare,
> And ponderous hammers lifted high in air.   (*Ec.Veg.* I 167–70)

Blake describes the same process in *The Four Zoas*, in even more detail –

> Then were the furnaces unseal'd with spades, and pickaxes
> Roaring let out the fluid: the molten metal ran in channels –

but his attitude is diametrically opposite:

> With trembling horror pale, aghast the Children of Man
> Stood on the infinite Earth and saw these visions in the air.[41]

This difference deserves to be emphasized, because my pursuit of similarities between Blake and Darwin has tended to give the impression that they were more in tune than they really were. Darwin was all in favour of mills driven by the 'Giant-Power' of steam:

> There the vast mill-stone with inebriate whirl
> On trembling floors his forceful fingers twirl,

Whose flinty teeth the golden harvests grind,
Feast without blood! and nourish human-kind.

(*Ec.Veg.* I 275–8)

Spinning-mills were not quite so admirable, but Darwin was scarcely less enthusiastic. The huge Albion Mill in London was, he thought, 'a grand and successful effort of human art',[42] a monument to the great talents of his friends Boulton and Watt; and he was much grieved when the Mill was burnt down during 1791. In contrast, Blake saw the Albion as a dark Satanic Mill that deprived workers of their livelihood and enslaved them in the factory system. Blake's many condemnations of 'Albion' are usually intended for England: but he also sometimes seems to refer obliquely to the mill[43] where 'enslaved the Daughters of Albion weep'. Blake opposed the aims of the Lunar Society; but the suggestion that his *Island in the Moon* (1784?) was a satire on the Society seems to be unfounded.[44]

MILTON AND AFTER

As the years passed, Darwin's influence seems to have waned, but *Milton* shows that Blake still remembered Darwin's cosmogony and biogeny, and the empathy with plants and insects.

Memories of Darwin's words may also possibly have flared up in the most famous lines of *Milton*:

Bring me my Bow of burning gold:
Bring me my Arrows of desire:
Bring me my Spear: O clouds unfold!
Bring me my Chariot of fire. (Preface)

Darwin often tells us about Cupid with his bow, shooting golden arrows of desire, and all Blake's words can easily be found, in relevant contexts. On one occasion Darwin brings on Cupid as

IMMORTAL LOVE, his bow celestial strung;
O'er the wide waste his gaudy wings unfold,
Beam his soft smiles, and wave his curls of gold.

(*Ec.Veg.* I 416–18)

which gives the *bow* and the *gold/unfold* rhyme. On another occasion we see Cupid letting fly:

LOVE culls a flaming shaft. . . .
Loud twangs the steel, the golden arrow flies.

$$(Ec.Veg. \text{ III } 235, 239)$$

It needs only one of these flaming golden arrows of desire to wing his target, Jupiter, who soon 'with kindling rapture burns'. In *The Loves of the Plants* Cupid is kept so hard at work that he might almost be called the leading character, and the plants are shown *burning* with *desire* all too frequently, e.g.,

With vain desires the pensive ALCEA burns.   (*Lov.Pl.* I 69)

Blake's Chariot is an aerial one which emerges from clouds, and recalls Darwin's 'flying-chariot' (*Ec.Veg.* I 292) powered by a 'fire engine' – for that was the usual name for a steam engine in the eighteenth century, and Darwin called his own projected steam-car a 'fiery Chariot'.[45] If this link seems contrived, there are several fiery flying cars in Darwin's poem, e.g.,

On wheels of fire, amid a night of clouds,
Drawn by fierce fiends arose a magic car.   (*Lov.Pl.* III 162–3)

This supplies the *clouds* and a car with wheels of *fire*. We now have all the nouns and adjectives in Blake's lines, except *Spear*, which seems to be from the same armoury as the spears thrown down by the stars in 'The Tyger' – a line already linked with Darwin. These parallels are not in themselves entirely convincing; the sceptic can still mumble about 'commonplaces of period diction'. But the suspicion remains that there may be some real reminiscences here.

In Blake's last and longest poem, *Jerusalem*, I have found nothing beyond repetition of previous parallels such as the Mundane Shell and the poison-tree. But A. S. Roe has drawn attention to 'the unexpected appearance of the Botanic Goddess's train of Nymphs, Gnomes and Sylphs' in one of *Jerusalem*'s 'most significant and terrific parts', the Gates of Golgonooza.[46] Since there are nymphs and sylphs aplenty to be found elsewhere, e.g. in *The Rape of the Lock*, this identification is arguable. Still, I would not disagree with Roe's conclusion that 'Darwin's poem did remain in Blake's memory in a remarkable way'.[46]

A similar view – that Blake had *The Botanic Garden* 'often in mind in later years when he was writing his great symbolic poems'[47] – was expressed by Bernard Blackstone, who pointed to a different type of 'influence'. Darwin treated the Rosicrucian machinery of nymphs and sylphs in a frivolous manner, and thereby destroyed the usefulness of this machinery for a serious poet like Blake, who consequently had to invent a new team of supernatural characters – Urizen, Los and their kin. However, it may be that Blake had an innate urge to create such characters, so Blackstone's thesis cannot be proved.

My own conclusions take a different form. Until recently, I had tended to regard Darwin and Blake as distinctly divided by temperament and belief: Darwin was a rationalist and approved of technology; Blake was a mystic and disapproved of it. But now I am inclined to see these as minor differences among wide areas of agreement, and I am convinced that 'Blake was an appreciative and attentive reader of Darwin', as Hilton stated.[37] In view of Blake's fellow feeling with Darwin, his attentive reading of *The Botanic Garden*, and the accumulated verbal parallels in this chapter, I would conclude that Darwin had an important influence on Blake in his most creative years. Blake was 'an original', and he might have ignored Darwin. But he did not, and as a result his poems are appreciably different to what they would have been if Darwin had never written. Not even the most original mind can selectively censor material lodged deep in the unconscious, and that seems to have been the situation with Blake's remembrance of Darwin.

NOTES

1. D. V. Erdman (ed.), *The Illuminated Blake*, pp. 33–4 and 39.
2. See *Thel*, Pl. 2, line 13, and *Lov.Pl.* I 231; *Thel*, Pl. 1, line 18, and *Lov.Pl.* IV 172. (In the third edition of *Lov.Pl.* 'dewy vale' becomes 'marsh'.)
3. Mona Wilson, *Life of William Blake*, p. 34. See also J. Lindsay, *William Blake*, pp. 52–3, and H. Bloom, *The Visionary Company*, p. 53.
4. G. Keynes, *Blake Studies*, p. 60. For Johnson, see G. P. Tyson, *Joseph Johnson* and C. Tomalin, *The Life and Death of Mary Wollstonecraft*.
5. J. Beer, *Blake's Humanism*, p. 254 and Figs 26–9.
6. For Fuseli, see *The Mind of Henry Fuseli*, ed. E. C. Mason.
7. W. Blake, *Complete Writings*, p. 551.
8. *Letters of Erasmus Darwin*, p. 139. Darwin wrote verses for a print of 'The Nightmare' in 1783.
9. J. Beer, in *William Blake, Essays in Honour of Sir Geoffrey Keynes*, ed. M. D. Paley and M. Phillips, pp. 246–55.
10. K. Raine, *William Blake*, pp. 32, 69. See also *William Blake*, ed. A. H. Rosenfeld, p. 159.
11. A. S. Roe, in *William Blake*, ed. A. H. Rosenfeld, p. 166.
12. D. Worrall, 'William Blake and Erasmus Darwin's *Botanic Garden*', *Bulletin of New York Public Library, 78*, 397–417 (1975).

13. *America*, Pl. 3, lines 15–17; *Ec. Veg.* I 342–3.
14. S. Foster Damon, *A Blake Dictionary*, p. 98.
15. See J. Beer, in *Interpreting Blake*, ed. M. Phillips, pp. 255–7.
16. D. Worrall, *Bull. New York Pub. Lib.*, *78*, 409–10.
17. D. V. Erdman (ed.), *The Illuminated Blake*, p. 107.
18. D. Worrall, *Bull. New York Pub. Lib.*, *78*, 401.
19. *Visions*, Pl. 6, line 23; Pl. 7, line 1.
20. *Lov. Pl.* IV 471–90. See Worrall, *op. cit.*, pp. 401–5, for a much fuller treatment of *Visions of the Daughters of Albion*, on which my account is largely based.
21. See D. G. Gillham, *William Blake*, p. 147, and *Blake's Contrary States* (CUP, 1966), p. 163.
22. *Ec. Veg.* II 561. Cf. also *Ec. Veg.* III 315–16, IV 511–18, E. Young, *Night Thoughts* I 353–7 – and *Twelfth Night* II iv 111–13.
23. From *Lov. Pl.* IV 303–24 and note.
24. *America*, Pl. 8, line 13; *Tem. Nat.* IV 427.
25. See G. Grigson, *The Harp of Aeolus* (Routledge, 1947) pp. 59–60.
26. For the key words in Blake's fourth verse – hammer, chain, furnace, anvil, dread grasp and deadly terrors – see *Ec. Veg.* I 170, 286, I 442; II 71; I 159; I 208 and 216; I 222. See also *Ec. Veg.* II 187–8, *Lov. Pl.* IV 62–4, 161–3.
27. *Ec. Veg.* I 596; see also *Ec. Veg.* IV 373. Note also the 'long beamed spears' in *The Four Zoas*, Night the Ninth, 41.
28. See H. Bloom, *The Visionary Company*, p. 38, and W. Blake, *The Four Zoas*, Night the Fifth, 224.
29. R. E. Simmons, in *Blake's Visionary Forms Dramatic*, ed. D. V. Erdman and J. E. Grant, p. 153.
30. D. Worrall, *Bull. New York Pub. Lib.*, *78*, 411–17 (1975).
31. N. Hilton, 'The Spectre of Darwin', *Blake*, *15*, 36–48 (1981).
32. D. C. Leonard, 'Erasmus Darwin and William Blake', *Eighteenth Century Life*, *4*, 79–81 (1978). See also S. F. Damon, *Blake Dictionary*, p. 452.
33. Quotations are from *Ec. Veg.* I 399–410 and note.
34. Darwin probably drew on Girtanner's description, translated by Beddoes in his *Observations on . . . Calculus* (Murray, 1793) pp. 202–12.
35. See D. V. Erdman, *Blake*, p. 333, and *Ec. Veg.* Note VI, 'Central fires'.
36. See W. Blake, *Complete Poems*, ed. A. Ostriker, p. 1048.
37. N. Hilton, *Blake*, *15*, 36–8 (1981).
38. *The Four Zoas*, Night the First, 24–5.
39. *Ibid.*, Night the Ninth, 604–5.
40. *Ibid.*, Night the Ninth, 846–8
41. *Ibid.*, Night the Second, 117–18, 121–2.
42. *Letters of Erasmus Darwin*, p. 211. For the story of Albion Mill, see L. T. C. Rolt, *James Watt* (Batsford, 1962) pp. 97–9.
43. E.g. *Jerusalem*, Pl. 32 [46], lines 4–9. See D. V. Erdman, *Blake*, p. 332, and B. Blackstone, *English Blake*, p. 19.
44. See D. V. Erdman, *Blake*, pp. 92–107.
45. *Letters of Erasmus Darwin*, p. 27.
46. A. S. Roe, in *William Blake*, ed. A. H. Rosenfeld, p. 168.
47. B. Blackstone, *English Blake*, p. 20.

REFERENCES

John Beer, *Blake's Humanism* (Manchester Univ. Pr., 1968).

Bernard Blackstone, *English Blake* (CUP, 1949).

William Blake, *Complete Poems*, ed. Alicia Ostriker (Penguin, 1977).

William Blake, *Complete Writings*, ed. Geoffrey Keynes (OUP, 1979).

Blake, an Illustrated Quarterly, vols 1–18 (1966–84).

Harold Bloom, *The Visionary Company* (Cornell Univ. Pr., Ithaca, New York, 1971).

S. Foster Damon, *A Blake Dictionary* (Thames and Hudson, 1973).

D. V. Erdman, *Blake: Prophet against Empire*, 2nd edn (Princeton Univ. Pr., Princeton, New Jersey, 1969).

D. V. Erdman and J. E. Grant (eds), *Blake's Visionary Forms Dramatic* (Princeton Univ. Pr., Princeton, New Jersey, 1970).

D. V. Erdman (ed.), *The Illuminated Blake* (OUP 1975).

D. G. Gillham, *William Blake* (CUP, 1973).

Nelson Hilton, 'The Spectre of Darwin', *Blake*, *15*, 36–48 (1981).

Geoffrey Keynes, *Blake Studies*, 2nd edn (OUP, 1971).

Zachary Leader, *Reading Blake's Songs* (Routledge, 1981).

Jack Lindsay, *William Blake: his Life and Work* (Constable, 1978).

Eudo C. Mason (ed.), *The Mind of Henry Fuseli* (Routledge, 1951).

M. D. Paley and M. Phillips (eds), *William Blake, Essays in Honour of Sir Geoffrey Keynes* (Clarendon Press, Oxford, 1973).

M. Phillips (ed.), *Interpreting Blake* (CUP, 1978).

Kathleen Raine, *William Blake* (Thames and Hudson, 1970).

A. H. Rosenfeld (ed.), *William Blake: Essays for S. Foster Damon* (Brown Univ. Pr., Providence, R.I., 1969).

Claire Tomalin, *The Life and Death of Mary Wollstonecraft* (Weidenfeld and Nicolson, 1974).

Gerald P. Tyson, *Joseph Johnson: a Liberal Publisher* (Univ. of Iowa Pr., Iowa City, 1979).

Mona Wilson, *The Life of William Blake* (1927) (Hart-Davis, 1948).

David Worrall, 'William Blake and Erasmus Darwin's *Botanic Garden*', *Bulletin of New York Public Library*, *78*, 397–417 (1975).

4 Wordsworth

The sounding cataract
Haunted me like a passion.
W. Wordsworth, *Tintern Abbey*

Confounding coincidences as well as sounding cataracts begin to haunt us on looking at the life of William Wordsworth (Fig. 3), born in 1770 at Cockermouth on the fringes of the Lake District. He had the right surname for a poet, and lived his early years in a house beside the Cumbrian river Derwent; Darwin lived in a house beside the Derbyshire river Derwent, and also had the 'right' surname, because it derived from the river name. These coincidences are most improbable; but they happened.

Wordsworth grew up in the Lake District, and soon began to breathe the spirit of mountains, lakes and rivers:

> From Nature and her overflowing soul
> I had received so much, that all my thoughts
> Were steep'd in feeling,

as he saw it in Book II of *The Prelude*. The experience was overwhelming for him –

> Thence did I drink the visionary power

– and the events of his life sometimes seem almost an irrelevance, as random as the skips of a stone sent skimming across the surface of a lake and always destined to become one with Nature.

The demon of improbability pops up again in October 1787, when Wordsworth followed in Darwin's footsteps by entering St John's College, Cambridge. Hard on the heels of this coincidence comes another: one of the fifty-eight undergraduates of his year at St John's was Darwin's stepson Sacheverel Pole. They had the same tutor, and it is quite probable that they knew each other.

Cambridge was too urban and too flat to impress Wordsworth; but he lasted out four years, and duly graduated BA in 1791. He spent 1792 in France, where he caught the revolutionary fever, met that deep-dyed Jacobin, James Watt junior, and fell in love with Annette Vallon, who bore him a child in December 1792. By then he was back in England, and he passed the first half of 1793 in London[1] among the group of dissenters and radicals associated with Joseph Johnson, who had just published Mary Wollstonecraft's *Rights of Woman* and Darwin's complete *Botanic Garden*. The unknown Wordsworth had the privilege of being added to the list in February 1793, when Johnson published his first poems, *An Evening Walk* and *Descriptive Sketches*. The same month saw the outbreak of war with France, which perplexed Wordsworth, and the publication of Godwin's *Political Justice*. 'No work in our time gave such a blow to the philosophical mind of the country', Hazlitt justly said, also remarking that Wordsworth was among those influenced.[2]

In 1795 Wordsworth received a modest legacy, and thereafter, with help from friends, he was able to devote himself to poetry. In 1797 he and his sister Dorothy went to live at Alfoxden in Somerset, near Coleridge at Nether Stowey. Wordsworth and Coleridge reacted on each other to generate a marvellously creative year of poetry, which culminated in the publication of *Lyrical Ballads* in the autumn of 1798. Though the finest and longest ballad was Coleridge's *Ancient Mariner*, the epoch-making feature of the book was the idea of simplicity and truth to nature expressed by Wordsworth in the 'Advertisement' and in the preface to the second edition: as Hazlitt put it, 'We begin *de novo*, on a *tabula rasa* of poetry'.[3] The elegant rhyming couplets that Darwin turned out so skilfully were left as obsolete jetsam on the shores of the dying century – to be admired at times by beachcombing critics, but never again to sail the seven seas in glory.

In 1799 Wordsworth and Dorothy settled at Dove Cottage, Grasmere, and in 1802 Wordsworth married Mary Hutchinson. Nearly all his best poems were written between 1797 and 1807: *The Prelude* was begun in 1798 and completed at full length by 1805; *Tintern Abbey* was written in 1798, the 'Lucy' poems in 1799 and the Ode on 'Intimations of Immortality' was begun in 1802.

In 1813 the three Wordsworths moved to Rydal Mount, after William's appointment as Stamp-Distributor for Westmorland. Their subsequent life, described in Mary Moorman's excellent biography, was uneventful. Wordsworth became Poet Laureate in 1843 and died in 1850, at the age of eighty.

THE ATTRACTION OF DARWIN

Wordsworth was at Cambridge and just nineteen when *The Loves of the Plants* was published in 1789. The poem was based on the idea that plants can feel, plus the certain knowledge that most of them reproduce sexually through the pistils and stamens of their flowers – their most sensitive parts. The idea that plants feel was regarded as mere fiction by the hard-boiled, though Darwin stoutly defended his view five years later, in *Zoonomia*. We need not consider his defence now, because Wordsworth was not among the doubters. Darwin was a respected man of science, so why should the young Wordsworth cavil? He took over Darwin's idea and made it an essential part of his basic belief in Nature:

> 'Tis my faith that every flower
> Enjoys the air it breathes.[4]

With *The Loves of the Plants* Darwin also succeeded in winning warm applause from the literary world for a long poem largely devoted to detailed descriptions of Nature, and particularly flowers. This success gave Wordsworth the inner confidence that he could do the same; though his style was to be different, his first fine careless confidence endured, and served as the backbone of his whole career. But Wordsworth never followed Darwin into the sex life of plants. Presumably he felt that Darwin's 'chronicle of the lustful flowers' was sexploitation.

Wordsworth's first poem of any consequence was *An Evening Walk*, a narrative nature-poem in rhyming couplets, begun in 1787, probably finished in 1789, and published in 1793. The style is similar to Darwin's and, as Helen Darbishire remarked, Wordsworth 'is balancing his lines in the Darwinian manner with ornamental epithets'.[5] There is one curious parallel: Darwin has 'Eliza' struggling over 'Minden's plain' with 'her dear babes' trying to find her soldier husband as he fought in the battle; Wordsworth has a poor widow struggling wearily with 'her babes' and wishing for help from her soldier 'asleep on Minden's charnel plain'.[6] Even more curiously, this line is singled out by Wordsworth for an *erratum* note, asking for 'Minden's charnel plain' to be changed to 'Bunker's charnel hill'. But the long arm of coincidence is snapping its fingers at us again: the amendment was really made because 'Minden's plain' appears in John Langhorne's *Country Justice*, as noted by a reviewer. So this apparent link with Darwin is illusory.[7]

After this false start, it is a relief to find an apparently genuine echo of Darwin at the start of Wordsworth's next long poem, the 800-line

Fig. 1   Erasmus Darwin, from the portrait by Joseph Wright of
Derby, painted in 1770 when Darwin was thirty-eight.
The portrait was considered an excellent likeness.

Fig. 2 William Blake (1757–1827), as painted by Thomas Phillips in 1807.

Fig. 3 William Wordsworth (1770 – 1850), as painted by William Shuter in 1798.

Fig. 4 S. T. Coleridge (1772–1834), as painted by Peter Vandyke in 1795.

Fig. 5 George Crabbe (1754–1832), from an engraving of the painting by Thomas Phillips.

Fig. 6   The title-page of *The Book of Thel* (1789) by William
Blake, with a youth leaping from the flower on the right
to seize a girl rising from the flower in the centre.

Meadia.

Fig. 7 *Meadia,* from the first
edition of *The Loves of the
Plants* (1789).

Fig. 8 From Plate 5 of *The Book of Thel,* showing a plant like
Meadia on the right and Thel bowed over 'the matron
Clay'.

Fig. 9   *Dionaea muscipula,* from *The Loves of the Plants,* with its eyelid-like traps and eyelash-like spines.

Fig. 10   From Plate iii of Blake's *Visions of the Daughters of Albion* (1793), with a marigold emitting sparks of light and a human form rising from the flower.

Fig. 11   Henry Fuseli's painting 'The Nightmare' (1781), which impressed both Darwin and Coleridge.

Fig. 12 Percy Bysshe Shelley (1792 – 1822), as painted by Amelia Curran in 1819.

Fig. 13 John Keats (1795–1821), from a painting by W. Hilton after Joseph Severn.

Fig. 14 Lord Byron (1788–1824), as painted by Richard Westall in 1813.

Fig. 15 Mary Shelley (1797–1851), from a miniature by Reginald Eastman.

(a) Cupid and Psyche in procession to Hymen's bower; from Bryant's *New System* (1774) ii 392.

(b) Cupid and Psyche embracing; from Spence's *Polymetis* (1774), p. 82.

Fig. 16   Cupid and Psyche in relation to Keats's *Ode to Psyche*.

Descriptive Sketches (written 1791–2, published 1793). In line 33 Wordsworth refers to Memnon's lyre and adds a footnote:

> The lyre of Memnon is reported to have emitted melancholy or cheerful tones, as it was touched by the sun's evening or morning rays.

Darwin's long note on Memnon's lyre in *The Economy of Vegetation* includes the following:

> The statue of Memnon . . . is said for many centuries to have saluted the rising sun with cheerful tones, and the setting sun with melancholy ones.   (Note VIII)

Wordsworth may have finished *Descriptive Sketches* before he saw *The Economy of Vegetation*, the footnote being a late addition.

The loudest of the possible echoes of Darwin in *Descriptive Sketches* occurs when the 'Grison gypsey' hears at midnight

> The death-dog howling loud and long

at midnight, which may emanate from

> loud and long the dog of midnight howls,

a stock-Gothic image from *The Loves of the Plants*[8] – already parodied by Coleridge. In the next line of his poem Darwin introduces 'two imps obscene', who 'with hideous laugh' and 'mock devotion' bow 'to the cross'. This pre-empts Wordsworth's line 70,

> The cross with hideous laughter Demons mock.

Relegating some further parallels to a note,[9] we can turn instead to an example of similar phrasing, in Wordsworth's line 569,

> Dear and more dear the lessening circle grows,

which follows a form common in Darwin's verse:

> Bright and more bright the blazing deluge flows . . .
> Close and more close their writhing limbs surround . . .
> Near and more near your beamy cars approach.[10]

Stylistically too, we come 'near and more near' to Darwin as Wordsworth's poem clanks along clothed in the heavy chains of the heroic couplet: like Darwin, he sometimes has to compress events incongruously or resort to inept abstractions. In a competition for the worst couplet, what about this victim of plague:

> Sooths with soft kiss, with tender accents charms,
> And clasps the bright Infection in his arms.

Or these victims of war:

> Where bleeding Sidney from the cup retir'd
> And glad Dundee in 'faint huzzas' expir'd.

The first is by Darwin, the second by Wordsworth,[11] and there is not much to choose between them.

When Wordsworth read *The Economy of Vegetation*, he found it even more appealing than *The Loves of the Plants*, because it was a more serious and continuous celebration of Nature, expressed through each of the four Elements – Fire, Earth, Water and Air being the subjects of the four Cantos. Presumably Canto II was particularly attractive to Wordsworth because its subject was Earth, mainly in the form of rocks, minerals and mountains. For example, Darwin explains how limestone rocks were formed:

> The lime-stone rocks have had their origin from shells formed beneath the sea, the softer strata gradually dissolving and filling up the interstices of the harder ones; afterwards, when these accumulations of shells were elevated above the waters, the upper strata became dissolved by the actions of the air and dews, and filled up the interstices beneath, producing solid rocks of different kinds from the coarse lime-stones to the finest marbles.   (*Ec.Veg.* II 93, note)

Darwin believed the shells enjoyed life while alive, and he therefore came to call the mountains 'mighty monuments of past delight' in *Phytologia* a few years later. Wordsworth never carried mountain-animism so far, though he went beyond Darwin in crediting mountains with healing powers and in declaring they were to him

> An appetite; a feeling and a love.

But in 1792–3 Wordsworth's appetite for mountains was temporarily eclipsed by his enthusiasm for the French Revolution –

> Bliss was it in that dawn to be alive,
> But to be young was very heaven! (*Prelude* XI 108–9)

He was delighted to find the same enthusiasm in *The Economy of Vegetation*, in the long invocation to 'the Warrior, Liberty' asleep in France, 'unconscious of his chains' until,

> Touch'd by the patriot flame, he rent amazed
> The flimsy bonds, and round and round him gazed. (II 385–6)

These lines fairly reflect Darwin's attitude: he had both feet off the ground, as his letters show. To James Watt on 19 January 1790 he wrote: 'Do you not congratulate your grand-children on the dawn of universal liberty? I feel myself becoming all french both in chemistry and politics.'[12] This enthusiasm may have influenced Watt's son James, then twenty: he soon turned into an ardent Jacobin, and in 1792 became deeply involved with the revolutionary leaders – so much so that he prevented a duel between Danton and Robespierre. Darwin's enthusiasm did not wear off, for he wrote to Richard Dixon on 25 October 1792: 'The success of the French against a confederacy of kings gives me great pleasure, and I hope they will preserve their liberty, and spread the holy flame of freedom over Europe.'[13] Wordsworth would have known of Darwin's attitude from the young Watt, from *The Botanic Garden* and from Joseph Johnson.

So in 1793 Wordsworth was a fervent admirer of Darwin. As Emile Legouis put it in *The Early Life of William Wordsworth* (p. 138): 'Wordsworth had his period of infatuation for Darwin . . . he was among those who, for some years, extolled *The Botanic Garden* to the skies.' And H. W. Garrod wrote: 'Wordsworth's poetic theory and practice in this period are derived from Erasmus Darwin. . . . It is, I think, more than likely that . . . he was in part responsible for the revolutionary and free-thinking turn given to Wordsworth's mind in 1791 and the following years.'[14]

Surprisingly, Darwin returned the compliment. He read and admired *Descriptive Sketches*, and was apparently pleased to find Wordsworth supporting his view that images of material things were the very essence of poetry. Christopher Wordsworth in his diary for 5 November 1793 reports his brother's high repute with Darwin.[15]

Wordsworth also admired the energy and range of Darwin's specula
tions in *The Botanic Garden*, as Francis Klingender pointed out: 'How
deeply Wordsworth himself was stirred by the profound substance if not
by the form of Darwin's message is shown by the following lines which
he wrote in 1794.'[16] In these lines, intended as an addition to *An Evening
Walk*, Wordsworth seems to have Darwin in mind when he praises

> those to whom the harmonious doors
> Of Science have unbarred celestial stores,
> To whom a burning energy has given
> That other eye which darts thro' earth and heaven,
> Roams through all space and [gazing?] unconfined,
> Explores the illimitable tracts of mind,
> And piercing the profound of time can see
> Whatever man has been and man can be.[17]

If he is writing about Darwin, the last three lines refer to *Zoonomia*, just
published – and highly valued by Wordsworth and Coleridge, as we shall
see.

Fifty years afterwards, Wordsworth himself admitted that in the early
1790s 'my taste and natural tendencies were under an injurious influence
from the dazzling manner of Darwin'.[18]

THE REPULSION FROM DARWIN'S STYLE

But it was not long before Wordsworth recognized that Darwin's
dazzling manner was injurious, and he began to react against it. That
reaction led him to chart for English poetry a new course that was to last
for more than a hundred years. But without the forceful example of
Darwin before him, would he have reacted so swiftly and so strongly? I
doubt it; and I would agree with Arthur Beatty's judgment[19] that we
have to thank Darwin for demonstrating so vividly that the couplet-
form was a dead end, and forcing Wordsworth to seek a new road while
he was still young and flexible enough to change course.

Wordsworth began his escape from the straitjacket of Darwinian
verse in the 'Salisbury Plain' poems of 1793–4. Here he has moved away
from rhyming couplets to the Spenserian stanza (which is not an
altogether happy choice). But his phraseology still has muted hints of
Darwin. For example, Wordsworth's lines 103–4,

No moon to open the black clouds and stream
From narrow gulph profound one friendly beam,

may owe something to *The Loves of the Plants:*

> While from above descends in milky streams
> One scanty pencil of illusive beams,
> Suspended crags, and gaping gulphs illumes . . .[20]

Wordsworth particularly liked Darwin's account of Cambyses's army being overwhelmed by sand. These soldiers, Darwin tells us,

> To Demon-Gods their knees unhallow'd bend,

and then, as they flee,

> Pierce the deaf tempest with lamenting cries.
> *(Ec.Veg.* II 480, 483)

Echoes of these cries and Demon-Gods may be sounding in Wordsworth's lines 424–7,

> from huge wickers paled with circling fire
> No longer horrid shrieks and dying cries
> To ears of Demon-Gods in peals aspire,
> To Demon-Gods a human sacrifice.

Wickers, shrieks and human sacrifice also figure in Darwin's startling lines,

> Heard dying babes in wicker prisons wail,
> And shrieks of matrons thrill the affrighted Gale.
> *(Lov.Pl.* III 105–6)

Wordsworth ends his poem with strong praise of Truth and Reason, and fierce invective against Oppressors, Error and Superstition –

> Heroes of Truth, pursue your march, uptear
> Th' Oppressor's dungeon from its deepest base . . .
> . . . pursue your toils, till not a trace
> Be left on earth of Superstition's reign.

This is rather like Darwin's picture of the triumph of Liberty in the American and French Revolutions,

> Lo! Truth and Virtue range their radiant bands;
> Sad Superstition wails her empire torn.[21]

By the time he began his association with Coleridge in 1797, Wordsworth was intellectually free of Darwin's influence on his style. He went too far in the opposite direction with his many verses of too-childish simplicity, but he directed poets along the new route with a fine clarity.

The clearest signpost to the new route is the Advertisement to the first edition of *Lyrical Ballads* (1798), which is Wordsworth's reply to Darwin's discourse on the nature of poetry in the first Interlude of *The Loves of the Plants*. Wordsworth shoots straight at Darwin when he refers to the 'gaudiness and inane phraseology of many modern writers', and he may have been thinking of Darwin's clumsy couplet about the sunflower, whose every floret has 'five males surrounding one female':

> Marshall'd in *fives* each gaudy band proceeds,
> Each gaudy band a plumed Lady leads.   (*Lov.Pl.* I 223–4)

True poetry, says Wordsworth in the preface to the second edition of *Lyrical Ballads*, should be the 'real language of men in a state of vivid sensation' – not contrived couplets. 'For all good poetry is the spontaneous overflow of powerful feelings' – and not carefully manufactured phrases from the head rather than the heart. 'Personifications of abstract ideas rarely occur in these volumes; and are utterly rejected, as an ordinary device to elevate the style' – a device that Darwin exploited to the full. 'Poetry takes its origin from emotion recollected in tranquillity' – not from neutral and factual materials worked up into a lather by a mechanical stirrer. 'Poetry is the breath and finer spirit of all knowledge; it is the impassioned expression which is in the countenance of all Science'; here, for once, Darwin might have agreed. In *The Botanic Garden* the sciences most discussed are botany, geology and chemistry. So there is little doubt where Wordsworth is aiming when he tells us: 'The remotest discoveries of the Chemist, the Botanist, or the Mineralogist, will be as proper objects of the Poet's art as any upon which it can be employed, if the time should ever come when these things shall be familiar to us.' The note of disapproval here would have puzzled Darwin, for he was trying to make 'these things familiar to us'. The quotations I have given show how Wordsworth kept Darwin's style constantly in mind as the very antithesis of his own ideals.

The antithesis was well appreciated at the time. In reviewing *Lyrical Ballads* in 1799, the *British Critic* said, 'We infinitely prefer the simplicity, even of the most unadorned tale in this volume, to all the meretricious frippery of the *Darwinian* taste.' In 1818 the *Edinburgh Magazine* commented that 'in matter, and in manner, the Lake and Darwinian schools of poetry are the very antipodes of each other – hostile in all their doctrines, and opposite in every characteristic'.[22]

ZOONOMIA AND LYRICAL BALLADS

Wordsworth had thrown off Darwin's 'dazzling manner' by 1798, but he was about to suffer a serious infection from that cornucopia of diseases, *Zoonomia*. Wordsworth probably read Volume 1 on publication in 1794, and may have read Volume 2 (1796). Be that as it may, he was certainly very keen to see the book again early in 1798: 'I write merely to request (which I have very particular reasons for doing) that you would contrive to send me Dr Darwin's Zoonomia *by the first carrier*.'[23] This was in a letter to Joseph Cottle, written from Alfoxden, probably on 28 February. Wordsworth received the two volumes about 13 March and kept them for two months. He wrote a number of the *Lyrical Ballads* during this time.

Wordsworth's most obvious borrowing from *Zoonomia* concerns a striking case of insanity recorded by Darwin. 'A young farmer in Warwickshire, finding his hedges broken, and the sticks carried away during a frosty season, determined to watch for the thief.' After he had lain 'many cold hours under a hay-stack', he saw an old woman collect a bundle of sticks. Springing out, he seized her. After some altercation, she cursed the shivering farmer, 'Heaven grant, that thou never mayest know again the blessing to be warm.' All the next day he complained of cold and took to his bed covered with many blankets, 'and from this one insane idea he kept his bed above twenty years for fear of the cold air, till at length he died' (*Zoonomia* ii 359).

Wordsworth versifies this story[24] as 'Goody Blake and Harry Gill', written in the spring of 1798. He introduces the chilly Harry in the much-parodied lines:

> Oh! what's the matter? what's the matter?
> What is't that ails young Harry Gill?

> That evermore his teeth they chatter,
> Chatter, chatter, chatter still!

– despite wearing a wealth of waistcoats of 'duffle grey and flannel fine', a blanket and at least nine topcoats. Wordsworth tells us how an old dame, Goody Blake, suffering badly from the winter cold, gathered sticks from Harry's hedge to make a fire. Waiting behind a rick of barley in bitter cold, Harry watched her as she took the wood, and sprang out on her: 'fiercely by the arm he shook her'. She cursed him, 'O may he never more be warm'; and he never was, as the opening lines show. This deliberate plundering of one of Darwin's stories is unusual: a semi-conscious or unconscious borrowing is the usual mode.

Although 'Goody Blake and Harry Gill' is not highly regarded today, F. W. Bateson liked it[25] – he said the poem 'is *alive* and it *rings true*' – and pointed out that it was rated one of the best of the *Lyrical Ballads* by many readers, including George Crabbe, C. J. Fox, Hannah More, and the compiler of *Beauties of British Poetry* (1801).

The story of 'Goody Blake' comes from the chapter in *Zoonomia* on 'diseases of increased volition', which records many other examples of patients 'at the end of their tether'. Several of the *Lyrical Ballads* are medical case-histories in Zoonomian vein, as James Averill has pointed out.[26] On the page after the 'Goody Blake' story, Darwin discusses post-natal depression and suggests that 'the child should be brought frequently to the mother, and applied to her breast, if she will suffer it . . . as by a few trials it frequently excites the storge, or maternal affection' (ii 360). This idea seems to have found its way into Wordsworth's 'Mad Mother', for she is eased by nursing her child:

> Suck, little babe, oh suck again!
> It cools my blood; it cools my brain;
> Thy lips I feel them, baby! they
> Draw from my heart the pain away.   (31–4)

At the end of the same page of *Zoonomia* we read: 'When a person becomes insane, who has a family of small children to solicit his attention, the prognostic is very unfavourable' (ii 360). There is a parallel here, as Averill noted, with 'The Last of the Flock', where the shepherd is gradually driven mad until

> God cursed me in my sore distress;

I prayed, yet every day I thought
I loved my children less.   (86–8)

'The Idiot Boy' and 'The Forsaken Indian Woman' also portray people
in desperate psychological states, as in Darwin's case histories.

   In 'The Thorn', begun a week after he received *Zoonomia*, Wordsworth seems to have drawn on two of Darwin's books. The thorn,
Wordsworth tells us, stands alone and,

   Like rock or stone, it is o'ergrown
   With lichens to the very top.   (12–13)

This recalls Darwin's picture in *The Loves of the Plants* of the upper
slopes of Snowdon, where

   Lichen climbs the topmost stone,   (I 349)

and Wordsworth comes even closer in his next verse, where he says the
thorn stands 'high on a mountain's highest ridge', near 'the mountain
path' (Darwin has 'the steepy path'). Both poets harp on the weather.
Darwin tells us that

   round the rifted rocks hoarse whirlwinds breathe,

while the clouds sail beneath, 'dark with thunder'. Wordsworth picks up
the whirlwind in the repeated phrase

   the whirlwind's on the hill,

and his narrator battles through 'storm and rain' on the mountain.
   Near the thorn is a heap of coloured moss, 'green, red and pearly
white'. This variegation of colour might derive from Darwin's note that
lichen is the first plant 'that vegetates on naked rocks, covering them
with a kind of tapestry'. When the lichen dies, 'earth enough is left for
other mosses to root themselves' (and he points out that this may be how
'the whole earth has been gradually covered with vegetation'). Darwin
was keen on moss: in *The Loves of the Plants* the words *moss* or *mossy*
appear 12 times; in 'The Thorn' Wordsworth is even more moss-
encrusted – the words occur 12 times in its 253 lines.
   So much for the scenery in 'The Thorn': the human interest centres

obsessively on 'a woman in a scarlet cloak' who sits beside the thorn. Many years before, she was deserted by her lover:

> She was with child, and she was mad.   (139)

People thought she had buried her child under the mossy heap. 'Her name is Martha Ray'. The relevant section in *Zoonomia* is that on *Erotomania*, or sentimental love, six pages after the 'Goody Blake' story. 'When a lover has previously been much encouraged, and at length meets with neglect or disdain', Darwin tells us, the effects may be irremediable:

> the maniacal idea is so painful as not to be for a moment relievable by the exertions of reverie, but is instantly followed by furious or melancholy insanity; and suicide, or revenge, have frequently been the consequence. As was lately exemplified in Mr Hackman, who shot Miss Ray in the lobby of the playhouse.   (*Zoonomia* ii 365)

The murder of Martha Ray in 1779 is a celebrated *crime passionel* – details may be found in the *Dictionary of National Biography* under 'Hackman'. So Darwin's reference to the crime is no surprise. What *is* surprising is that Wordsworth should have appropriated the name for a fictional character suspected of child-murder, when he knew that his friend Basil Montagu was the son of the real Martha Ray. This curious love-and-murder link between Darwin and Wordsworth was pointed out by Averill.[27]

There are other verbal parallels, but I shall only quote one explicitly. Darwin's Lichen 'dwells alone' on the mountain by day and by night –

> Bright shine the stars unnumber'd o'er her head.
>
>   (*Lov.Pl.* I 287)

Wordsworth's Martha sits alone

>   on the mountain high
> By day, and in the silent night,
> When all the stars shone clear and bright.   (248–50)

The other parallels are merely two-word coincidences.[28]

I have already suggested that the success of Darwin's long poem about Nature gave Wordsworth the confidence to claim that Nature can 'feed the mind'. In *Lyrical Ballads* this theme is most effectively drummed home in 'Expostulation and Reply', where we are told to learn from Nature and not from books. This poem is often said to be influenced by the theory of association in Hartley's *Observations on Man*; but if any book is cited, *Zoonomia* has the best claim because Association is one of Darwin's four divisions of the sensorium and he offers 124 pages on 'Diseases of Association' – and also because the poem was probably written while Wordsworth had *Zoonomia* with him. 'Expostulation and Reply' was rightly placed as the first poem in later editions of *Lyrical Ballads*.

The second poem in later editions was 'The Tables Turned', with a similar message to 'quit your books' and 'let Nature be your teacher'. Darwin had, in a sense, already taken this advice ten years before: the word *book* does not appear in the 4368 lines of *The Botanic Garden*; instead he tries to teach us all about Nature. But Wordsworth may have been reacting against Darwin later in the poem:

> Sweet is the lore which Nature brings;
>   Our meddling intellect
> Misshapes the beauteous forms of things –
>   We murder to dissect.   (25–8)

Darwin's continuing emphasis on the Linnaean classification of plants and his analytical 'dissection' of other natural phenomena may perhaps have prompted this rebuke.

Wordsworth had no objection to Darwin's belief that plants have feelings, and he deftly celebrates the idea in 'Lines Written in Early Spring' – the poem where every flower 'enjoys the air it breathes'. Darwin's ideas, first expressed in *The Loves of the Plants*, are argued out in Chapter 13 of *Zoonomia*, entitled 'Of Vegetable Animation'. Darwin stresses the individuality of buds:

> The individuals of the vegetable world may be considered as inferior or less perfect animals; a tree is a congeries of many living buds, and in this respect resembles the branches of coralline, which are a congeries of a multitude of animals.   (*Zoonomia* i 102)

After reviewing the evidence he concludes

> that the buds of deciduous trees are so many annual plants; that the bark is a contexture of the roots of each individual bud; and that the

internal wood is of no other use but to support them in the air, and
that thus they resemble the animal world in their individuality.

(*Zoonomia* i 102–3)

Darwin's emphasis on buds finds a place in the 'Lines Written in Early
Spring':

> The budding twigs spread out their fan,
>   To catch the breezy air;
> And I must think, do all I can,
>   That there was pleasure there.   (17–20)

Darwin goes on the expound his view that plants enjoy 'the passion of
love' and have senses to distinguish variations of heat, moisture, light
and touch. So they can be said to have perceptions and consequently
may 'possess ideas' of the 'external world'. Or, as Wordsworth wrote in a
fragment about sympathy with all nature,

> In all forms of things
> There is a mind.   (*Poetical Works* v 340)

Wordsworth's 'Lines' also have some verbal parallels with *The Botanic
Garden* which I shall not pursue.[29]

The first edition of *Lyrical Ballads* ends with the 'Lines written a few
miles above Tintern Abbey', a more mature poem with deeper
reflections from *Zoonomia*. To begin with, the epigraph for *Zoonomia*,
from Book VI of the *Aeneid*, is thus translated by Darwin:

> Earth, on whose lap a thousand nations tread,
> And Ocean, brooding his prolific bed,
> Night's changeful orb, blue pole, and silvery zones,
> Where other worlds encircle other suns,
> One Mind inhabits, one diffusive Soul
> Wields the large limbs, and mingles with the whole.

As Averill has pointed out,[26] this is similar in spirit and cadence to
Wordsworth having felt

> a sense sublime
> Of something far more deeply interfused,
> Whose dwelling is the light of setting suns,

And the round ocean, and the living air,
And the blue sky, and in the mind of man,
A motion and a spirit, that impels
All thinking things, all objects of all thought,
And rolls through all things.   (*Tintern Abbey*, 96–103)

It seems to me, however, that this is only the beginning of Darwin's influence on the poem. It is probably from *Zoonomia* that Wordsworth took his central idea of uniting animal pleasure in nature (the 'glad animal movements') with tranquil recollection of images of natural objects, to create that 'sense sublime'. Among Darwin's 'diseases of volition', two pages after the 'Goody Blake' story, is *studium inane* or reverie, and he refers his readers to Chapter 19 of Volume 1, 'Of Reverie', which begins as follows:

> When we are employed with great sensation of pleasure, or with great efforts of volition, in the pursuit of some interesting train of ideas, we cease to be conscious of our existence, are inattentive to time and place, and do not distinguish this train of sensitive and voluntary ideas from the irritative ones excited by the presence of external objects, though our organs of sense are surrounded with their accustomed stimuli, till at length this interesting train of ideas becomes exhausted, or the appulses of external objects are applied with unusual violence, and we return with surprise, or with regret, into the common track of life. This is termed reverie or studium.
> (*Zoonomia* i 244)

(In reading this, it is well to remember the fourfold division of all bodily actions into irritation, sensation, association and volition.) Wordsworth was much taken by the idea of Reverie, so obviously linked with poetic inspiration: he suggested that the *Ancient Mariner* should be subtitled 'A Poet's Reverie'; and one of his own poems is called 'The Reverie of Poor Susan'.

Tintern Abbey is really one long reverie, beginning at line 22,

These beauteous forms
Through a long absence, have not been to me
As is a landscape to a blind man's eye.

This curious negative image may derive from Darwin's remark in *Zoonomia*, in the section on 'Motions of the Retina' (i 23) that it is rare

for the organ of vision to be entirely destroyed; but he had met two blind
men in this condition, and they never dreamt of visible objects.
Wordsworth is only saying circuitously that he *has* remembered the
'beauteous forms', and he goes on to declare that to them he has owed

> sensations sweet,
> Felt in the blood, and felt along the heart.

These lines seem to be inspired by a remark on the same page of
Zoonomia, that 'our ideas are animal motions of the organ of sense'.
Wordsworth seizes on this mechanistic notion and transmutes it into his
own imagery, creating an organic vision by linking images of nature
indissolubly with mental insights, where 'the burthen of the mystery' of
the world is lightened

> Until, the breath of this corporeal frame
> And even the motion of our human blood
> Almost suspended, we are laid asleep
> In body, and become a living soul.   (43–6)

The visual emphasis in *Tintern Abbey* continues, and it is with 'an eye
made quiet by the power of harmony' that 'we see into the life of things'.
Wordsworth contrasts this with the 'glad animal movements' of his
boyish days, a phrase reminiscent of Darwin's conclusion to his remarks
about the retina:

> If our recollection or imagination be not a repetition of animal
> movements, I ask, in my turn, What is it? You tell me it consists of
> images or pictures of things. Where is this extensive canvas hung
> up?   (*Zoonomia* i 29)

Wordsworth goes beyond the retinal images, and in his creative reverie
he not only sees 'into the life of things' but also hears the plangent tones
of 'the still sad music of humanity'.

Historians see the *Lyrical Ballads* as marking the end of the
'Augustan' era characterized by the rhyming couplets of Pope (and
Darwin), and signalling the new era of 'the Romantics'. Yet we have seen
that the volume depended doubly on Darwin. First, he seduced
Wordsworth and Coleridge into following him, and it was largely their
revolt against his 'gaudiness' that spurred them to develop a new style.
Second, Wordsworth and Coleridge both drew heavily on Darwin in the

individual poems: I have mentioned possible links with Darwin in ten of Wordsworth's twenty poems; and Coleridge's main contribution to the volume, the *Ancient Mariner*, is deeply indebted to Darwin, as we shall find later. The *Lyrical Ballads* are usually seen as really new: Helen Darbishire said 'it is hard to see in the *Lyrical Ballads* any literary influence at all except that of the [traditional] ballads'.[30] Even though this may be too strong a statement, no serious competitors for Darwin spring to mind, and it seems fair to say that Darwin's influence over *Lyrical Ballads* was greater than that of any other individual author.

STRENGTH IN WHAT REMAINS BEHIND?

Though Darwin's influence on Wordsworth gradually declined after 1798, there are still a number of echoes to be heard. The first of these are in the prologue to *Peter Bell*, written in the summer of 1798 and published in 1819. Here Wordsworth soars high above his usual habitat, not in 'a huge balloon' (line 2) but in a boat 'shaped like the crescent moon' (line 5). The boat takes him away from the Earth

> Through many a long blue field of ether
> Leaving ten thousand stars beneath her.   (lines 33–4)

During this interstellar voyage the boat passes 'the red-haired race of Mars', Jove's 'stately bowers', and Saturn's 'decayed' towns, en route to the stars of 'the Crab, the Scorpion and the Bull'. This is the realm of Darwin, and Wordsworth's reference to 'a huge balloon' seems to confirm that his boat-journey is based on Darwin's imaginative forty-two lines about the balloon-journey of the Montgolfiers –

> Rise, great MONGOLFIER! urge thy venturous flight
> High o'er the Moon's pale ice-reflected light;
> High o'er the pearly Star, whose beamy horn
> Hangs in the east, gay harbinger of morn;
> Leave the red eye of Mars on rapid wing,
> Jove's silver guards, and Saturn's dusky ring.
>   (*Lov. Pl.* II 47–52)

And so on to the stars of Cassiopeia and the Great Bear, and then to southern oceans where 'new stars' light 'the blue etherial plain'. Wordsworth brings on the magic boat only to dismiss it. Not for him a gaudy Darwinian extravaganza: no, he is writing a homely (but unlikely) tale about a dodecagamic potter and a faithful Ass – which we need not pursue here.

Instead we come to Wordsworth's major work, *The Prelude*, the 1799 text being more relevant than the much longer and heavily revised version of 1850. The *1799 Prelude* begins with an invocation to the river Derwent, and in line 4 Wordsworth refers to

> his alder shades and rocky falls.

Darwin wrote an 'Ode to the River Derwent', where he mentions

> dusky alders, leaning from the cliff

and the river's 'foaming tide';[31] also he has 'alders shade' in *The Economy of Vegetation* (I 28). But Wordsworth lived beside the Derwent as a boy, and Darwin was still living beside the Derwent: so the parallel is natural and of no significance.

The same conclusion seems to apply to most of *The Prelude*: Wordsworth reproduces some of Darwin's ideas, as in *Tintern Abbey*, but he has almost thrown off the infection of Darwinian wording. Perhaps there is a hint of Darwin's 'organic happiness' (transmitted via Coleridge) in Wordsworth's reference to 'drinking in a pure organic pleasure' (I 396); and perhaps, as Bernard Blackstone suggested,[32] Wordsworth's lines about 'the mighty flood of Nile' pouring from 'Abyssinian clouds'

> To fertilize the whole Egyptian plain,   (*1850 Prelude* VI 615)

may derive from the Fuseli–Blake plate 'Fertilization of Egypt' and Darwin's accompanying lines, which mention 'Dog of Nile' and 'Abyssinian sands' (*Ec.Veg.* III 129–38). But the only clear verbal link I have noticed is with Darwin's vivid picture of

> Stout youths and ruddy damsels, sportive train,

who, as they skate in winter darkness,

> Hang o'er the gliding steel, and hiss along the ice.
>   (*Ec.Veg.* III 565, 570)

Wordsworth has a similar picture of youngsters skating 'sportively' in darkness:

> All shod with steel
> We hissed along the polished ice in games
> Confederate.[33]

The Prelude reaches its 'apocalyptic conclusion'[34] with an ascent of Snowdon by night, and John Beer has suggested[35] that this passage, and even perhaps the climb itself (in 1791), may have been provoked by Darwin's picture of lichen on Snowdon in *The Loves of the Plants* (1789):

> Where frowning Snowdon bends his dizzy brow
> O'er Conway, listening to the surge below;
> Retiring LICHEN climbs the topmost stone,
> And 'mid the airy ocean dwells alone. –
> Bright shine the stars unnumber'd *o'er her head*,
> And the cold moon-beam gilds her flinty bed;
> While round the rifted rocks hoarse whirlwinds breathe,
> And dark with thunder sail the clouds *beneath*. (I 347–54)

Wordsworth does not mention lichen, but he brings in several of Darwin's other properties – the Moon, the stars, a sea of mist beneath, and the sound of roaring torrents (*1850 Prelude* XIV 40–62). Though the verbal parallels are not very close, climbing mountains by night was an unusual exercise, and Darwin's lines may have sparked off the idea, especially in view of their influence on 'The Thorn'. However, other sources may also have been influential, as Jonathan Wordsworth has noted.[36]

There are possible traces of Darwin in 'A Slumber did my Spirit seal' (1799). The 'slumber . . . seal' and the general sibilance may derive from Darwin's lines,

> In death-like slumbers seals my hapless race . . .
> And iron slumbers seal their glassy eyes.

Also Darwin's instruction to

> Watch with nice eye the Earth's diurnal way,

may have filtered into Wordsworth's image in line 7,

Rolled round in Earth's diurnal course,

and possibly the reference to Earth rolling 'her diurnal round' in *The Prelude*.[37]

Darwin's favourite adjective is *bright*, used 108 times in *The Botanic Garden*, and Wordsworth's famous line in the 'Westminster Bridge' sonnet (1802),

All bright and glittering in the smokeless air,

is very Darwinian in its construction and sharp-etched pictorial quality, as is shown by three separate lines in *The Loves of the Plants*,

All wan and shivering in the leafless glade . . .
And all the glittering pageant melts in air . . .
And shot all-radiant through the glittering sky.[38]

The one feature of Wordsworth's line that has no parallel in Darwin is the redundancy of 'bright' and 'glittering': this is one of Wordsworth's own mannerisms, most cogently analysed by Herbert Dingle.[39]

Wordsworth's Ode 'Intimations of Immortality from Recollections of early Childhood' was started in 1802 but probably not finished until 1804. The theme of the poem, Donald Hassler has suggested,[40] derives from Darwin's emphasis in *Zoonomia* on the continuity of life through many generations: 'the offspring . . . is in truth a branch or elongation of the parent . . . and therefore it may retain some of the habits of the parent-system' (i 484). Or, in Wordsworth's ringing phrases,

Though inland far we be,
Our Souls have sight of that immortal sea
Which brought us hither.   (Lines 166–8)

The concept of continuity is essential to Darwin's theory of evolution, and Wordsworth may be also taking a hint from *The Temple of Nature* (1803), where life is presented as originating in the sea, and then evolving through fishes and amphibia to reptiles and mammals. Darwin's theory of the continual *improvement* of species through evolution was attractive to Wordsworth, because nature would then be semi-actively rather than passively benevolent; and John Beer[41] has suggested that Darwin's theory contributed to Wordsworth's faith in the future of the human race. Wordsworth's continual harping on instinct and 'first affections' in the *Immortality* ode may also, as Hassler points out, derive from Darwin's chapter on instinct in *Zoonomia*, where he discusses at length the relation between a new-born baby and its mother.[42]

In the last two lines of this, his last great poem, Wordsworth can be seen as returning to the original source of his attraction to Darwin, *The Loves of the Plants*, and nodding his head in recognition to his predecessor:

> To me the meanest flower that blows can give
> Thoughts that do often lie too deep for tears.

Earlier in the poem Wordsworth had written,

> I hear the echoes through the mountain throng;

but from now onwards they are rarely echoes of Darwin. Wordsworth's devotion to Darwin was a thing of the past – and so was his great decade of poetry.

I shall mention only one more echo, which demands inclusion because it is the clearest of all. It comes from 'To Enterprise' (1821), and its source is Darwin's description of the army of Cambyses being overwhelmed by sand in a desert whirlwind:

> Now o'er their head the whizzing whirlwinds breathe,
> And the live desert pants, and heaves beneath.

So Darwin begins, and he concludes with the soldiers buried alive:

> awhile the living hill
> Heaved with convulsive throes – and all was still!

Wordsworth follows closely in his track:

> Or caught amid a whirl of desert sands –
> An Army now, and now a living hill
> That a brief while heaves with convulsive throes –
> Then all is still.[43]

Wordsworth mentions the resemblance in a note to the first edition of the poem and in a letter to Alexander Dyce in 1830:

You are quite correct in your notice of my obligation to Dr Darwin. In the first edition of the Poem it was acknowledged in a note, which slipped out of its place in the last, along with some others.[44]

For me that is a good note on which to slip out of my reading of Wordsworth's later poems. Other echoes there may be, but none will be clearer or gorier than the heaving hell of this living hill.

RETROSPECT

This chapter has shown, so it seems to me, that Wordsworth was deeply influenced by Darwin in the 1790s, both stylistically and philosophically. As the 1790s progressed, Wordsworth reacted against the Darwinian verse-style; and his own simple – sometimes over-simple – wording was the diametric opposite of Darwin's. By enchaining him so heavily, Darwin roused his spirit to break those chains. Without the incentive provided by Darwin's grip, it is probable that the revolution Wordsworth wrought in English poetry would have been later, less complete and less effective.

Darwin's influence on Wordsworth's ideas was long-lasting. Wordsworth already believed in the importance of natural objects, particularly plants and flowers, before *The Loves of the Plants* appeared. But the publication of Darwin's poem in 1789 greatly strengthened Wordsworth's faith, (a) because the poem won such acclaim, and (b) because Darwin was an eminent man of science who was lending authority to the idea that plants could feel. Wordsworth was also favourably impressed by Darwin's obvious delight in mountain scenery, and by his enthusiasm for the French Revolution, expressed in *The Economy of Vegetation* in 1792. When he read *Zoonomia*, Wordsworth was much taken by Darwin's ideas on Reverie, which permeate *Tintern Abbey*; and by his ideas on evolution, with the continuity of life through many generations and its gradual improvement – ideas which underlie another of his finest poems, the *Immortality* ode. Of Wordsworth's twenty poems in *Lyrical Ballads*, ten have plausible links with Darwin either verbally or via the medical case-histories in *Zoonomia*.

For Wordsworth 'the influence of natural objects' was paramount, and his other debts are mainly to people rather than books. Those who know Wordsworth might therefore expect this chapter to be abortive. I hope it is not, and my own view is that in the 1790s Wordsworth was influenced more by Darwin than by any other author. (Hazlitt said

Wordsworth was much indebted to Godwin, but this has been disputed;[45] also Godwin had no influence on his verse-style.) Of course, Darwin could not compete with the personal magnetism exerted by Coleridge; but, as we shall see in the next two chapters, Coleridge was himself deeply indebted to Darwin.

I do not wish to give the impression of exaggerating Darwin's influence. Wordsworth did outgrow Darwin: but the influence was there in his most creative years.

I should also stress that in this book I am pursuing only the links with Darwin. If I ignore links with other writers, that does not mean I deny or denigrate the other links. This cautionary note is especially relevant for a poem like *Tintern Abbey*, which draws on a wide range of eighteenth-century nature poetry.[46]

NOTES

1. For Wordsworth in 1793, see L. F. Chard, *Dissenting Republican*, Chaps III and IV. For Johnson and his circle, see G. P. Tyson, *Joseph Johnson* (1979).
2. See W. Hazlitt, *The Spirit of the Age*: 'William Godwin'.
3. W. Hazlitt, *ibid*: 'Mr Wordsworth'.
4. 'Lines Written in Early Spring', lines 11–12. Darwin's influence here is generally accepted: see *Lyrical Ballads 1805*, ed. D. Roper, pp. 320–1.
5. H. Darbishire, *The Poet Wordsworth*, p. 17.
6. *Lov.Pl.* (3rd edn) III 269–310; *Evening Walk* (1793 edn) 241–56.
7. It might seem that such a link could be ruled out because Wordsworth wrote the widow's story by 1788 (see J. Wordsworth, *The Music of Humanity*, pp. 50–2). But this road-block might be by-passed via yet another curious coincidence: Colonel Pole fought at Minden, where he was seriously wounded; his future wife's name was Eliza; and she had two 'babes' when Darwin first met her. So the drama of 'Eliza at Minden' might have been a time-warp fantasy-poem, written when he was courting her in verse. If so, Sacheverel Pole, the elder of the babes, might have known the lines. The idea that Wordsworth knew of the lines from him seems to me too improbable for credence.
8. *Descr.Sk.* (1793) 226–8; *Lov.Pl.* III 14. See Chap. 5 for Coleridge's parody.
9. Cf. *Descr.Sk.* (1793) 694–7 with *Lov.Pl.* II 285–6, III 341–2.
10. *Lov.Pl.* IV 61, III 351; *Ec.Veg.* IV 369.
11. *Ec.Veg.* IV 105–6; *Descr.Sk.* (1793) 344–5.
12. *Letters of Erasmus Darwin*, p. 200.
13. *Ibid.*, p. 225.
14. H. W. Garrod, *Wordsworth*, pp. 55–6.
15. See C. Wordsworth, *Social Life at the English Universities in the 18th Century* (Cambridge, 1874) p. 589.
16. F. D. Klingender, *Art and the Industrial Revolution*, p. 35.

17. W. Wordsworth, *Poetical Works*, i 13.
18. *Ibid.* iii 442.
19. A. Beatty, *William Wordsworth* (2nd edn, 1927) pp. 57–65.
20. *Lov.Pl.* III 97–9. In *Paradise Lost* (II 592) there is 'a gulf profound as that Serbonian Bog'; but Wordsworth's gulph, like Darwin's is vertical.
21. Lines 541–2, 547–8 in *The Salisbury Plain Poems*, ed. S. Gill (Cornell Univ. Pr., 1975). *Ec.Veg.* II 374–5. See also *Lov.Pl.* II 184, 'And dash proud Superstition from her base'.
22. *British Critic*, *14*, 365 (1799); *Edinburgh Magazine*, *2*, 313 (1818).
23. *The Letters of William and Dorothy Wordsworth* i 199.
24. See Mary Jacobus, *Tradition and Experiment in Wordsworth's Lyrical Ballads*, pp. 234–40.
25. F. W. Bateson, *Wordsworth*, pp. 17–21.
26. J. H. Averill, *Wordsworth and the Poetry of Human Suffering*, pp. 154–6.
27. *Ibid.*, pp. 166–8.
28. Cf. 'Thorn', 14 and *Lov.Pl.* III 229; 'Thorn', 40 and *Ec.Veg.* III 532; 'Thorn', 44 and *Lov.Pl.* I 376.
29. Cf. 'Lines', 17–18 and *Ec.Veg.* IV 421–2; 'Lines' 20 and *Lov.Pl.* I 36.
30. H. Darbishire, *The Poet Wordsworth*, p. 46.
31. *Gent.Mag.*, *55*, 62 (1785). Also A. Seward, *Memoirs of the Life of Dr Darwin*, p. 121.
32. B. Blackstone, *The Consecrated Urn*, p. 24.
33. *1799 Prelude* I 156–8; *1850 Prelude* I 433–5. Cf. also *Ec.Veg.* I 482 and *1850 Prelude* I 442.
34. H. Bloom, *The Visionary Company* (1971) p. 162.
35. J. Beer, *Wordsworth and the Human Heart*, pp. 20–1.
36. J. Wordsworth, *William Wordsworth: The Borders of Vision*, Ch. 10.
37. *Lov.Pl.* I 328, II 290; II 165; *1799 Prelude* I 181–2.
38. *Lov.Pl.* I 317; II 346; II 378.
39. H. Dingle, *Science and Literary Criticism* (Nelson, 1949) pp. 113–15.
40. D. M. Hassler, *Erasmus Darwin*, p. 99.
41. J. Beer, *Wordsworth and the Human Heart*, pp. 148–9.
42. D. M. Hassler, *The Comedian as the Letter D*, p. 53. *Zoonomia* i 146–7.
43. *Ec.Veg.* II 473–4, 497–8; 'To Enterprise', lines 113–16.
44. *The Letters of William and Dorothy Wordsworth* v 235.
45. For opposite views, see H. W. Garrod, *Wordsworth*, p. 92, and F. W. Bateson, *Wordsworth*, pp. 120–1.
46. See the pastiche poem by J. O. Hayden, *Wordsworth Circle*, *12*, 211–16 (1981).

REFERENCES

James H. Averill, *Wordsworth and the Poetry of Human Suffering* (Cornell Univ. Pr., Ithaca, New York, 1980).
F. W. Bateson, *Wordsworth: A Reinterpretation* (Longman, 1954).
A. Beatty, *William Wordsworth*, 2nd edn (Madison, Wisconsin, 1927).
John Beer, *Wordsworth and the Human Heart* (Macmillan, 1978).

L. F. Chard, *Dissenting Republican* (Mouton, The Hague, 1972).

Helen Darbishire, *The Poet Wordsworth* (OUP, 1950).

H. W. Garrod, *Wordsworth* (OUP, 1923).

Donald M. Hassler, *Erasmus Darwin* (Twayne, New York, 1973).

Donald M. Hassler, *The Comedian as the Letter D: Erasmus Darwin's Comic Materialism* (Nijhoff, The Hague, 1973).

Mary Jacobus, *Tradition and Experiment in Wordsworth's Lyrical Ballads* (OUP, 1976).

F. D. Klingender, *Art and the Industrial Revolution* (Paladin Books, 1972).

Emile Legouis, *The Early Life of William Wordsworth* (Dent, 1921).

The Letters of William and Dorothy Wordsworth, ed. E. de Selincourt *et al.*, 2nd edn, 6 vols (OUP, 1967–82).

Mary Moorman, *William Wordsworth*, 2 vols (OUP, 1957, 1965).

D. Roper (ed.), *Lyrical Ballads 1805* (Collins, 1968).

Jonathan Wordsworth, *The Music of Humanity* (Nelson, 1969).

Jonathan Wordsworth, *William Wordsworth: The Borders of Vision* (Clarendon Press, Oxford, 1982).

W. Wordsworth, *Poetical Works,* ed. E. de Selincourt and H. Darbishire, 5 vols (Clarendon Press, Oxford, 1940–9).

5　Coleridge the Poet

Once on the trail of Coleridge through Erasmus Darwin and especially *The Botanic Garden*, one can find almost anything one is looking for.

　　Kathleen Coburn, *Coleridge's Notebooks*, vol. 1, Notes, no. 132

Samuel Taylor Coleridge (Fig. 4) was born at Ottery St Mary, Devon, eleven miles east of Exeter, on 21 October 1772, the youngest of fourteen children of John Coleridge, the vicar of Ottery. His father, who hoped to see his youngest son enter the Church, died when the boy was only eight. From 1782 to 1791 Coleridge was at school at Christ's Hospital, then in London, where he became a fine scholar, particularly in Latin and Greek, an omnivorous reader and already something of a compulsive talker. From 1791 to 1793 Coleridge was at Jesus College, Cambridge, where he became a Unitarian and grew increasingly fretful at the reactionary attitudes of the dons and his own increasing debts. He made his exit by enlisting in the Army as a Trooper, and after a few months was rescued from this self-destructive act by his family and friends. In June 1794 he met Robert Southey, and soon they were planning to set up a small society with everyone equal in rank and social position – a Pantisocracy as he called it. The community would start with twelve gentlemen and twelve young ladies on the banks of the Susquehanna river in Pennsylvania. The prospect of Pantisocracy inclined Southey and Coleridge towards marriage, and during 1795 they married the two sisters Edith and Sara Fricker. As Coleridge foresaw, Sara was not really suitable for him – who would have been? – and the marriage eventually proved to be another of his self-inflicted wounds.

　　Pantisocracy gradually receded over the horizon, to be replaced by bread and cheese; and in 1796 Coleridge was trying to earn money by journalism. He toured Britain to promote his periodical *The Watchman* and had a long talk with Darwin at Derby in January 1796. But *The Watchman* collapsed in May, and Coleridge went to live in a cottage at Nether Stowey in Somerset, with his friend Thomas Poole as neighbour.

William and Dorothy Wordsworth came to live nearby from July 1797 to July 1798, and, as we have seen, the two poets collaborated to produce *Lyrical Ballads* in the autumn of 1798, with Coleridge's *Ancient Mariner* as the longest of the Ballads. He also wrote Part 1 of *Christabel*, 'Frost at Midnight' and 'This Lime-Tree Bower' in 1797–8.

But Coleridge was still very short of money, and in 1798 was thinking of becoming Unitarian minister at Shrewsbury when he received a generous offer from his friend Tom Wedgwood and Tom's brother Josiah – an annuity of £150. Coleridge accepted and promptly went on a visit to Germany with the Wordsworths. On returning to England in 1799, he was unwell and becoming more dependent on opium. He was also turning away from poetry, his last poem of consequence being written in 1802. After two years in Malta (1804–6), his opium addiction deepened and his health further degenerated. In these dark years most of his projects proved to be phantoms, but he gave lectures on the English poets in 1808 and in 1811–12, produced *The Friend* in 1809 and dictated *Biographia Literaria* in 1815. The last and more serene phase of his life began in 1816, when he went to live with the surgeon James Gillman at Highgate. He remained in Gillman's judicious care until his death in 1834, aged sixty-one.

FIRST REACTIONS, 1789–94

Coleridge was sixteen when *The Loves of the Plants* burst on the literary world in April 1789: he was impressed, but quite critical of the style, which he proceeded to satirize in his 'Monody on a Tea Kettle' (1790), a mock dirge on the loss of a trusty tea-kettle spoilt by overheating.

No more the Tea shall pour its fragrant steams around,

Coleridge tells us, pouring scorn on the tea-party at the end of Canto II of *Loves of the Plants*, where a Naiad

In gaudy cups the steamy treasure pours . . .
Presents the fragrant quintessence of Tea.

Darwin's all-too-numerous 'swains' and 'charms' provoke Coleridge's

Who tho' the swain did wondrous charms disclose.

The funereal Canto III of *Loves of the Plants* also stirs Coleridge to parody. His line,

> Whilst Bats shall shriek and Dogs shall howling run,

tilts at Darwin's Gothic couplet,

> Shrill scream the famish'd bats, and shivering owls,
> And loud and long the dog of midnight howls.[1]

Another early poem orientated towards Darwin is 'Happiness' (1791), where lines 42–65 derive from Darwin's tirade against alcohol-induced diseases, in *Loves of the Plants* (III 357–70). Coleridge's 'Effusion at Evening' (1792) also has hints of Darwin, and of Samuel Rogers's *Pleasures of Memory*.[2]

Coleridge confirms in *Biographia Literaria* that he took an early interest in Darwin's poem. 'During my first Cambridge vacation, I assisted a friend in a contribution for a literary society in Devonshire: and in this I remember to have compared Darwin's work to the Russian palace of ice, glittering, cold and transitory.' This is a telling image, deriving partly from Cowper's picture in *The Task* of the ice-palace, 'cold' and 'transient', built by the

> Imperial mistress of the fur-clad Russ,

and partly from Darwin's own picture of the mines of Cracow,[3] with their 'glittering domes' and 'sculptured ice'. Coleridge's description applies not to the frivolous *Loves of the Plants*, but to *The Economy of Vegetation*, published in June 1792 when Coleridge's first Cambridge summer vacation was beginning.

In the same section of *Biographia Literaria*, Coleridge also remarks that he had

> frequent amicable disputes concerning Darwin's *Botanic Garden* which for some years was greatly extolled, not only by the reading public in general, but even by those whose genius and natural robustness of understanding enabled them afterwards to act foremost in dissipating these 'painted mists' that occasionally rise from the marshes at the foot of Parnassus.[4]

This is a tortuous way of saying that Wordsworth and Coleridge both admired Darwin's poem in the early 1790s and then led the rebellion against it.

So Coleridge was an early reader of Darwin's poem, and he remembered what he read; for, unlike Wordsworth, he was influenced more by books than by people. Coleridge wrote in a notebook: 'Dr Darwin's Poetry, a succession of Landscapes or Paintings – it arrests the attention too often.' It certainly arrested his, as Livingston Lowes remarked.[5]

The first volume of Darwin's *Zoonomia* appeared in April 1794, and there is every indication that Coleridge soon read and absorbed it. At this time Coleridge was in process of abandoning Cambridge for Pantisocracy, and Darwin's fascinating speculative essays on such subjects as Instinct, Sleep, Reverie and Generation, remained with him as an abiding influence. Volume 2 of *Zoonomia* (1796) discussed the detailed treatment of diseases and was of less interest to Coleridge.

THE BRISTOL CIRCLE, 1794–5

Coleridge's contacts with Southey in 1794 brought him into the literary–scientific group of friends then centred at Bristol, and Coleridge spent much of 1795 there, giving courses of lectures on Politics and Religion.

The most scientific of his friends at this time was Dr Thomas Beddoes (1760–1808), an energetic radical who produced a stream of political and medical pamphlets. Beddoes was also Darwin's most frequent correspondent in the early 1790s and, with Darwin's encouragement, he was pursuing an ambitious plan for a 'Pneumatic Institution' at Bristol to cure diseases, especially consumption, by the administration of gases. Three of the Lunar Society members, Darwin, James Watt and Josiah Wedgwood, gave Beddoes intellectual, practical and financial help in his project; and he had just married Anna Edgeworth, the daughter of a fourth Lunar member. So Beddoes was, in a sense, reviving at Bristol the Lunar activity which had been snuffed out by the Birmingham riots in 1791, and his associations with Gregory Watt and Tom Wedgwood make the parallel closer.

In June 1794 James Watt's daughter Janet died of consumption at the age of fifteen, and a series of harrowing letters from Darwin to Watt record Darwin's unsuccessful attempts to save Janet.[6] After her death, Watt devoted much time and effort to designing and manufacturing the equipment for pneumatic medicine, and Darwin tried it on several of his patients, with mixed results. Without the practical aid of Watt and the financial aid of the Wedgwoods, Beddoes would never have succeeded in establishing his Pneumatic Institution, which opened in 1798. (Unfortunately pneumatic medicine proved ineffectual, but that does not concern us here – it seemed a good idea at the time.)

If he had found suitable friends to help, Beddoes could well have inspired a new Lunar Society: he had superabundant energy. But Tom Wedgwood (1771–1805), the brilliant but unhealthy son of Josiah I, and Gregory Watt (1777–1804), the equally brilliant but consumptive son of James Watt, were too wayward: like Coleridge, they failed to live up to the Lunar ideal of health, enterprise and energy typified by Boulton and Darwin. Tom Wedgwood had much in common with Coleridge, the strongest bond between them being their rather similar (and mysterious) psychosomatic illnesses. They met in 1795, or possibly in 1794, and soon became friends. Tom inherited a small fortune on the death of his father in January 1795; so did his brother Josiah II, and together they gave Coleridge a generous annuity in 1798. In the same year Gregory Watt, who had moved to Cornwall to combat consumption, recommended Beddoes to take on as an assistant a young man from Penzance – Humphry Davy, whose amazing series of chemical discoveries began at Beddoes's Pneumatic Institution when he prepared and exploited nitrous oxide ('laughing gas'). Davy became a close friend of Coleridge.[7]

So the Bristol circle was central in Coleridge's life in the mid 1790s, providing him with an influential lifelong friend in Davy, an essential benefactor in Tom Wedgwood, and a sympathetic doctor in Beddoes. But Beddoes was more than a doctor, he was almost a father-figure: when Beddoes died in 1808, Coleridge 'felt his death like a bodily blow'. Beddoes also had a good library of German scientific and philosophical books, and probably sparked off Coleridge's interests in this sphere.

Darwin was the Wedgwood family doctor, and he had often treated Tom Wedgwood as a child. The treatment continued sporadically through the 1790s, and among eleven long letters from Darwin to Tom is one written on 10 August 1794, when Tom was staying at Tallaton, three miles from Ottery St Mary. Coleridge and Southey were at this time on a walking tour in the west of England. They visited Thomas Poole at Nether Stowey, but it is not known whether they went on to Ottery. The letter from Darwin gave Tom general medical advice. Although fairly well for once, Tom seems to have been suffering from his usual indigestion, and he had obviously demanded some medicine from Darwin, who commented that the cicuta was not very effective and said 'a grain of opium taken every night for many months, perhaps during the whole winter, I think a medicine of much greater value in your situation'.[8] Darwin was right, in the sense that Tom was too acutely conscious of minor pain and would benefit from its suppression; but the prescribed nightcap of opium proved to be non-reversible, and Tom Wedgwood became an addict until his death at the age of thirty-four, in 1805.

Coleridge had previously received medicinal opium as a child and also at Cambridge in 1791. There is no further admission from him that he was using it until March 1796. But Tom Wedgwood suffered from many of the same symptoms as himself and shared his sensitivity to pain; so when Coleridge heard of (or perhaps read) this prescription from the greatest doctor of the day, whose *Zoonomia* he admired so much, he may well have decided to try it. He would no doubt have been encouraged by Beddoes, who thought so highly of Darwin and was not averse to prescribing opium himself.

Creativity is not much affected by opium until it gets out of control,[9] and in the 1790s Coleridge may have gained more from opium's power to relieve pain than he lost by his growing addiction. So perhaps Darwin's prescription was on balance beneficial for English poetry, though not for Coleridge, whose will to work was in the end destroyed by opium, so that he became a mere shadow of his former self.

POEMS OF 1795–6

In the years 1794–6 Coleridge was still struggling to express himself as a poet, and many of the poems have a gawkiness that exposes his debt to Darwin.

The first example is the sonnet 'To William Godwin', published in the *Morning Chronicle* on 10 January 1795, where Coleridge refers to the aurora borealis:

> In Finland's wintry skies the Mimic Morn
> Electric pours a stream of rosy light.

'Mimic' is a favourite word of Darwin, and 'electric ... stream' probably derives from Darwin's lines on the aurora,

> Dart from the North on pale electric streams,
> Fringing Night's sable robe with transient beams,
>
> (*Ec.Veg.* I 129–30)

because these lines seem by far the most likely source for Coleridge's knowledge that the aurora is electrical.

A longer and stronger poem is *Religious Musings*, begun at Christmas 1794 and finished in March 1796. The first parallel here is with Darwin's attacks on superstition and the slave trade. The Spanish conquests in America particularly appalled Darwin:

> Heavens! on my sight what sanguine colours blaze!
> Spain's deathless shame! the crimes of modern days!
> When Avarice, shrouded in Religion's robe,
> Sail'd to the West, and slaughter'd half the globe;
> While Superstition, stalking by his side,
> Mock'd the loud groans, and lap'd the bloody tide.
>
> (*Ec.Veg.* II 413–18)

He tells Britannia

> How Afric's coasts thy craftier sons invade
> With murder, rapine, theft – and call it Trade!
>
> (*Ec.Veg.* II 423–4)

He ends with the slave in chains asking, 'Are we not brethren?' Coleridge brings on the 'Fiends of Superstition', whose 'grisly idols' are 'stain'd with brother's blood' by an 'erring Priest', and links this with the slave traffic,

> where more hideous Trade
> Loud-laughing packs his bales of human anguish.   (140–1)

Coleridge then goes on to other subjects, and tells us how Franklin, the 'Patriot Sage',

> Called the red lightnings from the o'er-rushing cloud.

In *The Botanic Garden* Darwin calls Franklin a 'Sage', who lit the 'patriot flame' and

> Snatch'd the raised lightning from the arm of Jove;

Darwin also refers to 'red-tongued lightnings'.[10]

These examples leave room for a sceptic to wriggle, but the next one is straitjacketing. In Darwin's Canto on Air we meet the stifling blast of the Simoom 'in his realms of sand' –

> Fierce on blue streams he rides the tainted air.

The parallel in *Religious Musings* is

> Where oft majestic through the tainted noon
> The Simoom sails,[11]

and Coleridge confirms his source by adding a long footnote that is almost identical to the first 14 lines of Darwin's footnote on the Simoom (itself a quotation from Bruce's *Travels*).

There are several other parallels in *Religious Musings* that are probably significant. In lines 359–63 Coleridge versifies a notebook entry on the 'Millenium . . . brought about by a progression in . . . meteorology or science of airs and winds'. Both Kathleen Coburn and Herbert Piper[12] link this with Darwin's plea to the Sylphs to disclose to 'some favoured sage' the 'Golden Secret' of the talisman that 'guides the changeful pinions of the winds'; then the climate could be made equable everywhere and everywhen, and we should see

> Autumn and Spring in lively union blend,
> And from the skies the Golden Age descend.
>
> (*Ec.Veg.* IV 319–20)

In the same canto of *The Economy of Vegetation* (lines 195 and 200) there is a distinctive trio of words, 'Sage, Lo! . . . Priestley', which appears reordered as 'Lo! Priestley . . . Sage' in line 371 of *Religious Musings*.

In 'Lines at Shurton Bars' (1795) Coleridge is lured into extensive plagiarism by Darwin's fascinating note on flashes of light from flowers, notably marigolds at dusk. The relevant lines in *The Loves of the Plants* are:

> A saint-like glory trembles round her head;
> *Eight* watchful swains along the lawns of night
> With amorous steps pursue the virgin-light;
> O'er her fair form the electric lustre plays . . .

Coleridge's verses have a different wording:

> 'Tis said, in Summer's evening hour
> Flashes the golden-colour'd flower
>   A fair electric flame:
> And so shall flash my love-charg'd eye.

But Coleridge then gives a long footnote, which proves to be copied word for word from Darwin's long note (of 28 lines) on pages 183–4 o *The Loves of the Plants*. The only change Coleridge makes is to introduce some misprints,[13] and he does not acknowledge his source.

Coleridge's next poem is 'The Eolian Harp' (1795). This was a favourite image with Darwin: the Sylphs of Air

> melt in dulcet chords, when Zephyr rings
> The Eolian Harp, and mingle all its strings. (*Ec.Veg*. IV 245–6)

And one of his fortunate flowers, 'fair Chondrilla', is waited on by five swains who all sigh if she sighs:

> So, tuned in unison, Eolian Lyre!
> Sounds in sweet symphony thy kindred wire. (*Lov.Pl*. I 101–2)

John Beer[14] has suggested that Coleridge's poem is particularly indebted to Darwin for the idea that an insect or bird approaching a flower is a crucial juncture in Nature. Most relevant are Coleridge's lines 23–5:

> Where melodies round honey-dropping flowers,
> Footless and wild, like birds of Paradise,
> Nor pause, nor perch, hovering on untam'd wing.

Darwin's idea is in *Zoonomia*, and the nearest parallel in verse is in *The Economy of Vegetation* (IV 500–4), where he refers to the 'Night-moth' feeding on 'honey'd cells' and asks the Sylphs of Air to go

> where the Humming-bird in Chili's bowers
> On murmuring pinions robs the pendent flowers.

This parallel is not conclusive, but further signs of Darwin's influence may be found in an earlier version of Coleridge's lines:

> Light cargoes waft of modulated Sound

From viewless Hybla brought, when Melodies
Like Birds of Paradise on wings, that aye
Disport in wild variety of hues,
Murmur around the honey-dropping flowers.[15]

As Kathleen Coburn points out, this is very like the opening of Canto IV
of *The Economy of Vegetation*,

As when at noon in Hybla's fragrant bowers
CACALIA opens all her honey'd flowers . . .

And in a note Darwin states:

The cacalia suaveolens produces so much honey that on some days
it may be smelt at a great distance from the plant. I remember once
counting on one of these plants besides bees of various kinds
without number, above two hundred painted butterflies, which
gave it the beautiful appearance of being covered with additional
flowers.   (*Ec.Veg.* IV 2 note)

So here we have Coleridge's 'honey-dropping flowers' and also (butterflies') wings 'in wild variety of hues'. The next line of 'The Eolian Harp'
(line 26, added some time after the poem was written) refers to 'the one
Life within us and abroad', and this may derive from Darwin's belief
that all living creatures are descended from one original living filament,
'one family of one parent'.[16]

Another poem of 1795, 'The Hour when We Shall Meet Again', is
written in rhyming couplets as a parody of Darwin and was later
reprinted under the title 'Darwiniana'. Coleridge catches Darwin's style
admirably, and mimics him for eighteen lines without any slavish
copying. There is no need for me to go through the parallels in detail,
because they are intentional, but I will quote Coleridge's line 17,

New life and joy the expanding flow'ret feels,

because it so nicely summarizes Darwin's celebration of spring in Canto
IV of *The Economy of Vegetation*.

In more serious vein there is the poem about the French Revolution
printed in the first issue of *The Watchman* (1 March 1796), which
includes the lines

When slumbering FREEDOM rous'd by high DISDAIN
With giant Fury burst her triple chain,[17]

This probably derives from Darwin's lines about the 'Giant-Form' o
'LIBERTY', who had long 'inglorious slept' in France 'unconscious of his
chains' –

O'er his closed eyes a triple veil was bound.   (*Ec.Veg.* II 381

'Touched by the patriot flame', he 'rent' the 'flimsy bonds'. So Blake
Wordsworth and Coleridge all made use of these lines.

The only other poem of any consequence from this period is *The
Destiny of Nations* (1796). Coleridge presents Nature as animated by
'involvèd Monads', their tasks being as follows:

Some nurse the infant diamond in the mine;
Some roll the genial juices through the oak;
Some drive the mutinous clouds to clash in air,
And rushing on the storm with whirlwind speed,
Yoke the red lightnings to their volleying car.   (lines 50–4

These functions are just those of Darwin's Gnomes of Earth, Sylphs o
Air and Nymphs of Fire, as H. W. Piper pointed out.[18] Thanks to the
Gnomes, Darwin tells us,

Bright Rubies blush, and living Diamonds blaze,
                                        (*Ec.Veg.* II 228

to which he adds a long note on diamonds. Coleridge's second line
brings us to Darwin's Sylphs, who see 'the pulpy acorn' as containing

The Oak's vast branches in its milky veins;   (*Ec.Veg.* IV 386

and, when Spring's 'genial lustres' arrive, the Sylphs set in motion the
'juices' that 'swell the leafy vein'. Coleridge's third line has more echoes
of Shakespeare than of Darwin, but the fourth comes back to Darwin
who is keen on whirlwinds.[19] In Coleridge's last line, we have already
linked his 'red lightnings' with Darwin's 'red-tongued lightnings', and
the whole line probably derives from Darwin's request to the Etherea
Powers (the Nymphs of Fire) to

yoke the vollied lightnings to your cars.   (*Ec.Veg.* I 116)

Not content with red lightnings, Coleridge also conjures up a red aurora, and his 'mimic lustre', 'streamy banners of the North' and 'robes of rosy light' resemble Darwin's 'mimic lightnings', 'northern lustres' and 'pale electric streams'.[20]

Later in the poem, Coleridge brings on the Whale –

> Yet if Leviathan, weary of ease,
> In sports unwieldy toss his island-bulk . . .

The phrasing is curious and seems likely to stem from *The Loves of the Plants*, where Darwin refers to the 'gambols' of 'the unwieldy Whale', which he likens to 'floating islands'.[21] One further parallel in *The Destiny of Nations* is between Coleridge's

> When Love rose glittering, and his gorgeous wings
> Over the abyss fluttered with such glad noise,

and Darwin's

> When Love Divine, with brooding wings unfurled,
> Call'd from the rude abyss the living world.

But they may both derive from Milton's spirit that

> with mighty wings outspread
> Dove-like satst brooding on the vast Abyss.[22]

Coleridge's 'Ode on the Departing Year' (1796) has several vague resemblances to Darwin, and the nightmare-vision in lines 103–12 is quite like the picture of Nightmare in *The Loves of the Plants* (III 51–78). But I shall not give details because the passages are rather long to quote and the subject comes up again in the next chapter.

Among a list of projects entered in his notebook (probably in December 1795), Coleridge includes: 'Hymn to Dr Darwin – in the manner of the Orphics'.[23] It was a nice idea, but the Hymn was never written – and perhaps there was no need to write it when all the poems of 1795–6 were, in a sense, hymns to Darwin.

Pursuing the parallels through these poems has been a tedious business. But when we know that all the substantial poems of 1795–6 exhibit debts to Darwin, his influence on the *Ancient Mariner* is easier to accept.

THE MEETING WITH DARWIN

In the early months of 1796 Coleridge toured the Midlands to drum up enthusiasm and subscribers for his proposed periodical *The Watchman*. He arrived in Derby on 22 January, and either Beddoes or Tom Wedgwood gave him an introduction to Darwin, who courteously made time for a long talk with him, probably on 24 January.[24] Their conversation, though it may have been a mere courtesy on Darwin's side, left an indelible impression on Coleridge, giving him a beau ideal for depth and breadth of knowledge, and a shining example for him to try to rival and outdo.

Though they differed radically about religion, Coleridge's respect for Darwin at this time comes out clearly in his letters. To Josiah Wade on 27 January 1796 he wrote:

> Derby is full of curiosities, the cotton, the silk mills, Wright, the painter and Dr Darwin, the everything, except the Christian! Dr Darwin possesses, perhaps a greater range of knowledge than any other man in Europe, and is the most inventive of philosophical men. He thinks in a *new* train on all subjects except religion. He bantered me on the subject of religion. I heard all his arguments, and told him that it was infinitely consoling to me, to find that the arguments which so great a man adduced against the existence of a God and the evidences of revealed religion were such as had startled me at fifteen, but had become the objects of my smile at twenty.[25]

He goes on to castigate Darwin for condemning revealed religion and boasting that 'he had never read one book in defence of such stuff, but he had read all the works of infidels'.[25] Obviously the banter was flowing freely!

Two days later he wrote in a similar vein to Revd John Edwards:

> Dr Darwin is an extraordinary man, and received me very courteously – He had heard that I was a Unitarian, and bantered incessantly on the subject of Religion – on which subject he confessed he had never read a single page. He is an Atheist – but has

no new arguments and does not seem acquainted with many *ingenious* old ones. When he talks on any other subject, he is a wonderfully entertaining and instructive old man.[26]

Calling Darwin 'an Atheist' was going rather too far: Darwin still passed as a deist, though he had atheistic leanings.

In the summer of 1796 Coleridge returned to Derby with Sara, originally with the intention of acting as tutor to the daughter of the recently widowed Mrs Elizabeth Evans of Darley. The scheme fell through because of objections by relatives – presumably the Strutts, since Elizabeth was the daughter of Jedediah Strutt. However, Coleridge thoroughly enjoyed going 'to see the beauties of Matlock' for five days in August, followed by a visit to Dovedale and Ilam with Mrs Evans, whom he described later as 'without exception the greatest WOMAN I have been fortunate enough to meet with in my brief pilgrimage thro' Life'.[27] Though the tutoring fell through, Darwin's friend Dr Peter Crompton offered to help Coleridge financially (to the tune of £100 a year) in setting up a school in Derby, and promised to send his own three children. Coleridge accepted, and said he would return to Derby in November. But the plan did not materialize.

Still, Derby had certainly done its best for Coleridge, with three job-offers (including one from Darwin, to be mentioned later), about fifty subscribers to *The Watchman* and some enjoyable excursions. That is why Coleridge was enthusiastic when John Thelwall was about to visit Derby in 1797.

> You are going to Derby! I shall be with you in Spirit. Derby is no common place; but where you will find *citizens* enough to fill your lecture room puzzles me. – Dr Darwin will no doubt excite your respectful curiosity. On the whole, I think, he is the first *literary* character in Europe, and the most original-minded Man.[27]

After this stunning tribute to Darwin, Coleridge continues in generous mood:

> Mrs Crompton is an Angel; and Dr Crompton a truly honest and benevolent man, possessing good sense and a large portion of *humour*. . . . Perhaps you may be so fortunate as to meet with a Mrs Evans whose seat is at Darley, about a mile from Derby. Blessings descend on her! Emotions crowd on me at the sight of her name – We spent five weeks at her house – a sunny spot in our Life![27]

Emotionally, Coleridge was indebted to Mrs Evans; but intellectually he was under Darwin's spell. In the previous twenty years Darwin had acquired 'a greater range of knowledge than any other man in Europe', and had worked that knowledge into a poem of epic length: it was an irresistible target for Coleridge to aim at. In April 1797 he wrote to Cottle:

> I should not think of devoting less than 20 years to an Epic Poem. Ten to collect materials and warm my mind with universal science. I would be a tolerable Mathematician, I would thoroughly know Mechanics, Hydrostatics, Optics, and Astronomy, Botany, Metallurgy, Fossilism, Chemistry, Geology, Anatomy, Medicine – then the *mind of man* – then the *minds of men* – in all Travels, Voyages and Histories. So I would spend ten years – the next five to the composition of the poem – and the five last to the correction of it.[28]

This was his great plan, never executed because opium addiction destroyed his will; but even if the opium had been kept in check it seems unlikely that his mind would have been capable of mastering 'Mechanics, Hydrostatics, Optics, and Astronomy' or even 'Botany, Metallurgy, Fossilism'. He lacked the exact, concrete and patient approach required of the successful scientist. Still, the Darwin-model remained as an ideal and his 'great poem' was a beacon towards which he continually stepped forward – only to slip back within weeks or days. But at least it helped to keep him from complete despair.

Despite his near-idolatry of Darwin, there were two points where they differed radically. The first was religion, as we have already seen. Coleridge called Darwin an atheist in one of his lectures at Bristol in 1795,[29] and saw no reason to change his mind as a result of their talk. When Darwin said that Unitarianism was 'a feather-bed to catch a falling Christian', it was the levity as much as the content of the remark that upset Coleridge.

The second point of difference between them was on the question of poetic style. Though Coleridge was only twenty-three when he met Darwin, he had never approved of the disciplined tread of Darwin's rhyming couplets. The meeting with Darwin no doubt provoked Coleridge to reread *The Botanic Garden*, and in May 1796 he suddenly ends a letter with: 'and I absolutely nauseate Darwin's Poem'.[30] Within about a year Coleridge had met Wordsworth and they were formulating the new style that made *Lyrical Ballads* a landmark in English poetry.

But Coleridge could not escape Darwin's dominion over his imagery and ideas, as we shall now see.

THE ANCIENT MARINER

When Darwin and Coleridge discussed religion and philosophies of life at their meeting in 1796, Darwin would have put forward his own philosophy of organic happiness, or universal sympathy, as expounded in *Phytologia*, the book he was then writing. Coleridge absorbed the idea, despite its atheism (or pantheism), and he amply repaid his debt to Darwin in *The Rime of the Ancient Mariner*, where he presents Darwin's guiding principle of universal sympathy for the living world, clothed in marvellous verse.

Darwin's philosophy of universal sympathy flows from his belief in biological evolution, via two channels, one direct, the other more subtle. Darwin was confident that all living creatures are descended from a common microscopic ancestor – that 'imperious man'

> Arose from rudiments of form and sense,
> An embryon point, or microscopic ens!   (*Tem.Nat.* I 313–4)

So we should look on all living creatures as our cousins and treat them kindly. That is the direct route to universal sympathy: to repeat the vital couplet already quoted in Chapter 2, man

> Should eye with tenderness all living forms,
> His brother-emmets, and his sister-worms. (*Tem.Nat.* IV 427–8)

The second channel, via organic happiness, is less direct but proves stronger once it has been explored. At first sight the struggle for existence in nature seems cruel, and in *The Temple of Nature* Darwin gives a vivid picture of the web of slaughter. But he sees beyond, and points out that the 'survival of the fittest' is also, by and large, the survival of the happiest. Darwin believed that all creatures and plants enjoy life and are 'happy', with the more highly organized animals having a correspondingly greater capacity for happiness. Thus every living creature contributes to the total of organic happiness, though the contribution of each creature depends on its complexity. And when a creature dies, often because it has become incapable of further happiness, it gives pleasure to a myriad of smaller creatures, especially those 'sister-worms', so that the sum of happiness is again increased. 'Is this not a consoling idea to a mind of universal sympathy?' Darwin asks. We have to answer, 'Yes', with the proviso that minds of universal sympathy seem to be in short supply. Darwin's idea of organic happiness extends to geological strata, many of which (e.g. limestone or coal) are formed from the remains of once-happy creatures or plants, and are 'mighty monuments of past delight'.

The presumption that Darwin offered this prescription to Coleridge is amply confirmed in the *Ancient Mariner*, written two years later. If we forget its beguiling poetry for the moment and look at the underlying theme, we find a story about a Mariner who wantonly shoots an albatross that is following the ship. When the ship is becalmed, the albatross is hung around his neck to remind him of his guilt. A 'spectre-bark' approaches, with Death and Life-in-Death dicing for the ship's crew; and then departs. The crew die one by one; but Life-in-Death won the Mariner, and he is left alone, in agony but unable to die. The crisis of the story comes when he watches the ship's wake at night, made luminous by microscopic sea-creatures: the Mariner suddenly feels universal sympathy with all living creatures. Immediately the Albatross falls from his neck, he sheds his guilt, and the ship is supernaturally guided back to his home country; it sinks in a whirlpool and he is taken aboard the Pilot's boat.

Many interpretations of the *Ancient Mariner* have been proffered,[31] but the main message, it seems to be generally agreed, is that we must have sympathy with the whole of organic nature:

> He prayeth well, who loveth well
> Both man and bird and beast.

This is just Darwin's philosophy, though Coleridge gives it religious wrappings, saying that we should love all God's creatures, whereas Darwin in effect says we should love all evolution's creatures.

All this would still apply if Darwin had never written any verse: his philosophy is best expressed in *Zoonomia* and *Phytologia*. But since Darwin wrote *The Botanic Garden* and Coleridge was steeped in it, we might expect to find echoes in crucial passages of the *Ancient Mariner*. And so it proves.

We can look first at the experience that 'converted' the Mariner – watching the luminous creatures in the ship's wake:

> Beyond the shadow of the ship,

I watched the water-snakes:
They moved in tracks of shining white,
And when they reared, the elfish light
Fell off in hoary flakes.

Within the shadow of the ship
I watched their rich attire:
Blue, glossy green, and velvet black,
They coiled and swam; and every track
Was a flash of golden fire.

O happy living things! no tongue
Their beauty might declare:
A spring of love gushed from my heart,
And I blessed them unaware.   (lines 272–85)

As soon as the Mariner experienced this sympathy with organic life, the Albatross fell from his neck.

Darwin provides a model for this scene in *The Economy of Vegetation* (I 199–200):

Or gild the surge with insect-sparks, that swarm
Round the bright oar, the kindling prow alarm,

to which he adds the note:

In some seas, as particularly about the coast of Malabar, as a ship floats along, it seems during the night to be surrounded with fire, and to leave a long tract of light behind it. Whenever the sea is gently agitated, it seems converted into little stars, every drop as it breaks emits light, like bodies electrified in the dark.   (Note IX)

The light arises, Darwin tells us, partly from 'microscopic insects' and partly because 'fish-slime in hot countries may become in such a state of incipient putrefaction as to give light, especially when by agitation it is more exposed to the air'. Darwin may have told Coleridge about his experiences as a medical student in Edinburgh, where fish heads thrown out into the streets were so strongly luminous that 'I have on a dark night easily seen the hour by holding one of them to my watch' (*Phytologia*, p. 208). We may add to all this discussion of putrefaction the note in *The Loves of the Plants* (IV 334), which states that 'prodigious quantities of sea-fish, dead and dying, were seen floating for leagues on the sea' near Sumatra in 1775. This may be the source of the 'slimy rotting' sections of the *Ancient Mariner*:

> The very deep did rot: O Christ!
> That ever this should be!
> Yea, slimy things did crawl with legs
> Upon the slimy sea . . .   (lines 123–6)

and

> And a thousand thousand slimy things
> Lived on; and so did I.
> I looked upon the rotting sea . . .   (lines 238–40)

'Slimy' (and 'scaly') are Darwin's stock adjectives for sea creatures: for example, in the ludicrous scene where St Anthony preaches to the fishes, they

> Ope their wide jaws, and bow their slimy heads,
> And dash with frantic fins their foamy beds.   (*Lov.Pl.* II 265–6)

As H. W. Piper noted,[32] Coleridge's curious phrase 'crawl with legs' may also derive from *The Loves of the Plants*. Darwin's note on Zostera, a type of sea-weed, states that 'numberless animals' – a 'thousand thousand slimy things'? – 'live on the under surface', and some of these creatures, he says, being lighter than sea water, 'have legs placed as it were, on their backs for the purpose of walking under it [Zostera]' (I 266 note). Marine luminescence had of course been described by many other writers[33] but since the parallels in Darwin are so close, and since we know from the poems of 1795–6 that Coleridge had Darwin's words stored in his capacious memory, I think it would be perverse not to admit Darwin's influence here.

If I may seem to have laboured this point, it is because some commentators have treated Coleridge's 'water-snakes' as actual animal snakes; there is no need to import such mythical monsters when the real snaking luminous wake of the ship fills the bill so well, especially with Darwin's notes in support.

The Mariner's blessing of the sea creatures, 'O happy living things!', has a simplicity and directness far removed from Darwin's elaborate images. Yet even here Coleridge's third line,

A spring of love gushed from my heart,

is suspiciously like a line in *The Loves of the Plants* (I 138),

And life and love gush'd mingled from his heart.

In the rest of the poem, needless to say, Coleridge did not altogether forget Darwin, and there is a fair sprinkling of Darwinian images, though some may be only chance likenesses. As Kathleen Coburn noted, Darwin's sonorous lines about the polar ice-fields,

And ever and anon with hideous sound
Burst the thick ribs of ice, and thunder round,

seem to be echoing in Coleridge's

The ice was all around:
It cracked and growled, and roared and howled,
Like noises in a swound . . .
The ice did split with a thunder-fit.[34]

Darwin had the idea of navigating icebergs from the Antarctic to ameliorate the climate in the tropics – it was an excellent idea, because we now know that placing an iceberg at the eye of a hurricane would greatly reduce its ferocity. Darwin comments on huge icebergs seen in the southern ocean, 'involved in mist' and rising 'about fifty fathoms above the surface of the water'. Part of one of these 'broke off and fell into the sea', he says, 'causing an extraordinary commotion in the water and a thick smoke all around it' (*Ec.Veg.* I 529 note). Coleridge's memories of this note may have filtered into the lines already quoted, and into lines 133–4:

Nine fathom deep he had followed us
From the land of mist and snow.

Darwin also goes to the other extreme in climate when telling us about the tropics, where

from his golden urn the Solstice pours
O'er Afric's sable sons the sultry hours.   (*Lov.Pl.* IV 325–6)

H. W. Piper has suggested that Darwin inspired Coleridge's picture o
the tropics in the *Ancient Mariner*:

> All in a hot and copper sky,
> The bloody sun, at noon,
> Right up above the mast did stand,
> No bigger than the Moon.[35]

Piper refers particularly to Darwin's note, where he says that when th
Harmattan wind blows, 'the sun appears through it only about noon
and then of a dilute red'; Darwin also refers to a darkness at Detroi
when 'the sun appeared as red as blood, and thrice its usual size' (*Lov.P*
IV 328 note). Not everyone will find these parallels convincing, but it i
possible that Coleridge subconsciously drew on Darwin's note.

We are now ready for the approach of the spectre-bark, seen far off a
'a little speck',

> A speck, a mist, a shape, I wist! . . .
> [I] cried, A sail! a sail!

As Kathleen Coburn pointed out, this is rather like Darwin's lines:

> Now dim amid the distant foam she spies
> A rising speck, – " 'tis! 'tis he!" she cries.[36]

Coleridge probably also remembered the opening lines of the sam
Canto of *Loves of the Plants*,

> Now the broad Sun his golden orb unshrouds,
> Flames in the west, and paints the parted clouds,

because he makes the spectre-bark arrive when

> The western wave was all aflame,

with the 'broad bright Sun' resting almost upon it. Coleridge's spectre
bark has sails 'like restless gossameres'; Darwin has ships 'harnesse
with gossamer'.[37]

Darwin's discussion of dreams and nightmares was of great impor
tance to Coleridge, as we shall see in the next chapter. So it is wortl
mentioning the possibility that Coleridge's 'Nightmare LIFE-IN-DEATH

with skin 'white as leprosy' may derive from the picture in *Loves of the Plants* of the 'Fiend' of 'NIGHTMARE', sitting on the breast of a sleeping girl with 'snow-white limbs'.[38]

To return to clearer parallels, Darwin describes the aurora borealis several times, and comments on the stars shining through aurorae and the tails of comets, his line

The wan stars glimmering through its silver train

being accompanied by a note saying that 'small stars are seen undiminished through both the light of the tails of comets, and of the aurora borealis'. Coleridge also brings in the aurora again, and this time with 'the wan stars' shining through:

The upper air burst into life!
And a hundred fire-flags sheen,
To and fro they were hurried about!
And to and fro, and in and out,
The wan stars danced between.[39]

Another possible echo of Darwin may be audible when the pilot's boat approaches the Mariner's vessel, to the accompaniment of a strange sound:

Under the water it rumbled on,
Still louder and more dread.

It reached the ship, which 'went down like lead', and

Upon the whirl, where sank the ship,
The boat spun round and round.

If 'the whirl' is a whirlpool, we can look to Darwin's descriptions of the Maelstrom,

Where whirling MAELSTROME roars and foams below

and

Down his deep den the whirling vessel draws . . .
The booming waters murmuring o'er the mast.[40]

So the *Ancient Mariner* continues the pattern set by the poems o
1795–6, with numerous examples of Darwin's influence, as would b
expected from a poet who had stored *The Botanic Garden* in his memor
and looked on Darwin as 'the first *literary* character in Europe'. What i
more surprising, I think, and more impressive, is to see Coleridg
propounding Darwin's philosophy, and apparently in an unconsciou
way, as if still under deep Darwinian hypnosis from their meeting tw
years before.

THE OPIUM-EATER

We have not yet needed to take much notice of Coleridge's opium habit
His addiction may have started after Darwin's prescription for Tom
Wedgwood in 1794 (as I would guess), or possibly a year or two later. I
1797 Coleridge's use of opium was probably under control and ma
have been beneficial in giving him more time free from debility or pain
But now that we are approaching *Kubla Khan*, which Coleridge himsel
said came to him in an opium dream, the subject can no longer b
evaded.

Despite his rash prescriptions, Darwin himself knew a good dea
about the effects of opium. As Alethea Hayter pointed out, his 'filigre
outline of the imagery of opium visions' in *The Loves of the Plants* i
starkly factual in recording opium's 'power to stimulate dreams and th
feelings of intense cold which accompany withdrawal from it', as well a
reflecting current controversy 'as to whether opium excited or allaye
sexual passion'.[41] Darwin's account is so relevant to Coleridge that fo
once I shall give him the privilege of a long quotation:

> Sopha'd on silk, amid her charm-built towers,
> Her meads of asphodel, and amaranth bowers,
> Where Sleep and Silence guard the soft abodes,
> In sullen apathy PAPAVER nods.
> Faint o'er her couch in scintillating streams
> Pass the thin forms of Fancy and of Dreams;
> Froze by inchantment on the velvet ground,
> Fair youths and beauteous ladies glitter round;
> On crystal pedestals they seem to sigh,
> Bend the meek knee, and lift the imploring eye.
> – And now the Sorceress bares her shrivel'd hand,
> And circles thrice in air her ebon wand;

Flush'd with new life descending statues talk,
The pliant marble softening as they walk . . .
To viewless lutes aerial voices sing,
And hovering loves are heard on rustling wing.
– She waves her wand again! – fresh horrors seize
Their stiffening limbs, their vital currents freeze;
By each cold nymph her marble lover lies,
And iron slumbers seal their glassy eyes.

(*Lov.Pl.* II 267–80, 285–90)

To clear the verbal echoes first, perhaps we have here the inspiration for the brilliant opening scene of the *Ancient Mariner*, with the Wedding Guest rooted to the spot –

Froze by inchantment on the velvet ground

– compelled to listen under the spell of the Mariner's 'glittering eye' (Darwin's 'imploring eye'?) while

Fair youths and beauteous ladies glitter round

at the wedding feast. Though this parallel is not entirely convincing, the presence of the three separate components in Coleridge's scene is rather unnerving.

The other reverberations are in *Kubla Khan*, particularly 'circles thrice in air her ebon wand', and in Blake, Shelley and Keats.[42]

Darwin's note on these lines coolly sums things up. 'In small quantities', he says, opium 'exhilarates the mind, raises the passions, and invigorates the body; in large ones it is succeeded by intoxication, languor, stupor and death.' Just so. But he did not appreciate how easily addiction can arise, nor the chemical changes that make it so difficult to escape. In *Zoonomia* he recommends opium for dozens of diseases, and in his letters there are prescriptions of opium for many patients besides Tom Wedgwood.[43]

KUBLA KHAN

Coleridge did not publish *Kubla Khan* until 1816, and his famous prefatory note stated that he wrote it in 1797 at a lonely farmhouse between Porlock and Lynton. 'In consequence of a slight indisposition, an anodyne had been prescribed, from the effects of which he fell asleep in his chair.' He awoke after three hours, 'during which time he has the most vivid confidence, that he could not have composed less than from two to three hundred lines'. While eagerly writing them down, 'he was unfortunately called out by a person on business from Porlock', and afterwards found he had forgotten the remainder.

The authenticity of this account has been endlessly argued. It bears all the marks of the untruth that crept in whenever Coleridge and opium met: the 'anodyne' was 'two grains of opium', self administered rather than prescribed, according to the Crewe manuscript; Coleridge's later life was one long story of 'excuses, excuses' for not completing work; and the date he gives is wrong and, as usual with Coleridge, too early. Elizabeth Schneider[44] has argued strongly that the poem was not written until October 1799.

Kubla Khan is unique because it is in one sense entirely unoriginal, being a mere reflection of Coleridge's reading, plus perhaps some memories of his travels in Germany and the scenery round the farmhouse (near Culbone Church). In another sense, it is magically original, partly because it is such a pure reflection, apparently unsullied by manipulation from the poet, and also because it is so tantalizingly constructed, with loose ends and *non sequiturs* to deepen the enigma. Nearly every phrase in *Kubla Khan* can be tracked to a plausible source: so, to be fair, I shall first indicate echoes of Darwin and then undermine myself by mentioning other sources.

Coleridge states that he was reading Purchas's *Pilgrimage* when he fell asleep, having reached the lines:

> In Xamdu did Cublai Can build a stately Palace, encompassing sixteene miles of plaine ground with a wall, wherein are fertile Meddowes, pleasant Springs, delightfull Streames, and all sorts of beasts of chase and game, and in the middest thereof a sumptuous house of pleasure.[45]

Apart from the 'dome', a standard piece of furniture in eighteenth-century poems (*The Botanic Garden* has twelve), the first two lines of Coleridge's poem come straight from Purchas:

> In Xanadu did Kubla Khan
> A stately pleasure-dome decree.

The next two lines, and much else in the poem, rely heavily on two passages in *The Loves of the Plants*. In the first (III 85–130 and note) Darwin describes the 'Giant Cave' of Thor at Wetton in the Peak District, and the 'extensive and romantic common' below 'where the rivers Hamps and Manifold sink into the earth' and each flow three miles underground before emerging at Ilam and running into the river Dove as it leaves Dovedale:

> Where HAMPS and MANIFOLD, their cliffs among,
> Each in his flinty channel winds along.

In form and substance this is a model for Coleridge's underground river in lines 3–4,

> Where Alph, the sacred river, ran
> Through caverns measureless to man,

though Coleridge has opted for the river Alphaeus, revered in Greek myth for flowing underground. During his second visit to Derby, in August 1796, Coleridge visited Ilam and probably saw the 'boil-holes' where the rivers re-emerge; he also walked up Dovedale, where he dined in a cave. Darwin does not use Coleridge's word 'measureless', but he has 'unmeasured caves', 'wide caverns and unfathom'd cells', and often uses 'immeasurable'.[46]

Darwin also tells us how Hamps and Manifold, after their three miles underground, flow gently

> Through flowery meadows and impending woods

before joining the Dove 'by towering Thorp' (III 124, 130). Similarly Coleridge introduces pleasant meadow scenery:

> So twice five miles of fertile ground,
> With walls and towers were girdled round:
> And there were gardens bright with sinuous rills,
> Where blossomed many an incense-bearing tree;
> And here were forests ancient as the hills,
> Enfolding sunny spots of greenery.   (Lines 6–11)

The first line here is from Purchas, while the rest may be coloured by Coleridge's memories of his visit to the Ilam valley with the admirable Mrs Evans – he may have remembered his phrase 'a sunny spot in our

Life'.[27] Darwin's lines about Ilam may also have played a part, and indeed quite possibly inspired the actual excursion in 1796.

Coleridge also visited Matlock with Mrs Evans, and the second relevant passage from *The Loves of the Plants* is the picture of the gorge at Matlock and the Masson heights,

> Where, as proud Masson rises rude and bleak,
> And with misshapen turrets crests the Peak,
> Old Matlock gapes with marble jaws, beneath,
> And o'er scar'd Derwent bends his flinty teeth;
> Deep in wide caves below the dangerous soil
> Blue sulphurs flame, imprison'd waters boil.
> Impetuous steams in spiral columns rise
> Through rifted rocks, impatient for the skies;
> Or o'er bright seas of bubbling lavas blow,
> As heave and toss the billowy fires below;
> Condensed on high, in wandering rills they glide
> From Masson's dome, and burst his sparry side;
> Round his grey towers, and down his fringed walls,
> From cliff to cliff, the liquid treasure falls;
> In beds of stalactite, bright ores among,
> O'er corals, shells, and crystals, winds along;
> Crusts the green mosses, and the tangled wood,
> And sparkling plunges to its parent flood.   (*Lov.Pl.* IV 175–92)

Coleridge now moves into a 'deep romantic chasm', which a biased eye might see as the deep gorge of Matlock mated with the 'romantic common' of Wetton. It is

> A savage place! as holy and enchanted
> As e'er beneath a waning moon was haunted
> By woman wailing for her demon-lover!

This curious imagery may owe something to the 'inchanted dell' introduced in Canto III of *Loves of the Plants:*

> And now the Goddess sounds her silver shell,
> And shakes with deeper tones the inchanted dell. . . .
> The timorous moon withholds her conscious light;
> Shrill scream the famish'd bats, and shivering owls,

>   (III 1–2, 12–13)

– a line Coleridge parodied in his 'Monody on a Tea Kettle'. Darwin often has gods or demons seizing reluctant maidens, but the women wail *at* rather than *for* their abductors. For example, in Canto IV of *The Economy of Vegetation*, 'gloomy Dis' rushed in and 'seized the trembling maid' (Prosperine), while her attendant damsels 'clung round the struggling Nymph with piercing cries'. In the same Canto (line 122) Darwin has an 'enamour'd Demon' – Plague, a deadly lover indeed.

But Coleridge says no more about the demon-lover, and returns to the aquifers:

> And from this chasm, with ceaseless turmoil seething,
> As if this earth in fast thick pants were breathing,
> A mighty fountain momently was forced:
> Amid whose swift half-intermitted burst
> Huge fragments vaulted like rebounding hail,
> Or chaffy grain beneath the thresher's flail:
> And 'mid these dancing rocks at once and ever
> It flung up momently the sacred river.   (Lines 17–24)

There are some parallels here with the 'impetuous steams' rising 'through rifted rocks' in Darwin's lines about Matlock gorge, and also with his picture of the Polish salt-mines:

> Thus, cavern'd round in CRACOW's mighty mines,
> With crystal walls a gorgeous city shines;
> Scoop'd in the briny rock long streets extend
> Their hoary course, and glittering domes ascend;
> Down the bright steeps, emerging into day,
> Impetuous fountains burst their headlong way,
> O'er milk-white vales in ivory channels spread,
> And wondering seek their subterraneous bed.
>   (*Ec.Veg.* II 125–32)

Apart from the general resemblances of the caverns, domes, etc., Coleridge's line,

> A mighty fountain momently was forced,

is a paraphrase of Darwin's sixth line, and may also embody memories of the real boil-holes at Ilam. Perhaps Darwin can also be blamed for the earth 'breathing' in 'fast thick pants', which might derive from his lines about the whirlwind breathing and the live desert panting, or, if you prefer a technological touch, from

> Loud roar the flames, the iron nostrils breathe,
> And the huge bellows pant and heave beneath.[47]

Coleridge's image of rocks vaulting into the air may owe something to Darwin's picture of the power of steam in volcanoes –

> Last with wide arms the solid earth He tears,
> Piles rock on rock, on mountain mountain rears –

or the notes on the cave of Thor, where he refers to 'the numerous large stones, which seem to have been thrown over the land by volcanic explosions'.[48] Coleridge was probably also influenced by his visit to the Valley of the Rocks at Lynton and by his reading of Bartram's *Travels*.[49]

The next two lines of *Kubla Khan*,

> Five miles meandering with a mazy motion
> Through wood and dale the sacred river ran,

are both a summary and almost a parody of the poem. The only new words, 'meandering' and 'mazy', are stock adjectives of the time, but perhaps we might offer one relevant couplet from Darwin, which encapsulates the spirit of *Kubla Khan*:

> So from secluded springs, and secret caves,
> Her Liffy pours his bright meandering waves.[50]

This takes us almost half way through *Kubla Khan* and you will be glad to know that I shall now abandon these tedious and detailed comparisons, because I have already inflicted more than flesh and blood can stand. The parallels with Darwin in the second half of the poem are relegated to a note.[51]

Having traced the resemblances to Darwin so assiduously – some might say fanatically – I shall now sabotage my thesis by indicating parallels with other authors pointed out by Elizabeth Schneider, J. L. Lowes and others. English literature in the 1790s was, as Schneider remarks, 'honeycombed with caverns and bursting at the seams with fountains, springs, cataracts, rills and "meanderings", not to mention also chasms and fragrant groves'.[52] So, even though Coleridge was quite strongly fixated on Darwin, he would have received more recent influences. The obvious suspects are Landor's *Gebir* (1798) and, above all, Southey's *Thalaba*, which he was writing in 1799, sometimes at the same table as Coleridge. Though Landor wallows in streams running through caverns, close parallels are few: he has a dulcimer, but no damsel to play it, and the closest resemblance is his picture of the Sun's 'chariot wheel', which 'stands midway in the wave', and may be the model for Coleridge's 'sunny dome', also semi-circular, which

> Floated midway on the wave,

(to quote the line as given in the Crewe MS).

With Southey's *Thalaba*, we stand on firmer ground. The poem was at first called 'The Destruction of Dom Danyel', where 'Dom' is pronounced 'dome', and the Domdaniel (to give it its final spelling) was a cavern beneath the roots of the sea, where evil magicians were educated. The poem's hero, Thalaba, is destined to destroy the Domdaniel, and after many adventures set amid oriental scenery, he eventually does so. Southey luxuriates in paradisal gardens at the slightest excuse, and his poem is riddled with caverns, subterranean or submarine. In the first book of *Thalaba* (line 103) the hero sees

> high in the air a stately palace,

to parallel Coleridge's 'stately pleasure dome' in line 2 of *Kubla Khan*, and his wish, in line 45, to 'build that dome in air'. Near the stately palace (lines 106–7),

> Trees of such ancient majesty
> Tower'd not on Yemen's happy hills,

which telescope into Coleridge's 'forests ancient as the hills' (line 10 of *Kubla Khan*). In lines 441–2 Southey brings us voices which

> like the ocean roar,
> One deep confusion of tumultuous sounds,

and reminds us of line 28 of *Kubla Khan*, 'And sank in tumult to a lifeless ocean'. As a boy, Thalaba lived with Moath and his daughter Oneiza, who in Books II and III is repeatedly called 'The Damsel' and the 'Arabian maid':

Peerless among Arabian youths was he . . .
The loveliest of Arabian maidens she.   (Book III, lines 209, 226)

Needless to say, Thalaba is separated from 'the damsel' and in Book VI
he calls up 'the voluntary vision' of 'His own Arabian maid'. A slight
change of nationality produces Coleridge's 'damsel', who

> In a vision once I saw:
> It was an Abyssinian maid.   (lines 38–9)

In Book VI, lines 110–12, Southey's hero heard the sound of waters

> from the fountain caves
> In mingled melody,

while Coleridge, in lines 33–4 of *Kubla Khan*,

> heard the mingled measure
> From the fountain and the caves.

These examples (several of them from Chapter 3 of Schneider's book)
show that Southey's poem was revolving in Coleridge's mind – or
possibly vice versa. This literary symbiosis is not surprising in view of
their close association: the surprise is that Southey's influence is not
stronger – *Thalaba* had more influence on Shelley's *Queen Mab* and
Alastor than on *Kubla Khan*.

Another literary ancestor is from an earlier era – Milton. In Book 4 of
Paradise Lost he pictures the paradise garden as a 'verdurous wall' with
'goodliest trees' laden with odoriferous fruits and blossoms, and he also
mentions the false Abyssinian paradise of Mount Amara – the source of
Coleridge's 'Abyssinian maid' singing 'of Mount Abora', as Lowes
demonstrated.[53] Coleridge's 'woman wailing for her demon lover'
probably derives from the story of Diocletian's fifty adulterous daughters and their devil-lovers described in Milton's *History of Britain*. This
story is mentioned in Coleridge's *Notebooks* in 1795 and was the subject
of comments from Coleridge, Southey and Davy in 1799.[54] To Milton,
Southey and Landor we must also add Purchas, some of the many travel
writers cited by Lowes, and Wieland's *Oberon*.[55]

Literary critics usually ignore the views of the taxpayers who provide
their salaries and grants but never read their books. This silent majority,
if obliged to listen to *Kubla Khan*, usually favour a different interpreta-

tion, treating the first half as a detailed disguised description of sexual congress and climax, and the second half as imaginative titillation by the exhausted poet. Literary sophisticates find this view difficult to refute and tend to subsume it into the canon as an earthier layer of meaning which adds to the stature of the poem.

From my decidedly Darwinian viewpoint, I would sum up by saying that in *Kubla Khan*, Darwin had several rivals for Coleridge's affections, and one of them, Southey, had the advantage of sitting across the table from him. If we set aside the overt copying of Purchas, the chief unconscious influences on *Kubla Khan* were, in my view, first Southey, second Darwin and third Milton; then Wieland's *Oberon*, Landor's *Gebir*, Bruce's and Bartram's *Travels*, the *Arabian Tales*, etc. Southey began writing *Thalaba* in 1799, and Coleridge read Books I and II, and possibly Book III, in September 1799. My listing of influences assumes that *Kubla Khan* was written in October 1799 (or possibly in 1800), as argued by Schneider. If *Kubla Khan* was written in 1798, the situation is reversed, and Southey was indebted to Coleridge, leaving Darwin as the prime influence.

THE LATER YEARS

Coleridge wrote little verse after 1800, and that little is not highly regarded. So I shall call off my pursuit and just mention three further links.

The first is from *Dejection: an Ode* (1802), generally considered Coleridge's last major poem. There are several possible echoes of Darwin, such as Coleridge's picture of a 'host in rout' with 'trampled men'; eventually there is an end to the

> groans and tremulous shudderings – all is over.   (Line 116)

Here we are back with the rout of the army of Cambyses when, Darwin tells us, 'man mounts on man', 'hosts march o'er hosts', and Night 'listened to the groans', while 'the living hill'

> Heaved with convulsive throes – and all was still!
> > (*Ec.Veg.* II 491–8)

After wrestling with slippery subconscious echoes, it is refreshing to be able to conclude with two overt references to Darwin in Coleridge's poems for the *Morning Chronicle* in 1801. One is in the poem to Addington,[56] which has a note on the owl taken from Darwin's book on *Female Education* (1797): Coleridge was familiar with all Darwin's books, not just the popular ones.

My final example is a poem published on 22 June 1801, in which Coleridge uses *The Loves of the Plants* as a lash to attack loose women, implying that the poem rouses lady readers to what Darwin called 'unallowed desires':

> If plants and flow'rs with sexual charms,
> Fondly entwine their sentient arms,
>   Can flesh and blood be cool?

asked Coleridge. 'With philosophic Darwin soar', he sarcastically suggests, and quotes Genista, Meadia and Iris, where the wanton female enjoys ten, five and three 'unjealous husbands'. The obvious conclusion?

> Each fragrant plant, and blooming flow'r,
> In am'rous bliss enjoy the hour,
>   And various pleasures taste;
> So beauties sport away frail life,
> And scorn the dull domestic wife,
>   Unpolish'd, dull, and chaste.[57]

So, with Coleridge chastizing Darwin instead of raiding his orchard, we may pass from Coleridge the poet to a wider view of Darwin's influence over him.

NOTES

1. The quotations are from 'Tea Kettle', lines 16, 34 and 7; *Lov.Pl.* II 482, 484 and III 13–14. For a 'swain' and 'charms', see e.g. *Lov.Pl.* I 110–16.
2. See N. Fruman, *Coleridge, the Damaged Archangel*, pp. 49–56.
3. *Biog.Lit.*, p. 10; *The Task* V 127–76; *Ec.Veg.* II 125–42.
4. *Biog.Lit.*, pp. 9–10.
5. Coleridge, *Notebooks*, vol. 1, no. 132; J. L. Lowes, *Road to Xanadu*, p. 91.
6. *Letters of Erasmus Darwin*, pp. 238–50.
7. For Beddoes and Davy, see F. F. Cartwright, *The English Pioneers of Anaesthesia*, and D. A. Stansfield, *Thomas Beddoes*.
8. *Letters of Erasmus Darwin*, p. 256.
9. See Alethea Hayter, *Opium and the Romantic Imagination*.
10. *Religious Musings*, 235; *Ec.Veg.* II 367, I 387; *Ec.Veg.* I 390; *Lov.Pl.* III 174.
11. *Ec.Veg.* IV 67–8; *Religious Musings*, 268–9, and footnote; *Ec.Veg.* IV 65 footnote.

12. Coleridge, *Notebooks*, vol. 1, no. 133, and K. Coburn's note; H. W. Piper, *The Active Universe*, pp. 52–4. Piper also (p. 50) compares *Religious Musings*, lines 317–22 with *Ec.Veg.* II 387–8.
13. *Lov.Pl.* IV 46–9 and note; 'Lines at Shurton Bars', 91–4 and note.
14. J. Beer, *Coleridge's Poetic Intelligence*, pp. 65–6.
15. Coleridge, *Notebooks*, vol. 1, no. 51.
16. For further discussion of the harp and the poem, see G. Grigson, *The Harp of Aeolus*, and K. Everest, *Coleridge's Secret Ministry*.
17. S. T. Coleridge, *Collected Works, No. 2: The Watchman*, p. 28 and *Poems*, p. 64. (The lines are an adaptation from Coleridge's 'Destruction of the Bastile'.)
18. H. W. Piper, *Active Universe*, p. 41.
19. See *Ec.Veg.* II 473, IV 296; *Lov.Pl.* I 353.
20. *Destiny of Nations*, 69, 77, 80; *Ec.Veg.* I 204; *Lov.Pl.* II 442; *Ec.Veg.* I 129.
21. *Destiny of Nations*, 412–13; *Lov.Pl.* I 292–3. Noted by K. Coburn, Coleridge's *Notebooks*, vol. 1, no. 54.
22. *Destiny of Nations*, 283–4; *Ec.Veg.* I 101–2; *Paradise Lost* I 20–1 (cf. also VII 234–5).
23. Coleridge, *Notebooks*, vol. 1, no. 174.
24. Darwin does not mention Coleridge when writing to Tom Wedgwood on 23 January, and Coleridge left Derby on 25 January.
25. Coleridge, *Collected Letters*, ed. E. L. Griggs, i 177.
26. *Ibid.* i 178–9.
27. *Ibid.* i 305–6.
28. *Ibid.* i 320–1. Darwin mentions an incubation period of 'above 20 years' in the preface of *Zoonomia*.
29. S. T. Coleridge, *Collected Works, No. 1*, p. 349.
30. Coleridge, *Collected Letters*, i 216.
31. See particularly R. P. Warren, *Selected Essays*, pp. 198–305.
32. H. W. Piper, *The Active Universe*, p. 223.
33. See J. L. Lowes, *The Road to Xanadu*, pp. 35–59. For modern views on bioluminescence, see F. McCapra, *Proc. Roy. Soc.* B *215*, 247–72 (1982), and P. J. Herring, *Proc. Roy. Soc.* B *220*, 183–217 (1984).
34. *Lov.Pl.* IV 351–2; *Ancient Mariner*, 60–2, 69. See Coleridge, *Notebooks*, vol. 1, Notes, no. 174.
35. H. W. Piper, *The Active Universe*, p. 92; *Ancient Mariner*, 111–14.
36. *Ancient Mariner*, 153, 161; *Lov.Pl.* IV 371–2. K. Coburn, Coleridge's *Notebooks*, vol. 1, Notes, no. 174.
37. *Lov.Pl.* IV 1–2; *Ancient Mariner*, 171–2, 184; *Ec.Veg.* III 86.
38. *Ancient Mariner*, 191–2; *Lov.Pl.* III 51–2, 60.
39. *Ec.Veg.* I 134 and Additional Note IV; *Ancient Mariner*, 313–17. This parallel was pointed out by J. L. Lowes, *Road to Xanadu*, pp. 174–5.
40. *Ancient Mariner*, 546–7, 556–7; *Ec.Veg.* I 512, III 100–2.
41. A. Hayter, *Opium and the Romantic Imagination*, p. 102.
42. Blake, *Thel*, Pl. 3, line 6; Shelley, *Esdaile Poems*, p. 50; Keats, *Eve of St Agnes*, st. II.
43. See D. King-Hele, *Doctor of Revolution*, p. 247; *Letters of Erasmus Darwin*, pp. 245–6, 256, 276, 288, 291, 296, 305.
44. E. Schneider, *Coleridge, Opium and 'Kubla Khan'*, Chap. IV.
45. *Purchas his Pilgrimage*, London, 1626, Bk IV, Chap. xiii, p. 418.
46. *Ec.Veg.* I 149; *Lov.Pl.* IV 395; e.g. *Ec.Veg.* II 205.
47. *Ec.Veg.* II 473–4; *Lov.Pl.* IV 59–60. Cf. also *Lov.Pl.* II 281–2.
48. *Ec.Veg.* I 325–6; *Lov.Pl.* III 90 note.
49. See J. L. Lowes, *Road to Xanadu*, pp. 334–7.

50. *Ec.Veg.* III 459–60. See also *Ec.Veg.* IV 207; *Lov.Pl.* I 417; *Lov.Pl.* IV 218.
51. See *Ec.Veg.* III 24, 27–8, 39, 136–7, 175, 197, 518–20, 551–4, and *Lov.Pl.* II 278, IV 223–4.
52. E. Schneider, *Coleridge, Opium and 'Kubla Khan'*, pp. 120–1.
53. Lowes, *Road to Xanadu*, pp, 324–67.
54. Coleridge, *Notebooks*, vol. 1, no. 39; E. Schneider, *Coleridge, Opium and 'Kubla Khan'*, pp. 294–5.
55. See W. W. Beyer, *The Enchanted Forest*.
56. S. T. Coleridge, *Collected Works, No. 3*, vol. 1, p. 260.
57. *Ibid.*, vol. 1, pp. 302–3.

References for Chapters 5 and 6 are at the end of Chapter 6.

6   Coleridge in Prose

> Mr Coleridge has 'a mind reflecting ages past'; his voice is like the echo of the congregated roar of the 'dark rearward and abyss' of thought.
>
> W. Hazlitt, *The Spirit of the Age*

The echoes of Darwin in Coleridge's poems were subconscious memories rather than plagiarism, and the same applies with Coleridge's prose. But the question of Coleridge's plagiarism is a nettle I cannot ignore, because it is so close to my path.

For the past century Coleridge has been highly regarded as a critic. Arthur Symons acclaimed *Biographia Literaria* as 'the greatest book of criticism in English'; Herbert Read regarded Coleridge as 'head and shoulders above every other English critic'; and W. J. Bate said that 'in philosophical profundity he excels every other English critic'.[1]

But there has always been another view. Hazlitt thought his conversation was sheer genius, but referred to his prose as 'dreary trash' and 'utterly abortive', and warned us of his addictive plagiarism.[2] Modern scholars have tracked down extensive plagiarism from German authors, in particular F. W. J. Schelling, F. Schiller, and A. W. Schlegel, and also several lesser-known philosophers like Maass and Tennemann, and from Kant. The evidence has been judiciously summarized by René Wellek,[3] while the case for the prosecution has been presented, with much detail and little mercy, by Norman Fruman,[4] who also discusses the deliberate but unacknowledged borrowings in Coleridge's poems, from Brun, Lessing, Jonson and Wordsworth among others. Coleridge falsely accused many well-known writers of plagiarism – Hume, Gray, Rogers, Maturin, Locke, Hazlitt, Mackintosh, Schelling, Scott and of course Darwin. Yet he was himself passing off translations of German philosophers as his own original thoughts. It is all psychologically curious, but consistent with Lamb's report of Coleridge being 'in the daily and hourly habit of quizzing the world by lyes most unaccountable'.[5]

Coleridge's reputation as a critic may now be on a slippery slope, and may possibly vanish from view over a precipice. But it takes decades to reverse entrenched literary opinions and, since conventional wisdom still rates Coleridge highly, I shall take the trouble to outline his relationship with Darwin – which is also rather fascinating in itself – on the assumption that Coleridge will continue to be regarded as an important figure in criticism until the end of the twentieth century, or the end of civilization, whichever is sooner.

We should expect Coleridge as a critic to be indebted to Darwin. Coleridge's addiction to *The Botanic Garden*, even though he was 'absolutely nauseated' by its style, suggests that he might be even more influenced by *Zoonomia*, where the ideas are not packaged in 'nauseating' verse.

The demonstration of a strong subconscious debt to Darwin would help Coleridge's reputation: he has been severely mauled in recent years for his plagiarism of German writers, and his defence – that he knew it all before he read them – has seemed rather a threadbare cover-up. But we know that he read *Zoonomia* soon after it was published in 1794, and any ideas that appealed to him would have been inscribed into his memory then, to be hoisted out subconsciously during his lectures in 1810–20. If so, he *would* already have held the ideas in the 1790s, before Schlegel's or Schelling's publications appeared; and if he used their wording, that 'genial coincidence' arose through laziness (or opium-induced lack of will, or whatever you wish to call it). So parallels with Darwin would reduce the crime of plagiarism to the peccadillo of subconscious imitation.

Before looking at the resemblances, however, I must clear the decks by examining – and throwing overboard when necessary – the comments Coleridge made (or is alleged to have made) about Darwin. Some of these pronouncements are fair, some are poisonous, and some are mere fiction.

COLERIDGE ON DARWIN

We have seen in the previous chapter how Coleridge drew on the phraseology of *The Botanic Garden* and on Darwin's ideas, such as the philosophy of universal sympathy in the *Ancient Mariner*. Until 1797, when he called Darwin 'the first *literary* character in Europe, and the most original-minded Man', Coleridge's attitude was generally respectful, though he disapproved of Darwin's irreligion and verse-style. After 1798, it was downhill all the way: most subsequent references to Darwin are derogatory, while some are vicious and demonstrably false. Why the change? I think the reason is clear. For the young Coleridge, Darwin's depth and breadth of knowledge – 'a greater range of knowledge than any other man in Europe' – stood as a shining ideal. Coleridge had a mind capable of encompassing all knowledge, and he knew he was a better poet than Darwin. So the idea of a great poem embracing all knowledge remained before him as an ideal, alas never to be realized. As the years passed, from the bright hopes of 1798 to the dejection of 1802 and the despair that followed, his hopes of actually writing his great work receded farther and farther over the horizon. He would never rival Darwin, after all, even though he was well capable of it. He lacked the will power, which had been destroyed by his opium addiction. And if Darwin is to blame for his opium addiction – either through the prescription for Tom Wedgwood, or merely by the frequent recommendation of opium in *Zoonomia* – it is no wonder that Coleridge turned bitterly against Darwin. In Coleridge's eyes, Erasmus Borgia had prescribed a slow but infallible poison for his only rival in the struggle for omni-knowledge.

Coleridge's rude remarks about Darwin need to be examined because they have often been quoted, maliciously and uncritically, by those seeking to smear Darwin. Perhaps the best known is Note 2325 in Kathleen Coburn's edition of the *Notebooks*:

> Darwin's Pain from Milk! O mercy! the blindness of the Man! – and it is *Imagination*, forsooth, that misled him! too much *poetry* in his philosophy!

In fact, of course, Darwin says just the opposite, that babies derive *pleasure* for their mother's milk, and Coleridge must have been in a rambling and incoherent state when he wrote this rough note (during his visit to Malta). Darwin's comments on milk come in the long chapter on 'Instinct' in *Zoonomia*, and their tenor is sufficiently indicated by the following excerpt:

> When the babe, soon after it is born into this cold world, is applied to its mother's bosom; its sense of perceiving warmth is first agreeably affected; next its sense of smell is delighted with the odour of her milk; then its taste is gratified by the flavour of it: afterwards the appetites of hunger and of thirst afford pleasure by the possession of their objects, and by the subsequent digestion of the aliment; and, lastly, the sense of touch is delighted by the softness and smoothness of the milky fountain, the source of such variety of happiness.
>
> (*Zoonomia* i 146)

Darwin then goes on to explain his theory that the curving line of beauty derives from the female breast, and concludes: 'This animal attraction i love . . . the purest source of human felicity, the cordial drop in the otherwise vapid cup of life . . .' Pain is nowhere to be found, so Coleridge's comment is complete nonsense: yet it has been blindly quoted by several scholars and biographers whom I will not embarrass by naming. Since Coleridge refers to poetry, he may have been thinking of the recently published *Temple of Nature*; but there too, and in *The Economy of Vegetation*,[6] Darwin merely versifies the ideas of *Zoonomia*.

Darwin was one of the many well-known writers of his day accused of plagiarism by Coleridge. In a conversation he is reputed to have said Darwin 'was like a pigeon picking up peas, and afterwards voiding them with excrementitious additions'.[7] This well describes Coleridge's own borrowings from Darwin, and seems like a direct guilt-reaction: in matters of plagiarism Coleridge thought attack was the best means of defence, and he may have been provoked by a conversational suggestion that he had borrowed from Darwin.

This remark is from 1804, but age did nothing to mellow Coleridge's views on Darwin, and in 1821 he is reported as saying:

> Darwin was so egregiously vain that, after having given to his son a thesis upon Ocular Spectra, in itself an entire plagiarism from a German book published at Leipzig, he became jealous of the praise it received, and caused it to be given out that he was the real author Nay, he even wrote letters and verses to himself, which he affixed to his own Poems as being addressed to him, by (I think) Billsborough a young admirer of his. He asked his friends whether they had not frequently heard him express opinions like these twenty years ago?'

This tissue of falsehoods is a perfect example of Coleridge projecting his own misdeeds on to Darwin. As Fruman remarks, 'a German book published at Leipzig' is typical of Coleridge's false charges of plagiarism because no one can ever find these sources – except as sources for Coleridge's own borrowings. Here however, Coleridge has neatly scuppered himself – because Darwin could not read German!

A further irony is that Darwin has been condemned by others (and possibly with some justice) for passing off the thesis on ocular spectra as the work of his son, when he probably did much of the experimental work himself. This is of course just the opposite of Coleridge's complaint.

As for writing letters to himself, Darwin was not neurotic and was most unlikely to have done so; but Coleridge definitely did, as in the letter from an imaginary correspondent which he uses in *Biographia Literaria*.[9] So again Coleridge is trying to visit his own sins on Darwin. The poems by Cowper, Hayley and Polwhele, prefixed to *The Botanic Garden*, are authenticated by letters from the authors; but even if they were not, the accusation that Darwin himself composed the poems, and then openly published them under the names of three well-known living authors, is so absurd that it refutes itself. Dewhurst Bilsborrow (whom Coleridge knew at Cambridge) was a young disciple of Darwin and would be expected to write poems praising his mentor. And Coleridge himself liked to point out that he 'had said that twenty years ago'. So Coleridge's farrago applies quite well to himself, but when applied to Darwin is a mixture of fiction and anti-truth.

It is as if Coleridge, having tried to be a Darwin and failed, had identified himself with his model so thoroughly that he came to believe Darwin shared his own character-defects.

These are the wildest of Coleridge's attacks on Darwin; the others are milder, and more interesting because they are nearer the truth. For example, there is a nice medical–botanical critique in a notebook of 1817:

> Darwin possesses the *epidermis* of Poetry, without the cutis – The cortex without the liber or alburnum, lignum or medulla.[10]

Kathleen Coburn provides a translation for those who feel blinded by science: 'the outer skin of Poetry, without the true skin – The bark without the inner bark, wood or pith'. The worst Coleridge can be accused of here is pretentious jargon, and even that accusation fails because the jargon is appropriate for a medical–botanical writer and because the notebook entry was not intended for publication.

Another interesting reference to Darwin is in *Omniana*, where Coleridge says he would like 'to see Claudian's splendid Poem on the Phoenix translated into English verse in the elaborate rhyme and gorgeous diction of Darwin'.[11] So even Darwin's style was not all bad, it seems.

Coleridge's most serious comments on his meeting with Darwin occur during a digression in his lecture on Epicurus. Coleridge said 'it was Epicurus's pride that he was a self-taught man' and he enquired into the opinions of other philosophers 'only for the purpose of confuting them'. This is not so strange as it might sound, Coleridge goes on,

> for it has happened to me with a man of considerable eminence in the medical world who, just after I had quitted college, told me that

he had some wish to employ a young man of a metaphysical turn to
read the books of all former philosophers [for] him and to give him a
syllabus of their opinions which he was not acquainted with. 'For'
says he, 'I can reconcile the whole to my system and I think it will be
doing a great service to confute them when I establish the great
doctrine of physics and the understanding of man.' This took place
with a man who was deemed a great philosopher some time ago and
I believe in the hospitals and elsewhere you may hear his name now
and there was a time when he was a great poet likewise.[12]

It is very unlikely that Darwin would have spoken these words, or that
Coleridge would have remembered them accurately twenty years later in
an apparently impromptu digression in a lecture recorded only by a
shorthand writer. The general tenor of the remarks may be correct
however. Seeing that Coleridge was widely knowledgeable and very
short of money, Darwin may as a kindness have offered him a job as a
research assistant, or so it would seem. Coleridge's task would have been
to assess and assimilate the views of earlier philosophers, to provide
Darwin with a digest of their opinions for a future book on philosophy.
Today Professors often give research students such tasks, and Darwin's
offer seems generous rather than reprehensible; but Coleridge obviously
did not see it in that light.

The last comment I shall quote here – there are others later in this
chapter – is a subconscious tribute to Darwin in a notebook entry of
1805:

> Let England be Shakespere, Spenser, Milton, Bacon, Harrington,
> Wordsworth, and never let the names of Darwin, Johnson, Hume,
> *furr* it over! – If these too must be England, let them be another
> England – or rather let the first be old England . . . and the second
> . . . be representative of commercial G. Britain . . .[13]

So Coleridge gives Darwin first place in the 'other England', as
Shakespeare has first place in the 'old England', as if he still thought
Darwin 'the first literary character in Europe'.

DRAMATIC ILLUSION

Coleridge's theory of dramatic illusion is generally reckoned to be one of
his most important contributions to criticism. To summarize, and

grossly over-simplify, there are three strands in Coleridge's argument. First, he attacks the classical dramatic 'unities' of time, place and action. He was not alone in this attitude – the unities were often under fire in the late eighteenth century – but it was his attack that proved lethal to the unities. Second, he greatly admired Shakespeare, who was notorious for violating the unities and was therefore regarded in the eighteenth century as a flawed dramatist – not quite proper, as it were. Coleridge's perceptive detailed commentary on Shakespeare is regarded as his finest criticism,[14] and initiates the modern line of Shakespearean criticism. The third and most important strand of Coleridge's argument relates to the effect of drama on its audience. This is, he says in his comments on *The Tempest*, neither complete delusion nor complete detachment, but an intermediate state of 'illusion':

> In what this consists I cannot better explain than by referring you to the highest degree of it; namely, dreaming. It is laxly said that during sleep we take our dreams for realities, but this is irreconcilable with the nature of sleep, which consists in a suspension of the voluntary and, therefore, of the comparative power. The fact is that we pass no judgement either way: we simply do not judge them to be unreal, in consequence of which the images act on our minds, as far as they act at all, by their own force as images. Our state while we are dreaming differs from that in which we are in the perusal of a deeply interesting novel in the degree rather than in the kind.[15]

Coleridge's 'dramatic illusion' is almost identical to Darwin's idea of 'theatric reverie', expounded in the Interludes to *The Loves of the Plants* and in the chapters 'Of Sleep' and 'Of Reverie' in *Zoonomia*. And Darwin also arrives at his definition via an attack on the unities and admiration of Shakespeare.

The three Interludes between the cantos of *The Loves of the Plants* consist of conversations between the Bookseller and the Poet, the former being a stooge who feeds the right questions to the Poet. In answer to one such question, Darwin starts discussing dreams and 'waking reveries', when 'we are often so much absorbed in the contemplation of what passes in our imaginations, that for a while we do not attend to the lapse of time or to our own locality; and thus suffer a similar kind of deception as in our dreams'. In sleep, he says, 'the organs of sense are closed or inert', and 'there is a total suspension of our voluntary power'; hence, Darwin goes on, 'as the trains of ideas are passing in our imagination in dreams, we cannot compare them with our previous knowledge of things'. (This is a preview of Coleridge's 'sleep . . . consists in a suspension of the voluntary and, therefore, of the comparative power'. When we are deeply interested in 'the art of the Painter or Poet', Darwin says, 'a compleat reverie is produced', during which 'the objects themselves appear to exist before us', and this 'has been called by an ingenious critic "the ideal presence" of such objects (Elements of Criticism by Lord Kaimes)'. In producing 'the ideal presence of the object', he says, 'the great Shakespear particularly excels', and

> so far captivates the spectator, as to make him unmindful of every kind of violation of Time, Place, or Existence. As at the first appearance of the Ghost of Hamlet, 'his ear must be dull as the fat weed, which roots itself on Lethe's brink', who can attend to the improbability of the exhibition. So in many scenes of the Tempest we perpetually believe the action passing before our eyes, and relapse with somewhat of distaste into common life at the interval of the representation.[16]

So in Darwin's Interludes we have all three strands of Coleridge's argument: scorn of the unities; admiration of Shakespeare, particularly *The Tempest*; and the definition of 'theatric reverie', as Darwin calls it. And Darwin's phrase is on the whole more satisfactory than 'dramatic illusion', because 'reverie' is voluntarily entered into, whereas 'illusion' carries hints of deception.

We have already seen Coleridge repeating so many phrases from *The Loves of the Plants* that he must have known it almost by heart. He was familiar with the Interludes too – he says in a letter that 'Darwin and Wordsworth' have each given 'a defence of *their* mode of Poetry'[17] – and this familiarity is amply confirmed by his use of Darwin's arguments and phrases. Of course, there is no plagiarism here: Darwin's ideas became part of Coleridge's mental structure and moulded his thoughts in a subconscious manner.

Darwin discusses sleep and reverie much more fully in *Zoonomia*: pages 202–30 of Volume 1 supply most of Coleridge's material on these subjects. I can only offer a short quotation, and the obvious choice is a paragraph in Darwin's section 'Of dramatic time and place', where reverie, the unities and Shakespeare all occur:

> So when we are enveloped in deep contemplation of any kind, or in reverie, as in reading a very interesting play or romance, we measure time very inaccurately; and hence, if a play greatly affects

our passions, the absurdities of passing over many days or years, and of perpetual changes of place, are not perceived by the audience; as is experienced by every one, who reads or sees some plays of the immortal Shakespear; but it is necessary for inferior authors to observe those rules of the πιθανόν and πρέπον inculcated by Aristotle, because their works do not interest the passions sufficiently to produce complete reverie.

(*Zoonomia* i 210–11)

Here we find further resemblances to Coleridge. Darwin says we experience reverie

in reading a very interesting play or romance,

as compared with Coleridge's

in the perusal of a deeply interesting novel.

Eight lines after the passage quoted, Darwin refers to

sleep; which consists in a suspension of all voluntary power,

an obvious model for Coleridge's

sleep, which consists in a suspension of the voluntary . . . power.

Darwin and Coleridge also both contend that improbability in drama is only a flaw if it is perceived as improbable, and that skilled dramatists and actors can produce the illusion of reality.

Darwin was, of course, more concerned about the disease of compulsive reverie than the niceties of theatric reverie, and his standard treatment for the disease was opium. A girl who became absorbed in imaginary conversations for hours on end 'was cured by very large doses of opium'.[18] Darwin also tells us about a man who wrote in a deep reverie, opening his eyes only to locate the inkpot. Am I dreaming, or is this a preview of *Kubla Khan*?

There is another striking resemblance to Darwin when Coleridge refers to nightmare: the examples he chooses are curious – 'an assassin, for instance, stabbing at the side, or a goblin sitting on the breast, etc.'.[19] These images surely derive from Canto III of *The Loves of the Plants*, where a sleeping girl is the victim of Nightmare, and a 'squab Fiend'

> Alights, and grinning sits upon her breast,

and she imagines a

> stern-eyed Murderer with his knife behind.   (III 54, 67)

The image was based on Fuseli's striking picture of Nightmare (Fig. 11), which appears as an illustration in some editions of *The Loves of the Plants* and had impressed Coleridge: in 1794 he thought of writing a '*wild* Ode' about 'St Withold' meeting 'the Night Mare and her nine Foals', when in a mood 'to *abandon* myself to all the Diableries that ever met the Eye of a Fuseli!'[20]

Coleridge has been suspected of taking the theory of dramatic illusion from the lectures of Schlegel (after 1800), but his obvious debt to Darwin shows that he was aware of these ideas by about 1795. They were among the many ideas that became 'loosely folded up in Mr Coleridge's memory, like a rich, but somewhat tattered piece of tapestry' as Hazlitt put it,[21] to be extracted subconsciously when his mind became concentrated at the imperative of having to lecture.

Since Coleridge is suspected of plagiarizing the three 'Sch's – Schelling, Schiller and Schlegel – I should confess that my discussion of dramatic illusion is almost plagiarism of another 'Sch', namely Elizabeth Schneider, who said nearly all that I have said and more, in *Coleridge, Opium and 'Kubla Khan'*, published in 1953. To acknowledge my debt, I end with her conclusion, that 'Darwin developed almost the whole of Coleridge's theory of dramatic illusion, in brief form, through an almost identical train of thought'.[22]

SUBLIMITY, INTUITION AND VEGETABLE ANIMATION

Three weird sisters, you may think; and they appear hand in hand only because they are the subjects of overt references to *Zoonomia* made by Coleridge. So we can take a rest from the tedious business of tracing resemblances.

The first reference is from the notebooks in 1804 (no. 2093): 'I have marked down . . . an Idea from Darwin, meant to prove the entire dependence of all Sublimity on Association.' The relevant paragraph from *Zoonomia* is in the section on Instinct:

> There are indeed a few sounds, that we very generally associate

with agreeable ideas, as the whistling of birds, or purring of animals that are delighted; and some others, that we as generally associate with disagreeable ideas, as the cries of animals in pain, the hiss of some of them in anger, and the midnight howl of beasts of prey. Yet we receive no terrible or sublime ideas from the lowing of a cow, or the braying of an ass. Which evinces that these emotions are owing to previous associations. So if the rumbling of a carriage in the street be for a moment mistaken for thunder, we receive a sublime sensation, which ceases as soon as we know it is the noise of a coach and six.   (*Zoonomia* i 157)

Darwin's example is powerful, and applies with great force over a much wider range of human activities. 'Prestige' in the arts and the mass media depends on previous associations of names and ideas. A 'big name' enjoys a captive audience for his or her possibly silly sayings, while the wisdom of a sage unknown to the media goes unheard: thus silliness prevails over wisdom throughout the world. Strangely enough, Coleridge contests Darwin's argument, saying it is not dependence but substitution.

The second example is Darwin's interesting concept of 'intuitive analogy', as he calls it:

in our waking hours, whenever an idea occurs which is incongruous to our former experience, we instantly dissever the train of imagination by the power of volition, and compare the incongruous idea with our previous knowledge of nature, and reject it. This operation of the mind has not yet acquired a specific name, though it is exerted every minute of our waking hours; unless it may be termed INTUITIVE ANALOGY. It is an act of reasoning of which we are unconscious except from its effects in preserving the congruity of our ideas.[23]

Darwin's phrase is memorable, and curious because some phrase based on 'awareness' or 'consciousness' might be expected. Coleridge must have known of the term, because it appears just before the chapter 'Of Sleep', but his reference to it is typically topsy-turvy. In one of the many confused paragraphs of *Biographia Literaria* he says that in trying to develop abstractions for use in philosophy, an innovator has 'either to use old words with new meanings (the plan adopted by Darwin in his *Zoonomia*); or to introduce new terms'.[24] The latter, which does not require the unlearning of a previous meaning, is favoured by Coleridge

and also of course (despite Coleridge's remark in parentheses) b
Darwin with 'intuitive analogy'. Coleridge then applies the principle h
has propounded, or to be more accurate fails to apply it, by reviving old
words. The first is *sensuous*; the second is *intuition*, taken (he says) from
'Hooker, Sanderson, Milton and others', to designate 'the immediate
ness of any act or object of knowledge'. Although the (obscure) meaning
is not quite the same as Darwin's, *Zoonomia* is probably his source, as he
half-acknowledged by the mention of *Zoonomia* earlier in the
paragraph.

In the third example Coleridge really adopts his own maxim of coining
new names:

> So long back as the first appearance of Dr Darwin's Phytonomia
> the writer, then in earliest manhood, presumed to hazard the
> opinion, that the physiological botanists were hunting in a false
> direction; and sought for analogy where they should have looked
> for antithesis.[25]

Coleridge is referring to the chapter 'Of Vegetable Animation' in
Zoonomia, though the hybrid title 'Phytonomia' is apt, because Darwin
did elaborate the subject further in *Phytologia*. Darwin is of course
propounding his favourite idea that animals and vegetables are very
similar: 'the individuals of the vegetable world may be considered a
inferior or less perfect animals',[26] he says, and goes on to discuss
insectivorous plants, mimosa, and the way in which anthers and stigma
'find their paramours'. Coleridge is heading in the opposite direction
towards his favourite idea of polarity. This passage is discussed in detail
by John Beer, and the concept of polarity by Trevor Levere.[27]

THE NATURE OF POETRY

Darwin's view of poetry emerges early in the Interludes to *The Loves o
the Plants*. The difference between poetry and prose is not solely in 'the
melody or measure of the language', he says, 'for some prose has it
melody, and even measure'. The dialogue then continues:

> *Bookseller*. In what then consists the essential difference between
> Poetry and Prose?
> *Poet*. Next to the measure of the language, the principal distinction
> appears to me to consist in this; that Poetry admits of very few

words expressive of perfectly abstracted ideas, whereas Prose abounds with them. And as our ideas derived from visible objects are more distinct that those derived from the objects of our other senses, the words expressive of these ideas belonging to vision make up the principal part of poetic language. That is, the Poet writes principally to the eye, the Prose-writer uses more abstracted terms. (*Lov.Pl.* pp. 41–2, 1st edn; pp. 47–8, 3rd edn)

The bookseller points out that 'this may be done in prose' and Darwin agrees, but says that too much visual ornamentation becomes tedious in prose, whereas 'much ornament is expected' in a poem. Darwin frequently says that the aim of his own poem is merely to amuse, and compares it to 'diverse little pictures suspended over the chimney of a Lady's dressing-room, *connected only by a slight festoon of ribbons*' (p. vi).

To Wordsworth and Coleridge such a pictorial definition of poetry was disgracefully frivolous and trivializing. Wordsworth asks nearly the same question as the Bookseller in the 1800 preface to *Lyrical Ballads* – 'Is there then, it will be asked, no essential difference between the language of prose and metrical composition?' – but his reply is very different to Darwin's. And Coleridge in *Biographia Literaria* takes *The Botanic Garden* as his example of a poem 'characterized not so much by poetic thoughts as by thoughts *translated* into the language of poetry'.[28]

When Coleridge came to define poetry in his Lectures, he also reacted strongly against Darwin, but with a different emphasis, attacking the premeditated and uninspired origins of Darwinian verse. If Collier's shorthand notes of his Lectures are accepted, Coleridge gave this reply to the question 'What is poetry?'

It is the art of communicating whatever we wish to communicate, so as both to express and produce excitement, but for the purpose of immediate pleasure; and each part is fitted to afford as much pleasure, as is compatible with the largest sum in the whole.[29]

If he had heard this, Darwin would probably have growled, 'This is sexual congress, not poetry'; but, to be fair to Coleridge, he does offer an alternative wording, 'It is an art . . . of representing, in words, external nature and human thoughts and affections . . .' He still says, however, that 'it must be done for the purpose of immediate pleasure', and that a poet writing real poetry 'is in a continuous state of excitement'.[29]

Coleridge's next paragraph is an attack on Darwin for contravening this definition. In the whole of *The Botanic Garden*, he says,

> there are not twenty images described as a man would describe them
> in a state of excitement. The poem is written with all the tawdr
> industry of a milliner anxious to dress up a doll in silks and satin
> Dr Darwin laboured to make his style fine and gaudy, b
> accumulating and applying all the sonorous and handsome-lookin
> words in our language. This is not poetry . . .[29]

No; poetry has 'pleasurable excitement' as 'its origin and objec
pleasure is the magic circle out of which the poet must not dare t
tread'.[29]

There are several layers of irony lurking here. One of the greatest c
English literary critics is defining poetry; yet instead of thinkin
positively of, say, his much admired Shakespeare, Coleridge's mind is o
Darwin, seen as the *opposite* of what a poet should be, and the definition
are framed to exclude Darwin, who is then singled out for obloquy
Coleridge is appalled at the sight of Darwin masquerading as the soul c
Poetry, and offers us a negative mirror-image to cancel out the atrocity
It is strange that even in 1811 Darwin could still exert such power ove
him.

But beneath this irony is a deeper one. Coleridge ends up by agreein
with Darwin: 'pleasure is the magic circle out of which the poet must no
dare to tread' is well said, but is it so different from Darwin? The basis c
The Loves of the Plants is a magical transformation of plants to people
the reverse of Ovid's *Metamorphoses*, as Darwin tells us in the Proem
And his aim is to amuse, he tells us.

In fairness to Coleridge, three other points deserve to be mentioned
First, his criticism of Darwin was cogent and valid: Darwin's verse wa
manufactured, not turned out in the white heat of strong emotior
though I doubt whether he *laboured* to make his style 'fine' – it cam
naturally. Second, the shorthand notes of Coleridge's lectures may no
be accurate; and, even if they are, he might have wished to correct th
text if he had seen it. However, Coleridge's reputation as a critic depend
heavily on these lectures, so it is no crime to quote them as if they wer
completely authentic; and he repeats his definition of poetry as 'th
communication of immediate pleasure'[30] in his next lecture (reported b
a different hand). The third point is that Coleridge's definitions ar
closely connected with Wordsworth's 'the Poet writes under on
restriction only, namely, the necessity of giving immediate pleasure . . .
(Preface to *Lyrical Ballads*). But of course Wordsworth's preface wa

tself a blast against Darwin, whose influence has therefore still to be
eckoned with.

Another cogent comment by Coleridge on *The Botanic Garden*
appears in the Gutch notebook in 1796:

> Dr Darwin's Poetry, a succession of Landscapes or Paintings – it
> arrests the attention too often, and so prevents the rapidity
> necessary to pathos – it makes the great little.
> – seems to have written his poem as Painters who of beautiful
> objects – take – Studies.[31]

This is fair comment, consistent with Darwin's own view of *The Loves of
the Plants*, given in the Proem:

> Gentle Reader! Lo, here a Camera Obscura is presented to thy view,
> in which are lights and shades dancing on a whited canvas, and
> magnified into apparent life! . . .

THE NOTEBOOKS

Coleridge's *Notebooks*, so admirably edited by Kathleen Coburn, offer
us a wealth of disjointed comments on life and literature. The earliest
notebook, the Gutch Memorandum Book (1795–9), has always been
regarded as the most important. Livingston Lowes wrote that it 'is, in
my judgment, one of the most illuminating human documents even in
that vast treasure-house'[32] [the British Museum]. The first entry in this
highly praised notebook is 'The Vernal Hours' – which, as Lowes noted,
comes straight from Darwin, who uses the phrase three times in *The
Botanic Garden*.[33] The second entry in Coleridge's notebook is:

> Moon at present uninhabited owing to its little or no atmosphere
> but may in time . . .

This too is directly from Darwin, whose summary of his note on the
Moon reads:

> Moon has little or no atmosphere. . . . Is not yet inhabited, but may
> be in time.[34]

It is singularly appropriate that Coleridge should declare his debt to

Darwin so clearly in the first two entries of his most famous notebook.

The indexes of the Coleridge *Notebooks* have 52 references to Darwin, and there are also a few unindexed. Some of these entries are complex, and rightly receive lengthy editorial annotation. Here I shall pick out a few of the shorter entries, on a wide variety of subjects.

Coleridge is not strong on physical science, but in note no. 3802 he refers to 'the *necessity* which at length shews itself in all the apparent final causes of Nature – the Land and Sea Breezes for instance, the great Spiracles made by earthquakes and volcanos . . .' The topics chosen here may seem curious – but not if you know the notes to *The Economy of Vegetation*, where the fifteen-page Additional Note on 'Winds' has a section entitled 'Land and sea breezes', and another note states:

> As these Volcanos are supposed to be spiracula or breathing holes to the great subterraneous fires, it is probable that the escape of elastic vapours from them is the cause, that the earthquakes of modern days are of such small extent compared to those of antient times . . . and on this account may be said not only to be innocuous, but useful.[35]

Coleridge was fascinated by electricity, and his notebook entry no. 137, 'Electrical picture', probably refers to Darwin's dramatic picture of electrified lovers.[36]

> Or, if on wax some fearless Beauty stand,
> And touch the sparkling rod with graceful hand;
> Through her fine limbs the mimic lightnings dart,
> And flames innocuous eddy round her heart;
> O'er her fair brow the kindling lustres glare,
> Blue rays diverging from her bristling hair;
> While some fond Youth the kiss ethereal sips,
> And soft fires issue from their meeting lips.   (*Ec.Veg.* I 349–56)

This 'electric kiss' was famous in its time, and more recently has been enacted every 30 seconds or so for many years by a working model in the basement of the Smithsonian Museum of History and Technology at Washington.

Darwin's picture of the 'big-bang' origin of the Universe in *The Economy of Vegetation* (I 105 note), with the stars projected from a Chaos by explosions, inspired a skittish note by Coleridge (no. 3157):

> Bigness for Greatness – a Being so large, that accidentally passing
> by during the explosion of the Dr Darwin's Chaos of the whole
> System of the Milky Way, the Shot flew in his face, and *pock-fretted
> him.*

Since Darwin's face was pockmarked by smallpox and his figure was
'vast and massive', Coleridge's comment seems rather personal, a
Gillray cartoon in words.

Half-way between chemistry and biology is Coleridge's obscure note
(no. 3883) on 'introsusception in chemical combinations'. The *Oxford
English Dictionary* gives the meaning of 'introsusception' as 'the
inversion of one portion of intestine and its reception within an adjacent
portion', the first recorded use of the word being in *Zoonomia* ii 154.
This explains the origin of Coleridge's note, though not its meaning.

Another strange physical-biological entry in the *Notebooks* is no. 144:
'her eyes sparkled: as if they had been cut out of a diamond quarry'.
Professor Coburn rightly notes that Darwin has many sparkling
diamond eyes (see *Lov.Pl.* II 177 or IV 44); but the parallel may not be
significant.

Coleridge has a weird variety of biological comments deriving from
Zoonomia. Note 2331 mentions 'the Bees in Barbadoes that finding
flowers all the year round left off making honey' (*Zoonomia* i 184). Note
3370 discusses the possibility of two bodies filling one space, following
Zoonomia i 133–4. Note 4461 discusses excess of stimulation, and
mentions Darwin's suffering 'paroxysms of gout from half a pint of table
Beer' (*Zoonomia* ii 452–3).

The most interesting of these entries, however, and one of the most
obscure, is note 3744:

> I wish much to investigate the connection of the Imagination with
> the Bildungstrieb – Imaginatio = imitatio vel repetitio *Imaginis* –
> per motum? ergo, et motuum – The Variolae – generation – Is not
> there a *link* between physical Imitation and Imagination?

Professor Coburn does much to elucidate this, pointing out that
'Bildungstrieb' is from Blumenbach, and giving references to *Zoonomia*
(i 257 and i 519–21). Coleridge's questions about imitation and imagination probably derive from Darwin's remarks about imitation in
Zoonomia and *The Temple of Nature* which I have already discussed in
the Introduction.

From this mishmash of notebook entries, I now turn to the mos
important subject of this chapter – Darwin's evolutionary world-view
and Coleridge's counter-view.

BIOLOGICAL EVOLUTION VERSUS OPPOSITIONAL POLARITY

So far we have seen Coleridge benefiting from Darwin's ideas and
images, and repaying his benefactor with some praise and many hard
words. It may seem that Darwin's reputation gained nothing from his
powerful influence over Coleridge. But that is not so. To begin with, it is
impressive that Darwin had such power over a man who is still generally
regarded as an intellectual giant; equally impressive are Coleridge's
spontaneous tributes to Darwin in 1796–7.

But in the long run, I think, Coleridge's best service to Darwin will
prove to be in recognizing the importance of Darwin's theory of
biological evolution (as we now call it[37]), which I have already
summarized in Chapter 2 (pages 22–3). Coleridge often discussed
Darwin's theory, and always rejected it: but he still worried over the idea
of 'Man's having progressed from an Ouran Outang state' and pinned it
firmly to Darwin, using the words *Darwinian* and *Darwinizing*.

Coleridge was of course not alone in discussing and deploring
Darwin's evolutionary ideas. For example, there is the famous satirical
outline in 'The Loves of the Triangles' (1798). The primitive living
filament, Canning and his co-authors assure us,

> would begin to *ramify*, and its viviparous offspring would diversify
> their forms and habits, so as to accommodate themselves to the
> various *incunabula* which Nature had prepared for them.[38]

The first products were vegetables, which

> by degrees detached themselves from the surface of the earth, and
> supplied themselves with wings or feet. . . . Others . . . by a
> stronger effort of *volition*, would become men. These, in time,
> would restrict themselves to the use of their *hind feet*; their *tails*
> would gradually rub off, by sitting in their caves or huts . . .[38]

It is all good fun, and the best joke is that it comes so close to orthodox
modern ideas: Darwin has the last laugh, because Canning and his co-

authors, by specifying man's ancestry, said for Darwin what he himself had not dared to say in *Zoonomia*.

The publication of *The Temple of Nature* in 1803 offered further chances for sarcasm about evolution, and some of the reviewers enjoyed themselves at Darwin's expense. Among the most severe critics in 1803 was Joseph Priestley.[39]

Darwin's evolutionary theory is also exposed to sardonic humour in that bizarre ragbag of German 'romantic agony', *The Night Watches of Bonaventura* (1804). Here the clown explains that, fool though he may be, his role in speaking the prologue to the tragedy of Man is appropriate because,

> according to Dr Darwin, the ape, which is incontestably still more cloddish yet than a mere fool, is actually the introductory speaker and prologuist of the entire human race. . . . Dr Darwin, whom I present here as my representative and attorney, maintains namely that Man as man owes his existence to a species of ape on the Mediterranean Sea and that the latter, merely by learning so to make use of their thumb muscle that thumb and fingertips touched, gradually acquired refined feelings, made the transition from this to concepts in following generations and finally donned the costume of judicious men, as we still see them now marching about daily in their court and other uniforms.[40]

The black comedy continues with the comment that 'an ape mother even today loves her children more than many a prince's mother'. The clown is 'in agreement with Dr Darwin'; so he urges us 'to value more highly our younger brothers, the apes on all continents'.[40] The ideas here seem to derive from *The Temple of Nature*, but go beyond anything that Darwin published.

A rather similar scenario appears in Washington Irving's semi-spoof *History of New York* (1809). After referring to 'the renowned Dr Darwin . . . as much distinguished for rhyme as reason', Irving credits him with the conjecture 'that the whole human species are accidentally descended from a remarkable family of monkeys'.[41]

So Darwin was widely associated with biological evolution in the early nineteenth century. And it seems that the term *Darwinism* was used – and abused. At a scientific house-party in September 1856, three years before *The Origin of Species* appeared, the engineer Thomas Sopwith gave a talk on evolution, and the Revd J. B. Reade complained, 'That is rank Darwinism.'[42]

Though Coleridge was not the only critic of Darwin's evolutionar
ideas, he was foremost in recognizing and publicizing their importanc
and in refuting their implications for religion. The later Victoria
objections to Charles Darwin's theory sometimes seem like an amplifie
replay of Coleridge's objections to Erasmus Darwin's theory.

Coleridge was particularly nettled by *The Temple of Nature* becaus
Darwin left God out in his naturalistic picture of the development of lif
and the struggle for existence. Even worse was Darwin's analysis of th
observed fact that the males of many species, such as boars, stags, cock
and quails, have developed 'weapons to combat each other' for th
purpose of 'exclusive possession of the females':

> The final cause of this contest amongst the males seems to be, tha
> the strongest and most active animal should propagate the species
> which should thence become improved.   (*Zoonomia* i 507

'Final cause' meant the 'purpose' or 'end' intended by the Creator, an
was a familiar phrase in Darwin's day: he imported the phrase to cove
up the fact that his theory left the Creator without a role. (To expres
Darwin's intention in modern parlance, we need to replace 'final cause
by a neutral word such as 'outcome'.) Coleridge saw through the cover
up, of course, and was angry at the Creator being cast off like worn-ou
clothes.

The implications of evolution, which did not seem to strike Coleridg
when he first read *Zoonomia*, burst on him with full force in Januar
1796 during his traumatic talk with Darwin about religion an
philosophies of life. Darwin made it clear that he believed evolutio
proceeded 'by its own inherent activity': partly through 'blind chance'
as with the 'monstrosities' or milder mutations which gave rise t
variation; and partly through the chaotic struggle for existence, in whic
'the strongest and most active' survived. Coleridge was appalled at th
idea of humanity evolving by blind chance and natural causes. In th
letter he wrote immediately after their meeting, he condemns Darwin fo
reading the works of infidels and not taking any account of 'th
evidences of revealed religion', in deciding 'whether we be the outcasts o
a blind idiot, called Nature, or of an all-wise and infinitely good God'
Darwin was 'playing up' his young visitor with banter, and it had th
desired effect by making Coleridge very conscious of evolution and it
consequences: it was an idea he continued to agonize over.

Coleridge's train of thought is easy to follow. He believed in God
Evolution was a theory that dispensed with God and replaced Him with

blind chance' and the struggle for existence. Therefore Coleridge must fight against evolution. Fight against it he did, and his curious theory of polarity – that everything was a clash of opposites – can be seen as the antithesis of evolution, which draws its plausibility from the obvious similarities between different species of animals.

Coleridge devoted much thought to the question, and his *Theory of Life*, probably written about 1818 in collaboration with his benefactor Gillman, is in a sense his answer to Darwin. Coleridge sees the unceasing polarity of life as the form of its process, and its tendency to progressive individuation as the law of its direction'. For him 'the vegetable and animal creation' are 'its two great poles'. Yet Nature 'has created' as an 'intermediate link' the insects,

> an intenser life, that has struggled itself loose, and become emancipated from vegetation. *Florae liberti, et libertini!* If for the sake of a moment's relaxation we might indulge a Darwinian flight, though at the risk of provoking a smile (not, I hope, a frown) from sober judgment, we might imagine the life of insects an apotheosis of the petals, stamina, and nectaries, round which they flutter. . . . All plants have insects . . . though probably the mere likeness of *shape*, in the *papilio*, and the papilionaceous plants, suggested the idea of the former . . . to our late poetical and theoretical brother.[43]

So Darwin's cloven hoof has been forgotten for the moment, and even more so in subsequent paragraphs, where Coleridge refers to the fishes as 'a yet higher step' of life, and birds as 'a wonderful synthesis of fish and insect'. But in the making of Man, Coleridge says, Nature 'did but assist as handmaid under the eye of her sovereign Master, who made Man in his own image . . . and breathed into him a living soul'. Still, Coleridge refers to Man as 'at the apex of the living pyramid'.[44]

Coleridge's theory is full of contradictions, particularly the insistence on polarity, combined with recognition of the similarity of all nature. Although Coleridge was committed to opposing evolution, his mind seemed to gravitate towards evolution whenever he temporarily forgot his commitment. He often half-implies evolution without realizing it, as in this passage:

> From the Vermes to the Mammalia, Organic Nature is in every class and everywhere tending to Individuality; but Individuality actually commences in Man. This and many other problems must find their solution in the right 'Idea of Nature'.[44]

Another instance is when he draws attention to the flying lizards of the Indian archipelago described in Tiedemann's book (1811) and comments on a dragon, 'with the wings of the insect, and with the nervous system, the brain, and the cranium of the bird, in their several rudiments'.[44] His intelligence seized on many pointers towards evolution, but his religious commitment forced him to read in reverse the writing he saw on the signposts.

One of his strongest outbursts against evolution occurs in his letter to Wordsworth in 1815 about *The Excursion*. Coleridge had hoped that in the poem Wordsworth would

> have exploded the absurd notion of Pope's Essay on Man, Darwin, and all the countless Believers – even (strange to say) among Xtians – of Man's having progressed from an Ouran Outang state – so contrary to all History, to all Religion, nay, to all Possibility – to have affirmed a Fall in some sense, as a fact.[45]

In another passage Coleridge comes close to modern views, but they are only expressed as an antithesis to his own:

> I attach neither belief nor respect to the Theory, which supposes the human Race to have been gradually perfecting itself from the darkest Savagery, or still more boldly tracing us back to the bestial as to our Larva, contemplates Man as the last metamorphosis, the gay *Image*, of some lucky species of Ape or Baboon.[46]

For Coleridge the idea of biological evolution is

> an assertion of a universal process of Nature now existing (since there is the same reason for asserting the progression of every other race of animal from some lower species as of the human race) in contradiction to all experience.[46]

Instead he prefers to believe

> the History I find in my Bible . . . that Man first appeared with all his faculties perfect and in full growth.[46]

Coleridge states the alternatives starkly, and his arguments against Erasmus Darwin are just as passionate as those used against Charles Darwin fifty years later:

What! Did Sir Walter Raleigh believe that a male and female ounce (and, if so, why not two tigers and lions, etc?) would have produced, in course of generations, a cat, or a cat a lion? This is Darwinizing with a vengeance.[47]

This is not a Victorian bishop attacking Charles, but Coleridge swiping at Erasmus.

To sum up, Coleridge realized the importance of Darwin's theory of biological evolution; he worried over it and produced all the arguments he could muster against it; he seized on its religious implications, which were the real cause of his objections. Darwin's influence was longer-lasting on this subject than on any other, and Coleridge paid back some of his debts by keeping alive Darwin's ideas on biological evolution – and words like *Darwinizing* – through that evolutionary dark age, the early nineteenth century.

CONCLUSION

The examples given in this chapter have fully confirmed the idea that the great influence of *The Botanic Garden* on Coleridge's poems would be matched by the influence of *Zoonomia* on his prose. I feel it is only fair to end with a quotation from Elizabeth Schneider, who was the first to point out Coleridge's debt: 'Remarks of Coleridge that had seemed to spring full-fledged from his own brilliant and original insights prove to be in fact Darwin's insights, sometimes more subtly expounded or developed by Coleridge, sometimes not.'[48]

NOTES

1. A. Symons, Introduction to the 1906 Everyman's Library edition of *Biographia Literaria*, p. viii; H. Read, *The True Voice of Feeling* (Faber, 1967) p. 169; W. J. Bate, *Coleridge*, p. 143.
2. W. Hazlitt, *Lectures on the English Poets* ('On the living poets') and *The Spirit of the Age* ('Mr Coleridge').
3. R. Wellek, *A History of Modern Criticism* (Cape, 1955) ii 151–2.
4. N. Fruman, *Coleridge, the Damaged Archangel*.
5. *Letters of Charles and Mary Lamb*, ed. E. W. Marrs (Cornell Univ. Pr., Ithaca, New York, 1975) i 183.
6. *Tem.Nat.* III 165–76; *Ec.Veg.* III 353–76.
7. *Coleridge the Talker*, ed. R. W. Armour and R. F. Howes (Cornell Univ. Pr., Ithaca, New York, 1940) p. 211.

8. *Letters, Conversations and Recollections of S. T. Coleridge*, ed. T. Allsop (Moxon, 1836) ii 115.
9. See Coleridge, *Letters* iv 728.
10. Coleridge, *Notebooks*, vol. 3, no. 4342.
11. *Collected Works, No. 4*, vol. 1, p. 1.
12. S. T. Coleridge, *Philosophical Lectures*, ed. K. Coburn, pp. 213–14.
13. Coleridge, *Notebooks*, vol. 2, no. 2598.
14. Coleridge, *Shakespearean Criticism*, ed. T. M. Raysor, i Introduction.
15. *Ibid.* i 129.
16. All quotations in this paragraph are from *Lov.Pl.*, pp. 46–50 and 85 in the first edition, or pp. 51–4 and 90 in the third.
17. Coleridge, *Letters* ii 830.
18. *Zoonomia* i 227.
19. Coleridge, *Shakespearean Criticism* i 202.
20. Coleridge, *Letters* i 135. See also N. Powell, *Fuseli: The Nightmare* (Lane, 1973).
21. W. Hazlitt, *Spirit of the Age*: 'Mr Coleridge'.
22. E. Schneider, *Coleridge, Opium and 'Kubla Khan'*, pp. 97–8.
23. *Zoonomia* i 200; reprinted in *Tem.Nat.*, Add. Note XIII.
24. *Biog.Lit.*, p. 92.
25. *Collected Works, No. 4*, vol. 1, p. 469.
26. *Zoonomia* i 102.
27. See J. Beer, *Coleridge's Poetic Intelligence*, pp. 53–7 and T. Levere, *Poetry Realized in Nature*, pp. 108–14.
28. *Biog.Lit.*, p. 9.
29. Coleridge, *Shakespearean Criticism* ii 66–8.
30. *Ibid.* ii 76.
31. Coleridge, *Notebooks*, vol. 1, no. 132.
32. J. L. Lowes, *The Road to Xanadu*, p. 5.
33. *Ec.Veg.* I 428 (as noted by Lowes); *Ec.Veg.* II 45 (as noted by Coburn); and *Lov.Pl.* IV 174 (not noted by either). Coleridge uses 'vernal hours' in 'To William Wordsworth' (1807), line 90.
34. Coleridge, *Notebooks*, vol. 1, no. 10; *Ec.Veg.* p. 212.
35. *Ec.Veg.*, Add. Notes, pp. 88 and 124; *Ec.Veg.* I 152 note.
36. See Coleridge, *Notebooks*, vol. 1, no. 137 and note.
37. The word *evolution* had a different meaning in Darwin's day: see C. Singer, *Short History of Scientific Ideas to 1900* (Clarendon Press, Oxford, 1959) pp. 500–3.
38. *Poetry of the Anti-Jacobin*, ed. C. Edmonds (Willes, 1854) pp. 127–8.
39. J. Priestley, *Trans. Amer. Phil. Soc.*, 6(1), 119–29 (1804).
40. *The Night Watches of Bonaventura*, trs. G. Gillespie (Edinburgh University Press, Edinburgh, 1972) pp. 137, 139.
41. [W. Irving], *A History of New York* (1809) i 18, 37.
42. B.W. Richardson, *Thomas Sopwith* (Longman, 1891) p. 256.
43. Coleridge, *Theory of Life*, pp. 67, 74–5.
44. *Ibid.*, pp. 79, 83, 85. In the third quotation I have altered 'did not' to 'did but'.
45. Coleridge, *Letters* iii 574–5 (30 May 1815).
46. *Coleridge, Select Poetry and Prose*, ed. S. Potter (Nonesuch Press, 1971) pp. 469–70.

47. 'Notes on Stillingfleet by S. T. Coleridge', *The Athenaeum*, no. 2474, p. 423 (1875).
48. E. Schneider, *Coleridge, Opium and 'Kubla Khan'*, p. 105.

REFERENCES

W. J. Bate, *Coleridge* (Weidenfeld and Nicolson, 1969).
John Beer, *Coleridge's Poetic Intelligence* (Macmillan, 1977).
Werner W. Beyer, *The Enchanted Forest* (Blackwell, Oxford, 1963).
F. F. Cartwright, *The English Pioneers of Anaesthesia* (Wright, Bristol, 1952).
S. T. Coleridge, *Biographia Literaria* (1817), ed. G. Watson (Dent, 1975).
S. T. Coleridge, *Collected Letters*, ed. E. L. Griggs, 6 vols (OUP, 1956–71).
S. T. Coleridge, *Collected Works: No. 1: Lectures of 1795; No. 2: The Watchman; No. 3: Essays on his Times* (3 vols); *No. 4: The Friend* (2 vols); and others in course of publication (Routledge, 1969–).
S. T. Coleridge, *Notebooks*, ed. Kathleen Coburn, vol. 1 (text) and vol. 1 (notes) (Routledge, 1957); vol. 2 (text) and vol. 2 (notes) (1962); vol. 3 (text) and vol. 3 (notes) (1973).
S. T. Coleridge, *Philosophical Lectures*, ed. Kathleen Coburn (Routledge, 1949).
S. T. Coleridge, *Poems*, ed. E. H. Coleridge (OUP, 1912).
S. T. Coleridge, *Shakespearean Criticism*, ed. T. M. Raysor, 2 vols (Constable, 1930).
S. T. Coleridge, *Theory of Life* (1848) (Gregg Int., Farnborough, 1970).
Kelvin Everest, *Coleridge's Secret Ministry* (Harvester Press, 1979).
Norman Fruman, *Coleridge, the Damaged Archangel* (Allen and Unwin, 1972).
Alethea Hayter, *Opium and the Romantic Imagination* (Faber, 1968).
William Hazlitt, *Lectures on the English Poets* (1818) and *The Spirit of the Age* (1825) (Dent, Everyman's Library, 1910).
Trevor Levere, *Poetry Realized in Nature* (CUP, 1981).
John Livingston Lowes, *The Road to Xanadu* (Vintage Books, New York 1959; 1st edn 1927).
H. W. Piper, *The Active Universe* (Athlone Press, 1962).
Elizabeth Schneider, *Coleridge, Opium and 'Kubla Khan'* (Univ. of Chicago Pr., 1953).
Dorothy A. Stansfield, *Thomas Beddoes* (Reidel, Dordrecht, 1984).
Robert Penn Warren, *Selected Essays* (Eyre and Spottiswoode, 1964).
Reginald Watters, *Coleridge* (Evans, 1971).

7 The Wider World of Literature

The verse has afforded delight to all who delight in verse.
William Cowper on *The Economy of Vegetation*

After four chapters single-mindedly pursuing single poets through verbal jungles, we have now reached easier ground – a chapter that superficially surveys the wider literary scene. The poets assembled here were all born before 1780, but otherwise they are varied, and only about half are 'Romantics'. The 'top ten' are, in order of appearance: Cowper, Hayley, Anna Seward, Scott, Southey, Landor, Moore, Campbell, Crabbe and then, ranging wider still, Goethe. Some of these could not have been indebted to Darwin, because they wrote before him; but few of them ignored him, and I thought it would be useful to record their attitudes to him, which together made up the 'Spirit of the Age' *vis-à-vis* Darwin for the younger poets who appear in later chapters.

I should confess that, after looking at Blake, Wordsworth and Coleridge, I began to wonder whether I should find Darwin's imprint on every poet of the time. If so, would it mean that Darwin was omni-influential or that I was somehow being deluded? Fortunately this nightmarish scenario has not materialized: some of the poets here, though exposed to Darwinian infection, resisted it.

COWPER

First place goes to the most senior and perhaps the most respected of the English poets on my list, William Cowper (1731–1800). He was actually older than Darwin, though only by twenty-seven days. Cowper's major poem *The Task* was published four years before *The Loves of the Plants*, so there is no possibility that Darwin influenced him. But it is of interest to see how Darwin was viewed by this leading poet of his own generation, who was so very different in personality and beliefs: where

Darwin was bold, rather irreligious and mentally tough, Cowper was timid, religious and mentally fragile. But both poets shared a delight in Nature that tended to dominate their verse and brought them close.

So it is not surprising that Cowper was among the foremost admirers of *The Botanic Garden*. His review of *The Loves of the Plants* runs to eight pages, and is almost fulsome in its praise:

> The poetry itself is of a very superior cast, and whether we consider the author's management of his subject, his delicacy of expression, or the sweetness of his numbers, we feel ourselves equally called upon to commend him. He introduces his various objects of description (for they follow in long succession) with so much versatility of genius that we could not but admire the grace and ease, and the playfulness of fancy with which he conducts himself through this part of his business, perhaps the most difficult of all. His descriptions themselves are luminous as language selected with the finest taste can make them, and meet the eye with a boldness of projection unattainable by any hand but that of a master. Neither is this all the praise that belongs to him . . .[1]

And Cowper goes on to praise the humanization of the flowers, giving long quotations. These include the descriptions of Anemone and Cinchona, and the latter draws the comment, 'The personification of Ague in the above passage is singularly terrific, and a proof of a strong romantic imagination.'[1]

You may expect that Cowper's review of *The Economy of Vegetation*, nearly four years later, would be cooler: but not so. The superlatives continue throughout the seven-page review:

> Scripture and fable, the wonders of creation and the works of art, the discoveries of the philosopher and the inventions of the mechanic, are alike made to contribute to the splendour of his poem, which could not have been more highly finished, sweeter in the flow of its numbers, more exquisite in the expression, more diversified in the matter, or richer in every species of embellishment. . . . No poet since Pope has seemed so privileged in the *verborum curiosa felicitas*, or in delicacy and harmony of versification. Yet he is no imitator of Pope, or of any other, but his style and manner are unquestionably his own.[2]

'Could praise be higher?' seems the most appropriate comment.

Though the question is rhetorical, it has an answer: 'yes'. For Cowper not only went to the trouble of writing these long reviews but also composed a poem in praise of Darwin. 'In pursuit of your idea to compliment Darwin', he wrote to Hayley on 10 June 1792, 'I have . . . put a few stanzas together . . .'.[3] This, with some small amendments by Hayley, was Cowper's poem 'To Dr Darwin', which begins:

> Two Poets, (poets by report
>   Not oft so well agree)
> Sweet Harmonist of Flora's court!
>   Conspire to honour thee.
>
> They best can judge a Poet's worth,
>   Who oft themselves have known
> The pangs of a poetic birth
>   By labours of their own.
>
> We, therefore, pleas'd, extol thy song,
>   Though various yet complete,
> Rich in embellishment, as strong
>   And learn'd as it is sweet.[4]

There are three more stanzas, just as sugary, and Cowper concludes by saying that any bard unwilling to 'twine a wreath' for Darwin would be 'unworthy of his own'.

So we may conclude without fear of contradiction that Darwin won the whole-hearted approval of his gentle coeval William Cowper.

Darwin's own admiration of Cowper and Hayley emerges in his letter to Hayley on receiving the poems:

> Nothing is so flattering to a cultivator of any branch of art as the praise of those who best understand the value of his exertions. I am therefore particularly happy in the approbation of yourself and your valuable friend Mr Cowper; both whose works I have studied with great delight and improvement. . . . Go on, both of you! to instruct and amuse the world in variety of composition both of prose and verse, and believe me, with true regard and affection amongst your numerous admirers.[5]

This is perhaps the most effusive of Darwin's letters, but there is no reason to doubt his sincerity.

HAYLEY

Although little valued now as a poet, William Hayley (1745–1820) was very popular in his own day, and in 1791 he was offered the Poet Laureateship, which he declined. Hayley lived in Sussex, at Eartham and Felpham near Chichester, but one of his close friends was Dr John Beridge of Derby. Thus he came to meet Darwin in 1781, and he went on to visit Anna Seward at Lichfield. She and Hayley were soon indulging in strong mutual admiration of each other's poems. This is Anna applauding his *Essay on History* (1780):

> For now thy Genius, with a critic sway,
> O'er History's ample field extends her way . . .
> Come then, and dare th' Homeric pencil wield . . .[6]

To descend from the Homeric to the domestic, Hayley found his wife Eliza very difficult to live with, and, after the death of John Beridge in 1788, he persuaded Mrs Beridge to take Eliza as a lodger. She became friendly with the Darwins, particularly with Erasmus junior, and also wrote voluminous letters to her absent husband, 'My dear Hotspur . . .'.[7]

Hayley's admiration of Darwin is not in doubt, being fully declared in his poem 'To Dr Darwin':

> As Nature lovely Science led
>   Through all her flowery maze,
> The volume she before her spread
>   Of Darwin's radiant lays.

There follow three stanzas of coy dialogue between Nature and Science, and the poem ends as follows.

> Thus Nature and thus Science spake
>   In Flora's friendly bower;
> While Darwin's glory seem'd to wake
>   New life in every flower.

> This with delight two poets heard;
>   Time verifies it daily;
> Trust it, dear Darwin, on the word
>   Of Cowper and of Hayley.[4]

So Cowper, Hayley and Darwin offer us a triangle of mutual admiration.

Amid the exchange of pleasantries we might well expect to find some 'technology transfer' too. And this time it is Darwin who is technically indebted, to Hayley, and in particular to his six-canto poem in rhyming couplets, *The Triumphs of Temper* (1781). This poem, which went through twelve editions, is the story of the even-tempered Serena, whose reward was marriage to a nice young squire. Darwin's subject is of course completely different, but *The Botanic Garden* is similar to *The Triumphs of Temper* in format, in its personifications, in the general Nymph-machinery and occasionally in wording. Analysing Darwin's own models is not part of my plan, so I shall say no more and instead shall turn to look at Hayley's fair friend Anna Seward.

ANNA SEWARD

When Darwin arrived at Lichfield in 1756, carrying nothing more important than his letter of introduction to Canon Seward, Anna was fourteen and already writing verses. The Bishop's Palace, where she lived, is about 200 yards from Darwin's house, and, in the inward-looking society of the Cathedral Close, the Sewards and Darwins were sometimes too close for comfort.

As a poet, Anna had a special relationship with Darwin: she was his only pupil, and a very successful one. He continually encouraged her talent for verse, and soon she could 'lisp in couplets' with a facility much admired by the *literati* in her extensive circle of acquaintance. It is possible now to look on her as an archetypal 'completely literary person', almost cut off from real life yet writing endlessly out of limited experience. But that was not how she appeared in her own time, and in the 1780s she became known as 'the Swan of Lichfield', being judged the best poetess of her day. Her *Elegy on Captain Cook* (1780), 'Monody on Major André' (1781) and the 'poetic novel' *Louisa* (1784) in particular were highly regarded.

If you think Anna is more unknown than known as a poet today, and feel like skipping this section, let me remind you of her former glory. Southey tells us that 'George Washington said no circumstance in his life had been so mortifying to him as that of having been made the subject of her invective in her Monody on Major André'.[8] After the war, Washington sent an American officer to Lichfield to show her some papers which, Washington hoped, would reveal him in a better light.

Anna was won over and apologized to Washington 'for the rash injustice of my censure'.[9] Such was the Swan of Lichfield, a force taken seriously by the man who had engaged and overcome Britain's armed forces in their era of conquest. How many subsequent poets can claim such clout?

With Anna there is no denying Darwin's influence: she admitted that he was 'a sort of poetic preceptor to me',[10] and Miss Mitford unkindly called her 'a sort of Dr Darwin in petticoats.'[11] So we need not look for passages influenced by Darwin. But a deeper problem remains: how many lines were actually *written* by Darwin?

The most flagrant example is Anna's *Elegy on Captain Cook*, where we keep on meeting lines that sound like pure Darwin, such as

> Now the warm solstice o'er the shining bay,
> Darts from the north its mild meridian ray.[12]

'Solstice' and 'meridian' are favourite words of Darwin, but rather technical for Anna, and another parallel is Darwin's 'Dart from the North on pale electric streams' (*Ec.Veg.* I 129). A few lines later Anna has Cook 'ambushed' by coral, with a note about coral rocks being 'fabricated by sea-insects', which resembles Darwin's note about 'rocks built by the swarms of coral insects' (*Ec.Veg.* III 90). Next Cook sees 'a rock-built temple . . . unwrought by mortal hands', rather like Darwin's Temple of Nature 'unwrought by mortal toil' (*Tem.Nat.* I 67). Anna's description,

> Sublime the ponderous turrets rise in air,
> And the wide roof basaltic columns bear,[13]

has an obvious parallel in Darwin's 'Basaltic piers the ponderous roof sustain' (*Lov.Pl.* IV 437). The next few lines of the elegy bring us 'sister-virgins' and 'gentle Flora', who wears 'leaves of new forms' and 'folds of vegetable silk' that 'wanton in the wind'. Then we meet the fishes, described in real Darwinian cliché as 'scaly tribes' with 'diamond-eye'.

So we have to conclude either that Darwin wrote parts of Anna's *Elegy* or that Darwin copied Anna – or a little of both? The first conclusion seems the most likely, to judge from R. L. Edgeworth's account, in a letter to Walter Scott in 1812:

> Miss Seward's ode to Captain Cook stands deservedly high in the public opinion. Now, to my certain knowledge, most of the passages, which have been selected in the various reviews of that

work, were written by Dr Darwin. Indeed they bear such strong
internal marks of the Doctor's style of composition, that they may
easily be distinguished by any reader who will take the trouble to
select them. I remember them distinctly to have been his, and to
have read them aloud before Miss Seward and Doctor Darwin, in
presence of Sir Brooke Boothby, who will corroborate my assertion.[14]

One of the passages selected for praise by Dr Johnson was the
description of the polar regions, of which this is one couplet:

> Barb'd with the sleeted snow, the driving hail,
> Rush the fierce arrows of the polar gale.[15]

This has a sharpness characteristic of Darwin, who was accused of
chiselling his lines with a lancet.

But the story has a twist in the tail, because the first 58 lines of *The
Botanic Garden* incorporate 31 lines written by Anna Seward in
celebration of Darwin's botanic garden at Lichfield, lines which Darwin
kindly arranged to be sent to the *Gentleman's Magazine* for publication
(under Anna's name[6]). Anna complained – with justice – about Darwin
stealing her lines, and Edgeworth asked Darwin about it. 'He replied,
that it was a compliment, which he thought himself bound to pay to the
lady, though the verses were not of the same tenor as his own.'[14] Darwin
was usually scrupulous in acknowledging lines borrowed, such as those
from Jerningham (in *Ec.Veg.* III 367–72). Also, as Edgeworth remarks,
'I knew the late Dr Darwin well, and it was far from his temper and
habits, as it was unnecessary to his acquirements, to beg, borrow, or
steal, from any person upon earth.'[14] The matter was discussed between
Darwin and Anna beforehand,[16] so Anna knew that the lines would
appear – she was complaining about not being credited with the
authorship. Probably Darwin just forgot to insert an acknowledgment,
and his forgetting would have been aided by the subconscious feeling
that since he had provided lines for her, she could return the
compliment. As the literary relationship between them was so inces-
tuous, it also seems fair to conclude that Darwin's style must owe
something to Anna, most probably in its ornamentation, as Southey
suggested.[8]

Although I have been treating Anna Seward rather light-heartedly,
she was a capable critic as well as a successful poet. The six volumes of
her *Letters* have many acute comments on Darwin, but these are

ightweight compared with the 217-page exegesis of *The Botanic Garden* n her *Memoirs* of Darwin. Despite its painful verbosity, this is a udicious performance. One of her shortest and sharpest judgments is, Dr Darwin's poetry, while it delights the imagination, leaves the nerves it rest' (p. 174). By bringing in recent scientific discoveries, *The Botanic Garden* breaks new ground, she says, and 'forms an additional order in he fanes of the Muses' – so brilliantly that 'it will probably never have an :qual in its particular class' (p. 178). 'The genuine charms of his muse nust endure so long as the English language shall exist' (p. 208). She inalyses the verse, its accentuation, phraseology, mannerisms and weaknesses, with a skill that no one who is not an eighteenth-century poet can really hope to rival. She concludes that *The Botanic Garden* will :ome to enjoy 'the slowly-accumulating suffrages of those discerning ind generous readers who delight in fertile and daring Genius' (p. 381). Anna was rather scathing about Darwin as a man, so her tribute to the power of his poem was both discerning and magnanimous.

SCOTT

A young poet particularly admired by Anna Seward was Walter Scott (1772–1832), and he more than repaid any obligation by editing her 3-volume *Poetical Works* (1810). Scott has a tenuous link with Darwin too, because he is sometimes said to be Darwin's successor as a popular poet. However, his picaresque poems *Lay of the Last Minstrel* (1805) and *Marmion* (1808) had a much wider appeal than *The Botanic Garden*.

Scott was generous in judging his fellow poets, including Darwin. When in 1796 William Taylor criticized his poem 'The Chase' because it 'leans too much to the Darwin style', Scott replied that 'I do not . . . think quite so severely of the Darwinian style, as to deem it utterly inconsistent with the Ballad.'[17] As well as being generous, this is also one of the first instances of the adjective 'Darwinian', which soon became a standard literary term.

Scott also made a kind judgment on Darwin when writing to Edgeworth in 1812. Scott remarked that some passages in *The Botanic Garden*, such as 'the march of Cambyses' and the 'descent of Juno', ensure Darwin a 'ranking among British poets of the highest class'.[18]

I have found only one passage where Scott seems to lean on Darwin. That is in the Melrose-by-moonlight scene in *The Lay of the Last Minstrel* (Canto II, verses 7–11), when the Monk leads the Knight into the cloister-garden, where 'beneath their feet were the bones of the dead'.

There is a similar scene in Canto III of *The Loves of the Plants* (lines
15–38), when an imp leads Circe into a churchyard, where a sickly yew
sheds

> O'er many a mouldering bone its nightly dew.

In Scott's cloister-garden

> Spreading herbs, and flowrets bright,
> Glistened with the dew of night;

the first of these two lines recalls Darwin's

> Crops the young floret and the bladed herb,   (*Lov.Pl.* II 216)

especially as *bright* is Darwin's favourite adjective, used 108 times in *The
Botanic Garden*. When Scott's Monk raises his eyes, he sees the aurora
glowing in the north with 'bright . . . streamers' like 'glittering
squadrons' of soldiers, as if to rival Darwin's 'electric streams', of the
aurora and 'glittering bands' and 'bright squadrons' of Nymphs
(*Ec.Veg.* I 129, 93; III 201). Scott's visitors enter the church through a
'steel-clenched postern door', Darwin's through 'ponderous portals'
with 'hoarse' hinges. Scott has moonlight falling on the oriel window,
showing

> many a prophet, and many a saint,
> Whose image on the glass was dyed . . .
> The moon-beam kissed the holy pane,
> And threw on the pavement a bloody stain.

Darwin's church is also moonlit and 'the moon-beam falls', he tells us,
'through the coloured glass' into aisles lined with statues of 'protecting
saints' (*Lov.Pl.* III 20–7). Moonlight is not strong enough to throw
colours, as Scott implies, but Darwin's slightly ambiguous wording
could have misled him. In the absence of parallels elsewhere in Scott's
poems, these probable echoes of Darwin must be declared 'non-proven'.

SOUTHEY

Robert Southey (1774–1843) now shines less brightly than his fellow

'Lake poets' Wordsworth and Coleridge; but he was an admirable man, esteemed for his hard work and virtue, like Walter Scott. Born in Bristol, he caught the French Revolutionary fever at Westminster School, from which he was expelled for an article he wrote in a magazine. He entered Balliol College, Oxford, in 1792, met Coleridge in 1794, planned Pantisocracy with him and, partly in consequence, married Edith Fricker in 1795. He settled at Greta Hall, Keswick, in 1803 and lived there for the rest of his life, supporting his large family, and often Coleridge's too, by ephemeral writing for journals. Southey's long poem *Joan of Arc* (1795) was popular enough to go through five editions, and his later oriental epic poems *Thalaba* (1801) and *The Curse of Kehama* (1813) were much admired, particularly by Shelley. Though a radical in the 1790s, Southey became a conservative after 1800 and was Poet Laureate from 1813 until his death in 1843.

Southey was ideally placed to receive Darwin's influence: he was eighteen when *The Economy of Vegetation* appeared; he was an ardent supporter of the French Revolution at that time; he lived in Bristol and knew Thomas Beddoes, Darwin's keenest disciple in the 1790s. But even in *Joan of Arc*, written when he was twenty, he set himself at a distance from Darwin by writing in blank verse. And the gap was maintained in *Thalaba* and *The Curse of Kehama*, written in a complex 'free verse'.

It would be wrong to say that Darwin had no influence at all on Southey. The glittering jewels that go to make up Darwin's 'dazzling manner' can sometimes be glimpsed in Southey's poems, especially *Thalaba*. But there is nothing comparable with the clear echoes that leap from the pages of Coleridge. The resemblances are more general. For example, *Thalaba* has magic cars and underground rivers; and when in Book II Abdaldar is about to plunge a dagger into Thalaba, Southey suddenly brings in the 'Blast of the Desert', the Simoom, to save his hero. At another climactic moment, in Book IV when Thalaba is in desperate straits, a sandstorm rolls up:

> High . . . high in heaven upcurl'd
> The dreadful sand-spouts moved:
> Swift as the whirlwind that impell'd their way . . .
> Columns of sand came moving on,
> Red in the burning ray. (*Thalaba* IV 536–8, 527–8)

This may owe something to Darwin's well-known picture of the army of Cambyses overwhelmed by the sand (which also impressed Wordsworth and Scott):

> Now o'er their head the whizzing whirlwinds breathe,
> And the live desert pants, and heaves beneath;
> Tinged by the crimson sun, vast columns rise
> Of eddying sands.   (*Ec.Veg.* II 473–6)

Another possible but dubious parallel is Thalaba's vision of dancing girls:

> Transparent garments to the greedy eye
>   Exposed their harlot limbs,
> Which moved, in every wanton gesture skill'd.
>   (*Thalaba* VI 365–7)

This might be linked with some of Darwin's 'wanton beauties' in *The Loves of the Plants*, for example,

> O'er her light limbs the dim transparence plays,
> And the fair form, it seems to hide, betrays. (*Lov.Pl.* IV 343–4)

These possible echoes must be regarded as at most casual remembrances, however, because there is no other indication that Southey took notice of what he called 'the brocade fashion of Dr Darwin'.[8]

So we have to conclude that Southey was genuinely unimpressed by Darwin. This surprises me: of the three Lake poets, Southey was closest to Darwin, because both are intensely visual, both revel in outlandish scenery and mythical or magical stories, and both write to entertain. So I had expected Southey to draw on Darwin. But it is clear that Wordsworth and Coleridge profited far more than Southey from their acquaintance with Darwin's verse.

LANDOR

One unlikely oriental tale, *Thalaba*, leads us to another, Landor's *Gebir*. Circumstances conspired to ensure that Walter Savage Landor (1775–1864) was also ideally placed to receive Darwin's influence, for Landor was expelled from Rugby School in 1791 and continued his schooling for eighteen months with a tutor – William Langley, Rector of Fenny Bentley near Ashbourne. When *The Economy of Vegetation* appeared in June 1792, Landor was seventeen and living locally. Later in 1792 he went up to Oxford, where he became known as a 'Jacobin'.

Landor's epic poem *Gebir* (1798) was little read, but admired by Southey, Coleridge and Shelley. When I came to reread it listening for echoes of Darwin, I was surprised to find very few. There are some rather Darwinian nymphs and aerial journeys, but I found only one strong parallel, when an aquatic nymph wrestles with the shepherd Tamar; having vanquished him,

> She smil'd, and more of pleasure than disdain
> Was in her dimpled chin, and liberal lip,
> And eyes that languished, lengthening – just like love.
>
> *(Gebir* I 214–6)

The wording and the *l* alliteration recall Darwin's description of his aquatic Nymphs:

> Each dimpling cheek with warmer blushes dyes,
> Laughs on the lips, and lightens in the eyes.   *(Ec.Veg.* III 51–2)

But one swallow does not make a summer, and my expectation that Landor would be indebted to Darwin proved to be wrong. Nor did I find resemblances in any other of Landor's poems. This was another blind alley.

MOORE

I cannot ignore 'Ierne's sweetest lyrist', as Shelley called him, Thomas Moore (1779–1852), whose *Irish Melodies* (1808 onwards) won him a popularity rivalled only by Scott and Byron. But his lyrics have virtually nothing in common with Darwin; so no link is to be expected, and I have found none.

Moore's oriental extravaganza *Lalla Rookh* (1817) is written largely in rhyming couplets, with a strong scenic background and not a few nymphs. Here, if anywhere, echoes of Darwin might be heard. But there seem to be none, apart from random coincidences; nor is there any mention of Darwin in the hundreds of footnotes to the poem. So, symbolizing Moore by his favourite instrument, we may say that

> The harp that once through Tara's halls
>   The soul of music shed
> Ignored the siren Darwin's calls
>   And calmly cut him dead.

CAMPBELL

Thomas Campbell (1777–1844) was famous for his songs of battle – 'Ye Mariners of England', 'The Battle of the Baltic' and 'Hohenlinden' – and his patriotic virtue was rewarded by burial in Westminster Abbey. He seems likely to be poles apart from Darwin, who wrote, 'I hate war' (and really did).

But the young Campbell was not so martial. His first long poem, *The Pleasures of Hope* (1799), written when he was twenty-one, is heavily indebted to Darwin's *Botanic Garden*, and also to another poem published in 1792, Samuel Rogers's *The Pleasures of Memory*. Campbell's poem is in 539 rhyming couplets and his language can only be described as Darwinian pastiche. For example, Darwin's pet adjective, *glittering*, appears in line 2 of Campbell's poem and again in line 53; we also have *ethereal* (line 1), *viewless* (lines 38 and 51), *tiptoe* (line 28) and many more, including the unusual *sun-illumined* – which the *Oxford English Dictionary* credits to Campbell, but which was actually used twice by Darwin.[19] A young man writing his first poem in the 1790s might be half-expected to take Darwin as a model; so there is no need to follow the many parallels in detail. I shall limit myself to three examples.

The first four lines of *The Pleasures of Hope* declare the author's allegiance at once:

> At summer eve, when Heaven's ethereal bow
> Spans with bright arch the glittering hills below,
> Why to yon mountain turns the musing eye,
> Whose sunbright summit mingles with the sky?   (I 1–4)

This is like the opening of Canto IV of *The Loves of the Plants*, where the first two lines tell us that the sun 'flames in the West', and the next four depict a rainbow watched by a musing eye (or rather the eye of a Muse):

> O'er heaven's wide arch refracted lustres flow,
> And bend in air the many-colour'd bow. –
> The tuneful Goddess on the glowing sky
> Fix'd in mute ecstacy her glistening eye.   (*Lov.Pl.* IV 3–6)

Three of the four rhyme-words are the same, as well as *heaven* and *arch*, and Darwin's *glistening* is only an elegant variation on *glittering*, already pre-empted for use in line 23. Nearly all Campbell's other words are Darwinian: for example, the second half of his line 4 is supplied verbatim n Darwin's 'Fire . . . mingles with the skies';[20] and the most striking of Campbell's adjectives, *sunbright*, appears twice in *The Economy of Vegetation* – 'sun-bright showers' and 'sun-bright leaf'.[21]

A second similarity is Campbell's reliance on Darwin for his character-sketches. Darwin presents Elijah in lines which begin

Thus, when Elija mark'd from Carmel's brow . . .

and Campbell's approach is very similar:

Thus, while Elijah's burning wheels prepare
From Carmel's height to sweep the fields of air.

Darwin's Nymphs of Fire tell Franklin to

seize the tiptoe lightnings, ere they fly,

while Campbell's Hope tells Franklin to

grasp the lightning's fiery wing.

Darwin calls Linnaeus 'the Swedish sage'; and so does Campbell.[22]

My third example is Campbell's long attack on slavery (*Pleas.Hope* I 473–570), which has obvious similarities to Darwin's (*Lov.Pl.* III 435–56 and *Ec.Veg.* II 413–30).

Since Campbell's opening lines are so thoroughly Darwinian, it is of interest that the opening might have been quite different, because Campbell greatly altered it at a late stage. However, the original opening (published after his death) is even more Darwinian, because it includes a twenty-line description of Nightmare, which is very similar to Darwin's in Canto III of *The Loves of the Plants*. For example, Darwin stresses the paralysis of the nightmare-victim's limbs and voice:

Her snow-white limbs hang helpless from the bed . . .
In vain to scream with quivering lips she tries.   (III 60, 71)

Campbell follows with the flat (and rightly rejected) line:

No voice can call for aid, no limb can turn.[23]

Darwin's victim inhales only 'suffocative breath' so that her 'heart-pulse' is interrupted as if 'in death'. Campbell's victim inhales 'tortur'd breath', and is immured 'living in the vaults of death'.[24]

The merits of Campbell's poem were recognized by the reviewers, and so was his allegiance to Darwin: the *Critical Review* said 'we are sometimes reminded of Dr Darwin's versification', and gave examples; and Campbell was called the 'Darwin of Edinburgh'.[25] The young poet was none too pleased about this, but as his poem was very successful, going through five editions in two years, he was able to take quick action to dispel the impression that he was a disciple of Darwin. He could scarcely rewrite the poem in non-Darwinian phraseology, so instead he added 130 lines, which can be read as an attack on Darwin (though not by name, because he was still alive) for being a 'dark idolater of Chance' who with 'all his parting energy' dares to 'call this barren world sufficient bliss'. Though 'of cultured soul, and sapient eye serene', this deplorable sceptic treats Man as

> Spouse of the worm, and brother of the clay.   (II 306)

The wording is rather like Darwin's in *The Temple of Nature* (IV 427–8, 460); but that was not published until 1803, so Campbell's phrases probably derive from the caricature of Darwin's theory of evolution in 'The Loves of the Triangles' (1798).[26]

To most readers at the time, including Campbell, evolution without divine intervention was an appalling thought. Campbell states quite clearly his opinion that scepticism is a crime worse than murder:

> Ah me! The laurelled wreath that Murder rears,
> Blood-nursed and watered by the widow's tears,
> Seems not so foul, so tainted, and so dread,
> As waves the night-shade round the sceptic's head.[27]

When such a morality prevailed – and was approved by a well-educated young poet – it is easy to see why Erasmus Darwin was so viciously put down after 1800, and why Charles Darwin suffered such severe attacks, even in the relatively enlightened 1860s.

There is no need to say more about Campbell. Having grown to regret his early flirtation with Darwin, he tried to purge his style of Darwinian pollution. But none of his other long poems did so well as *The Pleasures of Hope*, and the success of that poem depended not a little on the glittering visual style he borrowed from Darwin.

CRABBE (Fig. 5)

I have been running through the poets in this chapter quite rapidly, but that is no longer possible with George Crabbe (1754–1832), whose ties with Darwin are many and complex.

Crabbe was born at Aldeburgh in Suffolk, where, after apprenticeship, he set up practice as a surgeon-apothecary in 1775. He had already written some poetry and was keenly interested in natural history, particularly botany, which he studied with 'insatiable ardour'. His practice was not a success, so in 1780 he decided to try his luck as a writer in London. In 1781 he found a patron in Edmund Burke and was able to publish his long poem in rhyming couplets, *The Library*. In 1782 Crabbe was ordained priest and became chaplain to the Duke of Rutland at Belvoir Castle. He married, published *The Village* (1783), and for the next thirty years held livings in the Vale of Belvoir, where he lived from 1782 until 1792 and again from 1804 until 1814. He returned to Suffolk between 1792 and 1804. His *Poems* published in 1807 included *The Parish Register* and a revised version of *The Library*. His poem *The Borough* appeared in 1810 and *Tales of the Hall* in 1819. In 1814 Crabbe became rector of Trowbridge, Wiltshire, where he lived for the rest of his life. Crabbe was an opium addict for forty years, but any ill effects were slight.[28]

There are obvious biographical parallels between Crabbe and Darwin. Both were medically trained and can be said to have 'practised medicine', one as a surgeon-apothecary, the other as a physician. Both became deeply interested in botany in the mid 1770s, and wrote botanical works *in English*: Darwin's were published, and so were some of Crabbe's, but one of his botanical contributions was burnt, being condemned by a Cambridge don who 'could not stomach the notion of degrading such a science by treating of it in a modern language' – or so Crabbe's son tells us.[29] Both wrote long poems in rhyming couplets in the 1780s and both were noted for bringing science into their verse: Crabbe has been called 'the most scientific of all English poets',[30] but this is surely one superlative that can scarcely be denied to Darwin – unless you deny that he is an English poet! So both Crabbe and Darwin were men of medicine very keen on botany who in the 1780s wrote long poems in rhyming couplets of scientific timbre.

The resemblances go deeper. Both were successful in their day as poets, and wrote in rather similar styles, which provoked similar complaints. Coleridge's notebook entry, 'Dr Darwin's Poetry, a succes-

sion of Landscapes or Paintings', is matched by Hazlitt's remark tha
Crabbe 'paints in words, instead of colours: there is no other dif
ference'.[31] Both poets were criticized for 'verbal photography', contrive
and lacking in passion. Because of these resemblances, and becaus
Crabbe's best-known poems appeared after 1800, it was widely believe
that Crabbe was influenced by Darwin: for example, Jeffrey said Crabb
was 'frequently misled by Darwin into a sort of mock-heroic mag
nificence', and Hunt made a similar accusation.[32] The opposite may als
be true, however: Crabbe's *The Library* and *The Village* (1783) may hav
influenced Darwin, for it was not until 1784 that he completed the firs
draft of *The Loves of the Plants*.[33] So to be fair to Crabbe, I must brea
my stated rule and look at the mutual interaction of Crabbe and Darwin

Although I do not know that Crabbe and Darwin ever met, they coul
easily have done so during the 1780s. In 1782 Crabbe went to live i
Belvoir Castle, which can be seen from Darwin's birthplace at Elston
ten miles away. For the next ten years Crabbe lived in the area as priest i
three parishes, Stathern, Muston and West Allington: among his fellow
clergymen in neighbouring parishes were Thomas Hall, Darwin'
nephew, rector of Westborough, and Darwin's brother John, rector o
Elston and Carlton Scroop.[34] All six parishes mentioned are within
circle of radius seven miles. Also within that circle, at Elston, wa
Darwin's eldest brother Robert, a dedicated botanist and author o
Principia Botanica (1787) – another botanical book written in English
Though evidence is lacking, it seems probable that Crabbe met some o
Darwin's close relatives during his first ten years in the 'Darwir
country'. So, whether or not Darwin met Crabbe, we can safely assum
that Darwin would have been aware of Crabbe's poems in the 1780s.

Anna Seward tells us that the idea and the name of Darwin's *Botanic
Garden* came from the botanic garden which he created 'about the yea
1777' in a previously 'tangled and sequestered scene' about a mile to th
west of Lichfield.[35] As soon as she saw the garden, Anna wrote som
verses about it (those later stolen by Darwin), and he remarked that th
Linnaean system was 'unexplored poetic ground, and an happy subjec
for the Muse': she encouraged him to write such a poem. Anna may hav
been a year or two early with the date, but the botanic garden wa
certainly in full flower well before Darwin left Lichfield in March 1781
So the subject of his poem was decided before the publication o
Crabbe's *The Library* in July 1781, and it is not possible that 'the very
germ of Darwin's botanical epic lies in Crabbe's *Library*', as Chamberlain suggested.[36]

Far more convincing is Chamberlain's suggestion that *The Loves o the Plants* was influenced in tone and technique by Crabbe's description in *The Library* of the 'vegetable tribes',

> Whose fruitful beds o'er every balmy mead
> Teem with new life, and hills, and vales, and groves,
> Feed the still flame, and nurse the silent loves;
> Which, when the Spring calls forth their genial power,
> Swell with the seed, and flourish in the flower:
> There, with the husband-slaves, in royal pride,
> Queens, like the Amazons of old, reside;
> There, like the Turk, the lordly husband lives,
> And joy to all the gay seraglio gives;
> There, in the secret chambers, veil'd from sight,
> A bashful tribe in hidden flames delight;
> There, in the open day, and gaily deck'd,
> The bolder brides their distant lords expect;
> Who with the wings of love instinctive rise,
> And on prolific winds each ardent bridegroom flies.[37]

The first five lines here are fairly standard spring-worship, except for the mention of 'silent loves'. The next four lines, however, have six words in common with Darwin's picture of the mimosa:

> Veil'd, with gay decency and modest pride,
> Slow to the mosque she moves, an eastern bride;
> There her soft vows unceasing love record
> Queen of the bright seraglio of her Lord.   (*Lov.Pl.* I 309–12)

In the last six lines of the passage from Crabbe, the 'bashful tribe' delighting in 'hidden flames' in 'secret chambers' refers to the Linnaean class *Cryptogamia*, as he remarks in a footnote. Darwin translates *Cryptogamia* as 'Clandestine Marriage', and gives as one example the plant Barometz, which feels 'the *secret* fire' produced by 'the flames of Love' (*Lov.Pl.* I 281–2). Crabbe's last four lines, so his footnote tells us, refer to the class *Dioecia*. Darwin translates this as 'Two houses', and one of his examples is mistletoe:

> Scorning the sordid soil, aloft she springs,
> Shakes her white plume, and claps her golden wings;
> High o'er the fields of boundless ether roves,
> And seeks amid the clouds her soaring loves!   (*Lov.Pl* I 261–4)

This is somewhat similar to Crabbe's last four lines, though Darwin h[
no 'bolder brides' or 'ardent bridegrooms'. These examples clearly sho
that *The Library* influenced the tone and technique of *The Loves of th*
Plants (but not *The Economy of Vegetation*).

I now turn to the other side of the coin, and my proper theme
Darwin's influence on Crabbe. This is easily proved because Crabb
like Campbell, reacted against Darwin after 1800 and, realizing that th
original version of *The Library* might be thought to resemble Darwin, h
altered the poem when it was reprinted in 1807, so as to distance himse
from Darwin. The 'husband-slaves', the 'gay seraglio' and the 'bolde
brides' all vanish, and this cheerful humanization is replaced by du
abstractions and negative sentiments more appropriate to a clergyman

> Where flow'ry Tribes, in Valleys, Fields and Groves,
> Nurse the still Flame, and feed the silent Loves –
> Loves, where no Grief, nor Joy, nor Bliss, nor Pain,
> Warm the glad Heart or vex the labouring Brain;
> But as the green Blood moves along the Blade,
> The Bed of Flora on the Branch is made;
> Where, without Passion, Love instinctive lives,
> And gives new Life, unconscious that it gives.[38]

The array of capital letters guarantees respectability. Crabbe could n
longer be accused of naughty thoughts; but the changes show how ver
much aware of Darwin he was.

Crabbe's long poem *The Parish Register* (1807) has some interestin
links with Darwin too. In form it is a mere catalogue of names of birth
marriages and deaths, just as *The Loves of the Plants* was a catalogue c
the names of plants with their 'births, marriages and deaths' as it were
'The Linnaean Register' would serve as an alternative title for Darwin
poem. This similarity is probably subconscious, unless Crabbe wante
to rival Darwin in making a poem out of unpromising material; but ther
are also conscious resemblances, as when Crabbe introduced th
gardener Peter Pratt, who named his first child *Lonicera*. Crabb
proceeds to poke fun at him:

> Not DARWIN'S self had more delight to sing
> Of floral courtship, in th' awaken'd spring;
> Than *Peter Pratt*, who simpering loves to tell,
> How rise the *Stamens*, as the *Pistils* swell;
> How bend and curl the moist-top to the spouse,

And give and take the vegetable vows;
How those esteem'd of old, but tips and chives,
Are tender husbands and obedient wives;
Who live and love within the sacred bower, –
That bridal bed, the vulgar term a Flower.[39]

There are deliberate echoes here of Darwinian phrases, such as 'woo and win their vegetable loves'. But Crabbe's mind was just as deeply botanic as Darwin's, and their affinity shines through the satire. Crabbe could not help admiring Darwin for having made such a success out of a subject Crabbe himself found so congenial – as shown by his (non-satirical) early poem about the courting of Mira in the Suffolk countryside:

When we pluck'd the wild blossoms that blush'd in the grass,
And I taught my dear maid their species and class.[40]

Crabbe continues his satire on Darwin in *The Parish Register* by making Peter Pratt into quite a *voyeur* of plant-sex as he performs his fertilizations:

'View that light frame where *Cucumis* lies spread,
And trace the husbands in their golden bed,
Three turged *Anthers*; – then no more delay,
But haste and bear them to their spouse away . . .
Then by thyself, from prying glance secure,
Twirl the full tip and make the marriage sure'.[39]

This may seem a little indelicate for a clergyman, but at least it is satire. No such excuse is possible when Crabbe comes to make his own comments, still seemingly quite carried away by the excitement:

'Tis good, 'tis pleasant, through th' advancing year,
To see unnumber'd growing forms appear;
What leafy-life from Earth's broad bosom rise!
What insect myriads seek the summer skies!
What scaly tribes in every streamlet move!
What plumy people sing in every grove!
All with the year awak'd, to life's great duty, Love.[41]

'scaly tribes' and 'plumy people' are satirical digs at Darwin; but the idea that Love is 'life's great duty' goes beyond even Darwin, and also beyond the sentiments proper for a clergyman. So in the 1808 edition of the poem Crabbe altered the last line to:

All with the year awaked to life, delight, and love.[42]

So love is now only the icing on the cake, not 'life's great duty'; as Crabbe indicates a few lines later, God is really in charge, and that is where our great duty lies.[43]

The fertilization of plants rears its head again in one of the *Tales of the Hall* (1819), entitled 'The Preceptor Husband', where the pedantic bridegroom tries to instruct his bride:

Now o'er the grounds they rambled many a mile;
He show'd the flowers, the stamina, the style,
Calix and corol, pericarp and fruit,
And all the plant produces, branch and root.[44]

But the husband carried his pedantry too far:

He show'd the various foliage plants produce,
Lunate and lyrate, runcinate, retuse;
Long were the learned words, and urged with force,
Panduriform, pinnatifid, premorse,
Latent, and patent, papulous, and plane –
'Oh!' said the pupil, 'it will turn my brain.'[44]

The discussion of leaf shapes and their terminology recalls Darwin's illustration, in *A System of Vegetables*, of 168 different leaf shapes with anglicized names – including several which appear in Crabbe's lines. More than thirty of Darwin's words predate the earliest usage cited in the *Oxford English Dictionary*.

Crabbe returned to the botanic theme in his late poem *The Flowers*, which is a catalogue comparing women he knew with particular flowers. The humanization and cataloguing of the flowers has an obvious similarity to *The Loves of the Plants*.

Crabbe the clergyman should have disapproved of evolution, but there are four lines in *Tales of the Hall* which indicate just the opposite when he describes a 'mountain-rock',

And in that rock are shapes of shells, and forms
Of creatures in old worlds, of nameless worms,

Whose generations lived and died ere man,
A worm of other class, to crawl began.[45]

Possibly Crabbe was remembering the passages in *The Temple of Nature* where Darwin expresses the hope

That man should ever be the friend of man;
Should eye with tenderness all living forms,
His brother-emmets, and his sister-worms,   (IV 426–8)

and then discusses fossil shells and his idea that 'the tall mountains', those 'isles of rock', are 'mighty monuments of past delight' (*Tem.Nat.* IV 426–8 and 447–50).

As Crabbe and Darwin were both 'photographers', their scenic effects have many similarities. An example is the picture of the aurora in *Sir Eustace Grey*.[46]

This brings us back to Crabbe's opium habit, because Alethea Hayter has suggested that *Sir Eustace Grey* was in part an opium-dream sequence. Crabbe's opium addiction apparently began about 1790, when he was living in the 'Darwin country' and when Darwin was dispensing opium rather freely. Was Darwin responsible? I would say not: there is nothing to implicate him and Crabbe's addiction could well have arisen from self-treatment. Since the opium seems to have had little ill-effect, I need say no more about it. [47]

GOETHE

Although I intended to discuss only poets who wrote in English, I must make an exception for Johann Wolfgang von Goethe (1749–1832), because he is such a major figure in European literature and is so often linked with Darwin.

They go together because both strode so easily across the border between science and poetry, and made substantial contributions on both sides of the border. What is more, their fields of science were similar. Goethe concentrated on botany and biology, particularly the morphology of plants, the theory of organic forms and the development of species, with a lesser contribution in optics and the appreciation of cloud forms.[48] Some of Darwin's main work was also in these areas, though he made discoveries in other subjects. Within these common fields Darwin and Goethe thought along similar lines. Both were 'Nature philosophers', deeply impressed by the similarities in form among living things, particularly plants; and they both devoted much attention to the forms of leaves and flowers.

Their commonality of interest is shown by the coincidence that Darwin's *Loves of the Plants*, based explicitly on Ovid's *Metamorphoses* (Darwin says he will metamorphose the plants back to people), was followed within a year by Goethe's *Metamorphosen der Pflanzen (The Metamorphosis of Plants)*. Although Goethe's *Metamorphosen* is intended to mean 'development' rather than 'metamorphosis' in Ovid's sense, the near-simultaneous publication of the two books is a natural outcome of the interest taken by Darwin and Goethe in Linnaean plant-classification, an interest that began for both in the mid 1770s and came to fruition in the 1780s. Indeed Goethe's essay, with its detailed descriptions of the development of leaves, calyx, corolla, fruits, etc.,[49] might well have served as an introductory chapter to Darwin's Linnaean translations, the *System of Vegetables* (1785) and *The Families of Plants* (1787).

Goethe's ideas on plant morphology were often intuitional rather than experimental, and sometimes he follows in Darwin's track. Goethe had the idea that the female parts of plants grow spirally while the males tend to be straight and vertical, and he cited *Vallisneria spiralis*, which figures as one of the Plates in *The Loves of the Plants*.[50]

I have not found any evidence that Darwin knew of Goethe's work, and such knowledge seems unlikely because he did not read German; but Goethe certainly knew of Darwin's work. There are references to the *Botanic Garden* or *Zoonomia* in Goethe's diary in 1795, 1798, 1810 and 1817; and, in a letter to Schiller in 1798, he gives a full description of *The Botanic Garden*, concluding that, with some reservations, 'I am basically favourable to Darwin'.[51] In 1810 he mentions his debt to the paper on ocular spectra, nominally written by R. W. Darwin, but with help from his father. Much of this information comes from the book *Goethe's Knowledge of English Literature*, by J. Boyd, who tells us that 'elsewhere Goethe expresses a high opinion of Darwin as a scholar and on several occasions admits some indebtedness to him, as in a letter to Clemens on 15 January 1826':

> The merits of this man have long been known to me, and through him I have been helped on my scientific paths in more than one respect.[52]

Goethe was fascinated by the forms of clouds, and when in 1820 he heard of Luke Howard's classification of cloud-forms, he wrote a long article on *The Shape of Clouds according to Howard*. This has a poem in honour of Howard, and several cloud poems, including four entitled 'Stratus', 'Cumulus', 'Cirrus' and 'Nimbus'.[53] Though these events occurred after Darwin's death, he is linked with them by his achievement in explaining scientifically how clouds usually form. So it happened that when in 1983 the Royal Meteorological Society formed a group for the History of Meteorology, the first talk at their first meeting was on Erasmus Darwin and the second talk was on Luke Howard and Goethe. (No, I was *not* the organizer of the meeting!)

Perhaps the most illuminating link between Darwin and Goethe is that described by Elizabeth Sewell, in her book *The Orphic Voice*. The legendary Orpheus had the power to make nature dance to his tune, and 'Orphic' poets are those who take natural history as their chief subject and become so deeply involved with nature that they half-imply that they have insight into, and power over, natural processes. Such Orphic minds are quite rare, Elizabeth Sewell says, but in the late eighteenth century 'the respective Orpheus figures of Erasmus Darwin and Goethe appear'. Part III of her book, running to more than 100 pages, is entitled 'Erasmus Darwin and Goethe: Linnaean and Ovidian taxonomy'. Darwin declares his Orphism, she says, by using the Eleusinian mysteries as a structure in *The Temple of Nature* and then relying on the Orphic creation myth. Goethe's Orphism is continually expressed through his preoccupation with form in nature, and more explicitly in his *Urworte: Orphisch* of 1820. Darwin's propensity to fly with clouds, and Goethe's cloud-poems, are further facets of their Orphism. These Orphic links are complex and interesting, but I cannot do more than mention them here.

To summarize, it is clear that Darwin and Goethe had 'Nature-philosopher' minds that ran on similar lines. As poets, both were very strong on visual imagery: Goethe was fond of 'picture-thinking' and Darwin was condemned for peppering his poems with pretty pictures. Both brooded over form in nature, especially in plants, and both were Orphic as poets, in seeing a special power and value in natural processes. Goethe acknowledged his debt to Darwin, but it was not so much an 'influence' as an encouragement to continue along the path Goethe was already taking.

SOTHEBY

From Goethe we can return to England via William Sotheby (1757–1833), well known for his translation from the German of

Wieland's *Oberon* (1798), which influenced Coleridge and Keats. Although Sotheby's *Oberon* is in Spenserian stanzas, he adopts Darwin's language and many of his favourite words. When Jeffrey reviewed Sotheby's later translation of *The Georgics*, he complained about 'the Darwinian modulation with which Mr Sotheby's versification is infected', and quoted examples of his '*Darwinianism*'.[54] Since the influence of Darwin is so obvious, I shall give only one quotation from *Oberon*, of Huon and Rezia enjoying their love:

> Not linked with closer twine young ivy wreathes
> Her flexile shoot the wedded stem around,
> Than with fond clasp her arms the youth enring.
> Where overshadowing palms cool shelter fling,
> Soft on the pillowy moss he seats his bride.

(Canto VI, stanza IV)

Sotheby's 'on the pillowy moss' is cited in the *Oxford English Dictionary* as the earliest example of the word *pillowy*. However, this is not correct because one of Darwin's heroines, 'the beauteous Aegle',

> Sinks on the pillowy moss her drooping head,   (*Ec.Veg.* IV 97)

and Darwin has an earlier *pillowy* in *The Loves of the Plants* (IV 410 in the first edition). Another obvious parallel is between Darwin's 'clasp with fond arms' (*Lov.Pl.* I 20) and Sotheby's 'with fond clasp her arms . . .'

MARY TIGHE

The Irish poet Mary Tighe (1772–1810) was well known for her *Psyche* which ran to 372 Spenserian stanzas and at least six editions. Completed in 1795 and much influenced by Darwin, *Psyche* was published in 1811 and has remained alive in literary history because of its influence on Keats.[55] Echoes of Darwin are apparent from the outset. Tighe introduces Psyche as 'Fair Psyche . . .' at the start of a line; and so does Darwin (*Ec.Veg.* IV 48). In *The Economy of Vegetation* (II 222–8) Darwin dazzles us with amethysts, agates, opals, 'blue' sapphire, rubies that 'blush' and diamonds that 'blaze': all these gemstones and their qualifying epithets reappear in stanzas 46 and 47 of Canto I of *Psyche*. There are also suspicious resemblances to Darwin in stanzas 17, 19, 21,

39 and 42 of Canto I, and from time to time thereafter until Psyche's final triumph in stanza 59 of Canto VI, when she drinks immortal love

Bathed in ambrosial showers of bliss eternally!

Bliss such as this outdoes even Darwin: the best he can offer in ambrosial vein is

Steep in ambrosial dews the Woodbine's bells. (*Ec.Veg.* IV 499)

CARY

Henry F. Cary (1772–1844) is best known for his translation of Dante, but in his early literary career he was a protégé of Anna Seward, whose correspondence with him is extensive. So he was well informed about Darwin and wrote a long essay 'On the Life and Writings of Erasmus Darwin', published in the *London Magazine* in December 1822. Cary was a clergyman and he disapproved of Darwin for his lack of religious faith and for his theory of evolution. He also condemned Darwin for suggesting an unsuitable subject to a serious painter he knew, namely 'a shower, in which there should be represented a redbreast holding up an expanded umbrella in its claws'. Cary may have been blind to banter, but his final summary of Darwin's verse is quite judicious:

> As the singularity of his poems caused them to be too much admired at first, so they are now more neglected than they deserve. There is about as much variety in them as in a bed of tulips . . . diversely streaked and freckled . . . in which the bizarre . . . prevails.[56]

In view of his disapproval, Cary would not be expected to follow Darwin; and I have found no obvious parallels.

BARLOW

Joel Barlow (1754–1812) used to be called 'the first American poet', and his lengthy epic in rhyming couplets, *The Vision of Columbus* (1787), may possibly have influenced Darwin. But Barlow's greatly revised version, *The Columbiad*, which came out in 1807, has many distinctly

Darwinian descriptions: 'that he resembles Darwin, no one, we think, will doubt', Jeffrey remarked in his review,[57] giving two pages of quotations to back up his pronouncement.

LESSER POETS LINKED WITH DARWIN

The poets so far discussed are quite well known, or were so in their day, but they are of course only 'the tip of the iceberg'. Many lesser-known poets have close connections with Darwin: among them are Brooke Boothby, Thomas Beddoes, Humphry Davy, Richard Payne Knight, Richard Polwhele, Dewhurst Bilsborrow, Thomas Busby, John Gisborne, Elihu H. Smith, William Stevens, and others 'whose names are dark' today. I shall give a paragraph or two to each of the first five of these, not because of their literary merit but because their links with Darwin are varied and interesting.

Brooke Boothby (1744–1824), a friend and disciple of Darwin, was a very civilized man, the eighteenth-century country gentleman at his best. His family lived at Ashbourne Hall, and as a young man he became friendly with Rousseau, who stayed at nearby Wootton Hall in 1766–7. Boothby made the Grand Tour and returned with an unpublished manuscript of Rousseau's that had been entrusted to him. He gravitated naturally into Anna Seward's literary circle at Lichfield in the 1770s. He was also one-third of Darwin's three-man Lichfield Botanical Society, and helped Darwin with the translations of Linnaeus in the 1780s. He succeeded to his father's baronetcy in 1787.

Boothby was a bantam-weight as a poet, and his longest poem, an imitation of Horace, is dedicated to Darwin. Here he offers us the 'bright example' of Darwin,

> whose ever-open door
> Draws, like Bethesda's pool, the suffering poor;
> Where some fit cure the wretched all obtain,
> Relieved at once from poverty and pain.[58]

This was to overstate Darwin's medical powers, as Boothby found in 1791, when his six-year old daughter Penelope died, despite Darwin's best efforts. As her splendid monument in Ashbourne Church truly records, 'the wreck was total'. Boothby and his wife separated, and he contemplated suicide, until diverted by Darwin, as he recalled in sonnet:

When the last efforts of thy art had fail'd,
And all my thoughts were wedded to the tomb,
Thy mild philosophy repell'd the gloom,
And bade me bear the ills on life entail'd.[58]

Still, it was downhill all the way for Boothby from then on. He sank in financial ruin and spent his last years as a penurious wanderer in Europe.

The second name on my list was also a friend of Darwin, but quite different in temperament and interests – not a languid literary man but a hyper-active doctor. Thomas Beddoes (1760–1808) was Darwin's most fervent disciple and most assiduous correspondent during the 1790s. He was almost a mentor to Coleridge, to whom he passed on his enthusiasm for Darwin. Beddoes published dozens of medical and political pamphlets in the 1790s, often after discussion in correspondence with Darwin and sometimes greatly influenced by him. But Beddoes earns his place here because of his spirited poem *Alexander's Expedition*, written in 1792. In the Advertisement to the poem, Beddoes says he has attempted to assume the style of the most elegant of modern poets': in other words, he is openly imitating Darwin, to prove that anything Darwin could do, he could do too. The poem describes Alexander's progress on his expedition down the rivers Hydaspes and Indus to the Indian Ocean, and there are lengthy notes, mainly about India. As the resemblances to Darwin are many and intentional, there is no point in quoting more than a few of the 562 lines. Here is Alexander's fleet of varied barks' heading for troubled waters:

Now, quick emerging, o'er the wondering vale
Peeps the proud beak, and gleams the illumined sail –
Now sudden horror chills the jocund course –
Impetuous rivers clash with headlong force.[59]

This is reminiscent of Darwin's

Down the bright steeps, emerging into day,
Impetuous fountains burst their headlong way,
                              (*Lov.Pl.*, 1st ed, IV 313–14)

especially since Darwin also has *vales* and *wondering* in the next two lines.

From Beddoes it is a natural transition to his young assistant Humphry Davy (1778–1829), who in his early twenties deeply impres-

sed Coleridge: 'living thoughts spring up like the turf under his feet'.
This mercurial chemist came to Bristol to work for Beddoes at hi
Pneumatic Institution in 1798 and quickly made the first of his man
chemical discoveries – nitrous oxide. Davy went on to the Roya
Institution in 1801, and from 1820 to 1827 as President of the Roya
Society he was the most famous man of science of his day. Bu
throughout his life Davy also wrote poetry. 'Had not Davy been the firs
chemist, he probably would have been the first poet of his age': this wa
Coleridge's opinion,[61] perhaps in response to the six poems published i
the *Annual Anthology* in 1799 and 1800, mostly written by 1796 whe
Davy was eighteen. The poems are all concerned with Nature, and th
wording sometimes evokes memories of Darwin, e.g.

> Rich in a thousand radiant dyes,
> Around her steps the flowrets rise.[62]

But the arresting feature of Davy's poems is their anti-Darwinian style
Davy took a great step forward by abandoning the heroic couplet i
favour of varied and lyrical verse forms. These are lyrical ballads tw
years before *Lyrical Ballads*, while Wordsworth was still battling wit
The Borderers and Coleridge with *The Destiny of Nations*: that i
presumably why Coleridge was so impressed by Davy. With their varie
verse forms and scientific attitude to Nature, Davy's poems seem lik
forerunners of Shelley's nature-lyrics. Davy's vocabulary still ha
Darwinian roots, however: for example, in his poem on the death o
Byron, Davy refers to a comet

> that through the mighty space
> Of kindling ether rolls,

and he may be echoing Darwin's line,

> Through all his realms the kindling Ether runs.[63]

A stronger link between Darwin and Davy arises from their scientifi
work in agricultural chemistry. Davy's *Agricultural Chemistry* (1813
was generally regarded as supplanting Darwin's *Phytologia* (1800)
though today *Phytologia* seems more advanced and precise on th
subject of plant nutrition – Darwin recognized the essential roles o
nitrogen and phosphorus, while Davy did not. Davy praised Darwin'
work on the physiology of vegetation, but he was scornful of Darwin'
evolutionary biology, as shown by some remarks in his conversation

piece on fishing, *Salmonia*, where all three speakers agree to condemn
Darwin. The first speaker, Halieus, mentions the possibility that
'differences of shape and colours' among fish might be 'transmitted to
offspring'. The second speaker, Physicus, says this reminds him 'of the
ingenious but somewhat unsound views of Darwin on the same subject'.
Halieus is appalled that he should be thought a disciple of an author
'who, however ingenious, is far too speculative'. The third speaker,
Poietes, then butts in to say that Darwin 'deduced the *genesis* of the
human being, by a succession of changes . . . from the *fish* . . . thus
endeavouring to give currency to an absurd romance'.[64] This section of
Salmonia was written in 1829 (it is not in the first edition), and it is
piquant that Britain's leading man of science, having just completed
seven years as President of the Royal Society, should so boldly condemn
biological evolution, thirty-five years after *Zoonomia* and thirty years
before *The Origin of Species*.

Now we meet a fish of quite different complexion, the dilettante
Richard Payne Knight (1751–1824).[65] A landed gentleman and Member
of Parliament, Knight became notorious in the 1780s for writing *The
Worship of Priapus* at the behest of the Society of Dilettanti. The link
with Darwin, however, arises through Knight's long poems in rhyming
couplets, *The Landscape* (1794) and *The Progress of Civil Society* (1796).
The first of these should really have been entitled *The Landscape Garden*,
for that is its subject; and since it was written soon after *The Botanic
Garden* appeared, some echoes of Darwin are to be expected. But I have
found none, and I strongly suspect that Knight had not then read *The
Botanic Garden*; this would not be surprising, for in the second edition of
The Landscape Knight rebuts charges of stealing from Mason's *English
Garden* by saying he had never read it.[66]

Darwin and Knight are firmly linked, however, as the chief victims of
the campaign of vilification by the *Anti-Jacobin* magazine in 1798. A
parody of Knight's *Progress of Civil Society*, entitled 'The Progress of
Man' and written chiefly by George Canning, appeared in the *Anti-
Jacobin* for 19 February, 26 February and 2 April 1798. The parody of
Darwin's *Loves of the Plants*, entitled 'The Loves of the Triangles' and
also written chiefly by Canning, began in the issue of 16 April 1798, and
both poems were said to have the same author, 'Mr Higgins, of St Mary
Axe'. Knight's poem was censured for its attack on the indissolubility of
marriage, and Canning seizes Darwin's picture of free love in Tahiti as a
stick to beat Knight:

> O! learn, what Nature's genial laws decree –
> What Otaheite is, let Britain be.[67]

This derives from Darwin's finale to *The Loves of the Plants*, where 'pleased VENUS'

> Sheds all her smiles on Otaheite's plain . . .
> And the Loves laugh at all but Nature's laws.
>
> (*Lov.Pl.* IV 488, 490)

Obviously Canning thought Knight and Darwin were terrible-twin Jacobins. In reality there was not much in common between the gentleman-connoisseur and the doctor-technologist, apart from a tendency to think for themselves; but there they stand, handcuffed together in the Tory pillory.

Knight's *Progress of Civil Society* was certainly worthy of Canning's attention: it was an ambitious idea to try to describe the progress of civilization from barbarism to the cultured society. Contemporary readers complained that the poem was extremely tedious, and perhaps Knight was not equal to the task; but he had some good insights. He upset the religious at the very start, by saying he would keep an open mind on whether life sprang 'from the wild war of elemental strife' or from the action of 'one great all-pervading soul'. He recognized and neatly summarized the war in nature:

> In every species of each living kind . . .
> Progressive numbers without end increase,
> While nature gives them safety, food, and ease . . .
> Each stands opposed to some destructive power,
> By nature form'd to slaughter and devour;
> And still, as each in greater numbers breeds,
> More foes it finds, and more devourers feeds.[68]

Knight reminded his readers of their near relatives:

> There, too, the next gradations of his kind,
> The links that to the whole his species bind,
> Baboons and monkeys through the forests stray,
> And all his native beastliness display.[69]

Knight does sometimes draw on Darwin; but it is also obvious that Darwin is indebted to him. In *The Temple of Nature; or Origin of Society* Darwin follows Knight's plan of displaying the progress of life and, although Darwin's idea of evolutionary development is beyond Knight's thinking, Darwin's picture of the war in nature is rather similar to Knight's.

From the irreligious Knight we move to a Devonshire clergyman, Richard Polwhele (1760–1838), a prolific versifier who declared his allegiance with a sonnet 'To Dr Darwin' in 1792:

> Behold! amidst the vegetable bloom,
>   O Darwin! thy ambrosial rivers flow;
> And suns more pure the fragrant earth illume,
>   As all the vivid plants with passion glow . . .
> And NATURE, in primordial beauty, seems
>   Inspir'd by thee to breathe a renovated SOUL![70]

High praise, but perhaps also with a touch of disapproval, which is fully grown in Polwhele's poem *The Unsex'd Females* (1797). Here he castigates Mary Wollstonecraft and other feminists for advocating open discussion of sexual matters; botany is particularly dangerous because girls studying a plant might

> Dissect its organ of unhallow'd lust.[71]

Polwhele reports that he himself has actually witnessed the ultimate horror: 'I have, several times, seen boys and girls botanizing together.'[71] Though Polwhele did not approve of the loves of the plants, he remained loyal to Darwin, and a long note in *The Unsex'd Females* praises 'that admirable poem' *The Botanic Garden*: Darwin's descriptions of plants, he says, 'are pictures glowing in the richest colors – the most beautiful, in short, that were ever delineated by the poetic pencil'.[72]

THE PARODISTS

There is nothing beautiful about my next subject, the parodies: they have a nasty smell, but they demand a mention because the parodists parasitic upon Darwin were more than influenced by him – they owe their existence to him. I shall discuss three parodies.

The first, in *The Pursuits of Literature* (1794), is significant because it was the first sign that Darwin was about to be persecuted and because it went through many editions. Its anonymous author, T. J. Mathias, attracted attention by attacking nearly everyone, and he accused Darwin of trying to achieve 'mere novelty' by '*prettinesses*, glittering words, turns of *points*, conceits'. Darwin's 'filmy, gauzy, gossamery lines', he says.

> Raise lust in pinks; and with unhallow'd fire
> Bid the soft virgin violet expire.[73]

This attack on the pervading sexuality of *The Loves of the Plants* was a shrewd way of undermining Darwin's respectability.

The second parody, the best and most vicious, is *The Golden Age* (1794), 202 lines in rhyming couplets, allegedly written by 'Erasmus D——n, M.D.' The poem is supposed to be addressed to Beddoes, and the most extreme ideas of Beddoes and Darwin are heaped together for ridicule. These two devilish doctors proclaim themselves Democrats of the deepest dye –

> Ranks and Distinctions cease, all reeking lie
> In the mean muck of low Equality!

Even worse, they are 'pious Atheists' who dare to defy

> The King of Kings, that Bugbear of the sky.[74]

So Darwin was tarred with the same brush as his more extreme associate. The libel was crude but effective: it certainly damaged him, and continues to do so today because *The Golden Age* is still listed as one of his own works in some bibliographies and library catalogues.

The third parody, which was by far the most influential at the time, was the spoof poem 'The Loves of the Triangles', published in *The Anti-Jacobin* magazine in 1798. The first number of *The Anti-Jacobin* was published in November 1797, and the aim was to produce each week during the sitting of Parliament a periodical which would be 'the avowed, determined and irreconcilable' enemy of 'JACOBINISM in all its shapes'.[75] The conduct of this openly political magazine was in the hands of George Canning, then Foreign Under-Secretary in Pitt's government and later Tory Prime Minister. Canning and two collaborators, Hookham Frere and George Ellis, set out to assassinate Darwin's reputation with a parody of *The Loves of the Plants*, written in ultra-Darwinian verse and with footnotes ridiculing Darwin's ideas. Their rather puerile poem exploits the sexual implications of mathematical terms, like the osculation of curves. The 'sly Rectangle's too licentious love' is sought by a parabola ('with virgin blush'), a hyperbola ('blue-eyed wanton') and an ellipse. Though their subject is silly and its execution is botched – they missed the obvious point that all three curves are conic sections (sexions) – Canning and his co-authors do often catch the true Darwinian style. The most telling couplet is the last, a very sharp engraving of the guillotine:

> The liberated head rolls off below,
> And simpering Freedom hails the happy blow.[76]

The style is Darwin's and so he is, at a stroke, linked with Jacobinism. The notes to the poem also ridicule his theory of evolution (as we have already seen), his belief in the future usefulness of electricity and his terrestrial time-scale of 'millions of ages'. All three ideas have proved to be well founded, so Darwin has the last laugh over the parodists. But at the time the parody punctured his over-inflated reputation, and the puncture was disastrous: it forced him off the road of fame, and he has had a struggle to get back.

Before leaving the parodies, I should mention 'Architectural Atoms' by Horace Smith (1779–1849), one of the *Rejected Addresses* of James and Horace Smith published in 1812. Though this witty *jeu d'esprit* is ostensibly aimed at Dr Busby's translation of Lucretius, Horace Smith obviously has *The Loves of the Plants* in mind when he brings on his amorous bricks:

> The oblong beauties clap their hands of grit,
> And brick-dust titterings on the breezes flit;
> Then down they rush in amatory race,
> Their dusty bridegrooms eager to embrace.[77]

This explains the indissoluble marriage of bricks in a house wall, and is also 'a very tolerable imitation of Darwin', as Jeffrey remarked.[78]

AT THE PROSAIC LEVEL

The guillotine must now fall on a chapter that is already too long, because it is not my intention to burrow into the main mass of the iceberg – the prose writers who were indebted to Darwin. His influence on fiction is difficult to guess. The Gothic novelists may have derived something from him, and Mary Shelley certainly did (see Chapter 10). He was a guide and mentor to Thomas Day.[79] Another obvious link is with Robert Bage,[80] his friend for forty years and business partner for fifteen years. Maria Edgeworth admired him exceedingly and her father was his closest friend in his last years: their *Practical Education* (1798) follows many of the precepts of Darwin's *Female Education*. Another admirer was R. J. Thornton, who in his *Philosophy of Botany* (1799) treats Darwin as an 'intellectual presiding deity'.[81] Darwin was able to return the compliment by commending the plates in Thornton's celebrated *Temple of Flora*: 'I very much applaud and beg leave to recommend to the attention of the Public, the superb picturesque botanical Plates, now publishing by Dr Thornton, which I suppose to have *no equal*.'[82]

Before proceeding *à la guillotine*, however, I shall take the chance to mention three important philosophical books whose authors are believed to have been much influenced, either positively or negatively, by *Zoonomia*.

The first is T. R. Malthus's *Essay on the Principle of Population* (1798). Although the book is largely concerned with human populations, Malthus adopts a similar stance to Darwin's in referring to the 'want of room and nourishment' for animals, and their 'becoming the prey of others'.[83] However, this could have come from other sources, such as Knight's *Progress of Civil Society* or Robert Wallace's *Various Prospects of Mankind, Nature and Providence* (1761).

My second book is William Paley's *Natural Theology* (1802), often regarded as the Establishment's riposte to *Zoonomia*, answering Darwin's speculations with the calm certainties of theo-zoology. Paley examines the anatomy of creatures in just as much detail as Darwin and sees every functional part as the work of an all-seeing Deity. Paley was certain: 'Design must have had a designer. That designer must have been a person. That person is GOD.'[84] The question, 'who was GOD's designer?' never seems to have bothered him.

The third book is Charles Darwin's *Origin of Species* (1859), which has so many strong links with *Zoonomia*[85] but is beyond my time limit.

CONCLUSIONS

Looking back over the poets, we find they have sorted themselves into seven groups:

1. Cowper and Hayley, who applauded Darwin excessively, but wrote too early to be influenced by him.

2. Darwin's literary disciples, such as Anna Seward, William Sotheby, Mary Tighe, Richard Polwhele, Thomas Beddoes and Brooke Boothby.

3. Those who could have succumbed to the Darwinian virus, but did not (or only suffered very mild attacks): Scott, Southey, Landor and Moore, together with Davy and Knight.

4. Campbell, who began in thoroughly Darwinian style in the 1790s, but renounced it after 1800.

5. Crabbe, a poet very close to Darwin in his 'verbal photography' and passion for botany; each learnt from the other.

6. Goethe, who admitted a debt to Darwin, and whose mind ran on similar lines as a Nature philosopher and Orphic poet.

7. The parodists parasitic on Darwin.

NOTES

1. *Analytical Review*, 4, 29–36 (1789).
2. *Ibid.*, 15, 287–93 (1793).
3. *The Correspondence of William Cowper*, ed. T. Wright (Hodder and Stoughton, 1904) iv 227.
4. From the version printed in the second and later editions of *The Botanic Garden*.
5. *Letters of Erasmus Darwin*, p. 222.
6. *Gent.Mag.*, 53, 428 (1783).
7. Her extensive correspondence is in the Fitzwilliam Museum Library, Cambridge.
8. R. Southey, Preface to *Madoc* (*Poems*, p. 12).
9. A. Seward, *Letters* v 143. See also *ibid.* vi 3–5.
10. *Ibid.* ii 312.
11. *Letters of Mary Russell Mitford*, 2nd series (Bentley, 1872) i 29.
12. A. Seward, *Elegy on Captain Cook*, p. 10.
13. *Ibid.* p. 11.
14. R. L. and Maria Edgeworth, *Memoirs* ii 268.
15. J. Boswell, *Life of Samuel Johnson*, Everyman edition (Dent, 1906) ii 546. Seward, *Captain Cook*, p. 5.
16. See Anna's letter to Humphrey Repton of 15 July 1789 (Seward, *Letters* ii 311–13).
17. W. Scott, letter to W. Taylor, 22 January 1797. *Letters of Sir Walter Scott* (Constable, 1932) i 62.
18. MS in William Salt Library, Stafford.
19. For *sun-illumined*, see *Pleas.Hope* I 507; *Ec.Veg.* III 510; *Lov.Pl.* I 157.
20. *Ec.Veg.* II 150. (See also *Ec.Veg.* IV 316, 'mingle in the skies'.) Another possible parallel is with *Lov.Pl.* I 299–300, where the 'silvery arches' of 'transient rainbows' catch the sun's 'setting beams'.

21. *Ec.Veg.* III 8 and IV 31.
22. The quotations are from *Ec.Veg.* I 557; *Pleas.Hope* I 41–2; *Ec.Veg.* I 386; *Pleas.Hope* I 133; *Lov.Pl.* I 32; *Pleas.Hope* I 135.
23. T. Campbell, *Poetical Works*, p. 42.
24. *Lov.Pl.* III 61–2; Campbell, *Poetical Works*, p. 41.
25. *The Critical Review*, 27, 159 (1799). The examples given are *Pleas. Hope* I 58–60 and I 587–94. See also W. Beattie, *Life of Campbell* i 261, and *Edinburgh Magazine, 2*, 315–16 (1818).
26. *Poetry of the Anti-Jacobin*, pp. 127–8.
27. *Pleas.Hope* II 329–32 (5th edn).
28. For Crabbe and opium, see A. Hayter, *Opium and the Romantic Imagination*, Ch. VIII. For his life, see R. Huchon, *George Crabbe*.
29. G. Crabbe the younger, *Life of George Crabbe*, p. 128.
30. B. B. Jain, *Crabbe*, p. 263.
31. Coleridge, *Notebooks*, vol. 1, no. 132; Hazlitt, *The Spirit of the Age*, 'Mr Campbell and Mr Crabbe'.
32. *Edinburgh Review*, 16, 53 (April 1810), and L. Hunt, *The Feast of the Poets* (Cawthorn, 1814) pp. 46–7.
33. See *Letters of Erasmus Darwin*, pp. 139–40.
34. For biographical information on Hall and John Darwin, see *ibid.*, pp. 80, 226.
35. A. Seward, *Memoirs of Dr Darwin*, pp. 125–33, and D. King-Hele, *Doctor of Revolution*, pp. 110–12.
36. R. L. Chamberlain, 'George Crabbe and Darwin's Amorous Plants', *J. Eng. and Germ. Phil.*, *61*, 833–52 (1962).
37. G. Crabbe, *The Library* (1781) pp. 11–12.
38. G. Crabbe, *Poems* (1807) p. 149.
39. *Ibid.*, pp. 58–9.
40. G. Crabbe the younger, *Life of George Crabbe*, p. 34.
41. G. Crabbe, *Poems* (1807) pp. 59–60.
42. G. Crabbe, *Poems* (1905) vol. I, p. 175.
43. This telling change was noted by R. L. Chamberlain, *J. Eng. and Germ. Phil.*, *61*, 833–52 (1962).
44. G. Crabbe, *Poems* (1905) vol. II, p. 427.
45. *Ibid.*, vol. III, p. 27.
46. G. Crabbe, *Poems* (1905) vol. I, p. 244; *Ec.Veg.* I 129–30, 522.
47. For further discussion, see O. F. Sigworth, *Nature's Sternest Painter*, pp. 82–7, and A. Hayter, *Opium and the Romantic Imagination*, Ch. VIII. The story of Crabbe's seizure at Ipswich (*Life of George Crabbe*, pp. 153–4) is most implausible as the origin of his addiction.
48. A judicious summary of Goethe's scientific work is given by C. Singer, *Short History of Scientific Ideas* (Clarendon Press, 1959) pp. 386–9.
49. For a translation of, and commentary on, Goethe's essay, see A. Arber, 'Goethe's Botany', *Chronica Botanica*, *10*, 63–126 (1946).
50. See P. C. Ritterbush, *The Art of Organic Forms*, pp. 35–7 for *Vallisneria*, and Ch. I for Goethe's attitude to organic form.
51. J. Boyd, *Goethe's Knowledge of English Literature*, p. 286.
52. *Ibid.* (with excerpt from letter translated).
53. See K. Badt, *John Constable's Clouds*, Ch. II, for details – and a translation.
54. *Edinburgh Review*, *4*, 297 (July 1804).

55. See E. V. Weller, *Keats and Mary Tighe*, where *Psyche* is reprinted.
56. *London Magazine*, 6, 520–8 (December 1822).
57. *Edinburgh Review*, 15, 30–2 (1809).
58. B. Boothby, *Sorrows, Sacred to the Memory of Penelope* (Cadell, 1796) pp. 71 and 10.
59. T. Beddoes, *Alexander's Expedition* (Murray, 1792) lines 33–6. See also J. E. Stock, *Life of Beddoes*, pp. 52–62 and F. F. Cartwright, *The English Pioneers of Anaesthesia*, pp. 56–60.
60. J. Cottle, *Early Recollections* (Longman, 1837) i 329. For Coleridge on Davy, see A. Treneer, *The Mercurial Chemist* (Methuen, 1963) Ch. 5.
61. See J. Davy, *Memoirs of Sir H. Davy* ii 406. John Davy prints extracts from 33 of his brother's poems in the *Memoirs*. The poems from *The Annual Anthology* are reprinted in J. A. Paris, *Life of Davy*, pp. 25–39. Paris also states (p. 24) that Davy wrote a verse-epic called 'Tydidiad' at the age of twelve.
62. *Annual Anthology* (1799) p. 121.
63. J. Davy, *Memoirs of Sir H. Davy* ii 169; *Ec.Veg.* I 105.
64. H. Davy, *Salmonia* (4th edn, 1851) pp. 64–6.
65. See F. J. Messman, *Richard Payne Knight* (Mouton, The Hague, 1974) and M. Clarke and N. Penny (eds), *The Arrogant Connoisseur* (Manchester Univ. Pr., 1982).
66. R. P. Knight, *The Landscape* (2nd edn, 1795) pp. ix–xii.
67. *Poetry of the Anti-Jacobin*, p. 112.
68. R. P. Knight, *The Progress of Civil Society*, p. 27.
69. *Ibid.*, p. 101.
70. R. Polwhele, *Reminiscences in Prose and Verse* (Nichols, 1836) iii 153–4.
71. R. Polwhele, *The Unsex'd Females* (1797) pp. 8–9.
72. *Ibid.*, p. 4.
73. *Pursuits of Literature* (Owen, 1794) pp. 14–15.
74. *The Golden Age* (Rivington, 1794) pp. 11, 12.
75. *Poetry of the Anti-Jacobin*, p. 7.
76. *Ibid.*, p. 149.
77. James and Horace Smith, *Rejected Addresses* (Methuen, 1904) p. 102.
78. *Edinburgh Review*, 20, 446 (1812).
79. For Thomas Day, see G. W. Gignilliat, *The Author of Sandford and Merton* (Columbia University Press, New York, 1932).
80. For Bage, see P. Faulkner, *Robert Bage* (Twayne, Boston, 1979), and *Letters of Erasmus Darwin*, pp. 19–20.
81. C. Bush, *Eighteenth-Century Studies*, 7, 310 (1974).
82. *Thornton's Temple of Flora* (Collins, 1972) p. 4.
83. Cf. T. R. Malthus, *Essay on Population* (Penguin, 1970) p. 76, and *Zoonomia* i 507–8.
84. W. Paley, *Natural Theology* (6th edn, 1803) p. 473.
85. See D. King-Hele, *Erasmus Darwin* (Macmillan, 1963) Ch. V.

REFERENCES

Agnes Arber, 'Goethe's Botany', *Chronica Botanica*, 10, 63–126 (1946).
Kurt Badt, *John Constable's Clouds* (Routledge, 1950).

William Beattie, *Life and Letters of Thomas Campbell*, 3 vols (Moxon, 1849).

J. Boyd, *Goethe's Knowledge of English Literature* (OUP, 1932).

Thomas Campbell, *Complete Poetical Works*, ed. J. L. Robertson (OUP, 1907).

R. L. Chamberlain, *George Crabbe* (Twayne, Boston, 1965).

George Crabbe, *Poems* (Hatchard, 1807).

George Crabbe, *Poems*, ed. A. W. Ward, 3 vols (CUP, 1905).

George Crabbe the younger, *The Life of George Crabbe* (OUP, World Classics, 1932).

John Davy, *Memoirs of the Life of Sir Humphry Davy*, 2 vols (Longman, 1836).

Alethea Hayter, *Opium and the Romantic Imagination* (Faber, 1968).

René Huchon, *George Crabbe and his Times* (1907; Cass, 1968).

B. B. Jain, *The Poetry of George Crabbe* (Universität Salzburg, Austria, 1976).

Richard Payne Knight, *The Progress of Civil Society* (Nicol, 1796).

J. A. Paris, *The Life of Sir Humphry Davy* (Colburn, 1831).

Poetry of the Anti-Jacobin, ed. C. Edmonds, 2nd edn (Willes, 1854).

P. C. Ritterbush, *The Art of Organic Forms* (Smithsonian Inst., Washington, 1968).

Anna Seward, *Elegy on Captain Cook* (Dodsley, 1780).

Anna Seward, *Letters*, 6 vols (Constable, Edinburgh, 1811).

Elizabeth Sewell, *The Orphic Voice* (Routledge, 1960).

O. F. Sigworth, *Nature's Sternest Painter* (Univ. of Arizona Press, Tucson, 1965).

Robert Southey, *Poems*, ed. M. H. FitzGerald (OUP, 1909).

J. E. Stock, *Memoirs of the Life of Thomas Beddoes* (Murray, 1811).

E. V. Weller (ed.), *Keats and Mary Tighe* (1928; Kraus Reprint, New York, 1966).

8 Shelley

> Darwin made a profound impression upon Shelley's thought and imagination.
>
> Carl Grabo, *A Newton among Poets*, p. 200

Percy Bysshe Shelley (Fig. 12) was born at Field Place near Horsham, Sussex, on 4 August 1792, two months after the publication of Darwin's *Economy of Vegetation* and one month before the 'September massacres' started to stain the Revolution in France with blood. He was the eldest son of a solid Sussex landowner, Timothy Shelley, a Whig MP who inherited his father's baronetcy in 1815. The young Shelley was sent to Eton in 1804, where he suffered several years of baiting from his schoolfellows but benefited from the teaching of two remarkable men of science. The first was the itinerant lecturer Adam Walker, who gave regular courses and captivated Shelley: the boy liked to carry Walker's experiments to dangerous extremes – he gave his tutor severe electrical shocks, flew fire-balloons and dabbled with gunpowder.

The second man of science, who influenced Shelley more than anyone else he met, was Dr James Lind (1736–1812), who had for more than twenty-five years been Physician to the Royal Household at Windsor and a Fellow of the Royal Society. Despite these Royal connections, Lind was a deep-dyed radical, who had his own printing-press and was suspected of issuing subversive pamphlets. He was over seventy when he knew Shelley, white-haired, tall and thin – the very model of a modern sage to a schoolboy nurtured on Gothic romances. 'He was exactly what an old man ought to be, free, calm-spirited, full of benevolence, and even of youthful ardour. . . . I shall never forget our long talks.'[1]

James Lind had close links with Darwin's circle. Lind's father was Lord Provost of Edinburgh and the brother of Magdaline Lind, who was the mother of James Keir, Darwin's oldest friend. Like Keir and Darwin, Lind studied medicine at Edinburgh, and in the mid 1760s Lind became a close friend of James Watt: it is in his letters to Lind that Watt wrote the famous accounts of his invention of the improved steam engine in 1765. So Lind was in at the birth of the most important invention of the eighteenth century; and he kept up his friendship with Watt, who later came to stay with him at Windsor. After graduating in medicine at Edinburgh, Lind graduated in real life by going on a three-year voyage to China as a naval surgeon, from which he derived a fund of oriental stories – some taller than the teller – that fascinated Windsor (and Shelley). In 1772 Captain Cook was preparing for his second world voyage, and Lind was appointed as naturalist. But when Joseph Banks decided against going on the voyage, Lind also withdrew and instead went on an expedition to Iceland with Banks, who was soon to become the 'emperor' of British science and President of the Royal Society for forty-two years. Lind was also a friend of Sir William Herschel, the greatest of observational astronomers, who worked with his huge telescope at nearby Datchet. One evening when Lind and his wife were visiting Herschel, Mrs Lind saw a bright spot on the dark part of the Moon. This led to Herschel's series of observations of 'volcanos in the Moon', which in turn led to the modern study of transient lunar phenomena as well as to Coleridge's 'star within the nether tip' of the Moon in the *Ancient Mariner*. Though Lind and Darwin may never have met, they were kindred spirits, and were well known to each other by repute through Watt, Keir and Banks, and also through their scientific publications. Darwin refers to Lind's papers on meteorology in *The Botanic Garden*, and Lind admired Darwin's poem, which expresses so well the technological and enquiring 'Lunar' spirit. Lind would inevitably have commended Darwin's poems to Shelley, who had probably already come across them in the library at Field Place. Lind also led Shelley to Godwin's *Political Justice*, which became something of a bible to him for several years.

For the schoolboy Shelley it was a heady experience to be the confidant and protégé of a man who had such close links with the leaders in engineering (Watt), astronomy (Herschel), chemical technology (Keir) and all of science (Banks), as well as having entrée to the Royal Society and the Royal Household. But it was even more intoxicating to find that Lind was a radical socially and a sceptic in religion. Little wonder that, as Mary Shelley tells us, Lind's was a 'name he never mentioned without love and veneration'.[2]

Shelley went up to University College, Oxford, in the autumn of 1810, ready to follow Lind's example, including his habit of writing to leading authorities when he had a problem. Shelley's problem was religion, and he soon put together an essay expressing his scepticism. Meeting only opposition from his father, he wrote to various churchmen and men of substance, including Josiah Wedgwood II, whose benevolence was decisive in the lives of Coleridge and, later, Charles Darwin. Wedgwood, who had been a neighbour of Shelley's cousins the Groves in Dorset until 1806, made a long reply which stimulated Shelley and his friend T. J. Hogg to expound their views in the form of a mild pamphlet with a strong title, *The Necessity of Atheism*. As a result, Shelley was expelled from Oxford in March 1811 and partially disowned by his father. At the age of eighteen he began an unsettled and rather disastrous style of life, which continued until his death at the age of twenty-nine.

During the summer of 1811 Shelley was in a restless and morbid mood, feeling his life was ruined and not knowing how to repair it. In July he went off for thirty days into the wilderness, to the estate of his cousin at Cwm Elan near Rhayader in Wales, where, he told Hogg, 'I do not see a soul. All is gloomy and desolate. I amuse myself however with reading Darwin, climbing rocks and exploring the scenery.'[3] This was probably the most impressionable and critical month of his life, and the impression made by reading (or rereading) Darwin amid sublime scenery seems to have been indelible.

Shelley returned from Wales in August 1811, determined to dither no longer. On 28 August he married Harriet Westbrook, the sixteen-year-old daughter of a London coffee-house keeper, whose parents were about to 'persecute' her by sending her back to school for the autumn term. In the next two years Shelley and Harriet travelled widely, with two visits to Ireland and longer stays at Keswick, Lynmouth and Tremadoc. *Queen Mab*, Shelley's diatribe against the existing order in politics and religion, was the product of these years.

In 1814 Shelley met Mary Godwin, the sixteen-year-old daughter of the philosopher William Godwin and the pioneer of women's rights, Mary Wollstonecraft. Shelley fell violently in love with Mary Godwin, and in June 1814 they eloped to France. They soon returned, and in 1815 lived near Virginia Water. In 1816 they travelled to Switzerland and spent much time with Byron. After their return came the tragedy of Harriet's death by drowning. Shelley and Mary lived at Marlow in 1817, then left England in 1818 for Italy where Shelley wrote his best poems. After staying at Milan and near Venice, and visiting Rome and Naples, they settled in Tuscany in 1819, at Florence and then in and around Pisa, where Byron joined them in 1821. On 8 July 1822 Shelley was drowned in a storm while sailing in a small yacht from Leghorn to his summer house Casa Magni, near Lerici.[4]

SHELLEY'S FAITH IN SCIENCE

Dr Lind was deeply imbued with the Lunar spirit – the faith that the march of technology would bring great benefit to society – and he would have made a good member of the Lunar Society if he had lived near Birmingham. As it was, he infected Shelley with the Lunar spirit, and Shelley outdid his tutor.

At Oxford he turned his rooms into a laboratory. His friend Hogg tells us that he was liable

> to start from his seat at any moment, and seizing the air-pump, some magnets, the electrical machine, or the bottles containing those noxious and nauseous fluids, wherewith he incessantly besmeared and disfigured himself and his goods, to ascertain by actual experiment the value of some new idea that rushed into his brain.[5]

Once Hogg found himself pouring tea into a cup that was already half full of concentrated acid, and he retaliated by caricaturing Shelley's activities:

> His chemical operations seemed to an unskilful observer to promise nothing but disasters. His hands, his clothes, his books, and his furniture were stained and corroded by mineral acids. More than one hole in the carpet could elucidate the ultimate phenomenon of combustion. . . .[5]

This fusillade of contemptuous smoke-shells continues for several pages, but even Hogg admitted that

> I admired the enthusiasm of my new acquaintance, his ardour in the cause of science, and his thirst for knowledge.[6]

Shelley's burning faith that science could better the human condition also shines through Hogg's sarcasm:

> He discoursed after supper with as much warmth as before of the wonders of chemistry. . . . 'It is easy, even in our present state of ignorance, to reduce our ordinary food to carbon, or to lime; a moderate advancement in chemical science will speedily enable us, we may hope, to create, with equal facility, food from substances that appear at present to be as ill-adapted to sustain us. What is the cause of the remarkable fertility of some lands, and of the hopeless sterility of others? . . . The real difference is probably very slight; by

chemical agency the philosopher may work a total change, and may transmute an unfruitful region into a land of exuberant plenty'.[7]

All this is akin to Darwin's approach in *Phytologia*, though there are of course other possible sources for Shelley's ideas. Shelley was very keen on electricity, and Hogg reports him as saying:

> What a mighty instrument would electricity be in the hands of him who knew how to wield it. . . . How many of the secrets of nature would such a stupendous force unlock! The galvanic battery is a new engine . . . what will not . . . a well-arranged system of hundreds of metallic plates effect?[8]

Darwin's 34-page note on 'Chemical Theory of Electricity and Magnetism' in *The Temple of Nature* (pp. 46–79) is one possible source of these ideas.

Aerial navigation was another subject to which he was very likely led by Darwin. He told Hogg that

> the art of navigating the air is in its first and most helpless infancy; the aerial mariner still swims on bladders, and has not mounted even the rude raft. . . . It promises prodigious facilities for locomotion. . . . Why are we still so ignorant of the interior of Africa? – Why do we not dispatch intrepid aeronauts to cross it in every direction, and to survey the whole peninsula in a few weeks? The shadow of the first balloon . . . over that hitherto unhappy country would virtually emancipate every slave, and would annihilate slavery for ever.

The worldly-wise Hogg knew that the idea of aerial surveys was mere fantasy, of course; but even he was impressed by

> the zealous earnestness for the augmentation of knowledge, and the glowing philanthropy and boundless benevolence that marked them . . . for these high qualities, at least, I have never found a parallel.[9]

Such was Shelley at Oxford, as seen by one who scoffed at his prophecies.

What shines out clearly from all this is Shelley's zealous vision of the

advance of science and technology, and its power to improve society
Darwin could not have had a keener disciple, though many of the idea
would have arrived via Lind.

Shelley was also fully in sympathy with Darwin's radical line i
politics, his distaste for Christianity, and his emphasis on the link
between the human and the natural world. So it is not surprising tha
Darwin's influence on Shelley was deep and general.

THE 'ESDAILE POEMS' (1809–12)

Shelley's early poems in the Esdaile Notebook[10] are not of great merit
but we should sample a few of them to confirm that Shelley was indebted
to Darwin from the start of his career. Shelley never regarded technolog
as a fit subject for poetry and he had not yet absorbed the idea of man i
harmony with Nature. So the resemblances in these early poems centr
on Darwin's tirades against Tyrants and Superstition, as when he tells u
that

> Tyrants tremble on their blood-stain'd thrones,

and assures us that Time will

> dash proud Superstition from her base.

Very similar in its themes is Shelley's 'Falsehood and Vice' (1810?), wit
its attacks on such capital crimes as 'MONARCHY' and 'RELIGION'.[11]

Darwin has a whole Canto on Reproduction in *The Temple of Nature*
and explains how 'every pore of Nature teems with life'

> when a Monarch or a mushroom dies.   (IV 383

This was probably the origin of Shelley's poem 'The Monarch's Funera
(1810), where he informs us that

> The dross which forms the King is gone
> And reproductive earth supplies.   (57–8

The numerous probable echoes of Darwin in Shelley's 'Retrospect o
Times of Old' (1812) are too lengthy to discuss in detail here; so I lis
them in a note.[12]

The longest of the Esdaile poems is 'Henry and Louisa' (1809), whic

has the motto, 'She died for love – and he for glory'. Henry, a patriotic
youth, thinks he should seek glory in battle – 'Religion sanctifies the
cause' – so he becomes a soldier and goes to fight in North Africa. His
lover Louisa follows him there, finds him dead on the battlefield and
promptly dies herself. Probably written while he was still at Eton, this
fiercely anti-military but none-too-successful poem draws heavily on
Darwin. Shelley describes how the 'Genius of the South'

> Looked over Afric's desolated clime,
>> Deep wept at slavery's everlasting moan
>> And his most dear-belovèd nation's groan.　　(Lines 168–70)

Darwin's version is less moan-full and more powerful:

> E'en now in Afric's groves with hideous yell
> Fierce SLAVERY stalks, and slips the dogs of hell;
> From vale to vale the gathering cries rebound,
> And sable nations tremble at the sound.　　(*Lov.Pl.* III 441–4)

Shelley then makes a sudden switch of subject, from the groaning slaves
to

> The Boreal whirlwind's shadowy wings that sweep
>> The varied bosom of the northern world.　　(Lines 171–2)

With the scene set in the deserts of Egypt, Shelley has no reason to drag
in 'the northern world' or its 'varied bosom', whatever that may be. I
suspect he was fusing two passages from Darwin. The first is from *The
Economy of Vegetation*:

> No more shall hoary Boreas, issuing forth
> With Eurus, lead the tempests of the North;
> Rime the pale Dawn, or veil'd in flaky showers
> Chill the sweet bosoms of the smiling Hours.　　(IV 311–14)

Shelley may have meant to write *veilèd* (cloudy) rather than *varied*.[13] The
second passage is Darwin's famous picture of the army of Cambyses
being buried in the deserts of Egypt in a sandstorm driven by 'whizzing
whirlwinds'. Darwin liked writing about desert winds, and his image of
the Simoom that 'rides the tainted air' is echoed by Shelley in
'Retrospect of Times of Old', where he refers to 'the simoon's sigh' and
'the tainted blast'. Shelley would also have liked Darwin's note on the

Harmattan, which is based on Dr Lind's 'Account of the Harmattan' in
the *Philosophical Transactions* of the Royal Society.[14]

When Shelley tells us how Louisa searches the battlefield for Henry,
he closely follows Darwin's story of Eliza searching the battlefield of
Minden for her husband:

> So stood Eliza on the wood-crown'd height,
> O'er Minden's plain, spectatress of the fight,
> Sought with bold eye amid the bloody strife
> Her dearer self, the partner of her life. . . .
> Near and more near the intrepid Beauty press'd. . . .
> O'er groaning heaps, the dying and the dead. . . .
> So wings the wounded Deer her headlong flight. . . .[15]

Shelley's picture is very similar (and scarcely less ludicrous):

> When frantic o'er the waste Louisa sped
> To drink her dying lover's latest vow:
> Sighed mid her locks the sea-gales as they blew,
> Bearing along faint shrieks of dying men. . . .
> Silent she paused a space, and then again
> New-nerved by fear and hope sprang wild across the plain. . . .
> Fleet as the wild deer his Louisa came. . . .[16]

Shelley's letters confirm that he was familiar with Darwin's poems.
The idea of sentient plants figures in one of his letters to Hogg in the
traumatic summer of 1811: 'Perhaps the flowers think like this, perhaps
they moralize upon their state, have their attachments, their pursuits of
virtue; adore, despond, hope, despise. . . .'[17] A month later he was
reading Darwin in the wilds of Wales, and in 1812 we find Godwin
scolding him for his attachment to Darwin: 'You have what appears to
me a false taste in poetry. You love a perpetual sparkle and glittering,
such as are to be found in Darwin, and Southey, and Scott, and
Campbell.'[18] However, Godwin did advise him to read *Zoonomia*, which
he ordered a week later; he also ordered *The Temple of Nature* at this
time, but probably only to replace a copy he had lost.

QUEEN MAB (1813)

Shelley was twenty when he completed *Queen Mab*, the clearest and sharpest of his attacks on society-as-it-is. The poem owes much to Darwin, in form, in machinery, in opinion and in wording.

There are two obvious resemblances in form. First, the title-page of *The Temple of Nature* announces it as 'A POEM, WITH PHILOSOPHICAL NOTES'; the title-page of *Queen Mab* announces it as 'A PHILOSOPHICAL POEM, WITH NOTES'. Second, Shelley's decision to add scientific notes that were longer than the poem would have been bizarre, if he had not had the highly successful example of Darwin before him. (Shelley's science is not up to Darwin's standard, but he tries.)

Shelley adopts Darwin's machinery by bringing on a Goddess who descends in a 'magic car' and pronounces on the state of things, like Darwin's Goddess of Botany in *The Economy of Vegetation*. And Shelley's goddess speaks to a sleeping girl (Ianthe) in a dream, an idea that might have been inspired by one of the illustrations in *The Temple of Nature*, 'The Power of Fancy in Dream' by Fuseli.

The similarity in opinion arises because Shelley, like Darwin in *The Temple of Nature*, attacks superstition, tyrants, slavery, war, alcohol, avarice and luxury. Shelley also takes over some of Darwin's ideas on organic happiness.

Echoes of Darwin's wording are fairly numerous, as we shall see, and Shelley follows Darwin's technique of exploiting 'propaganda' words, such as 'Tyrant' and 'Superstition'.

Canto I of *Queen Mab* begins with a picture of the maiden Ianthe asleep. Then a rushing sound is heard, wilder than the notes

> Of that strange lyre whose strings
> The genii of the breezes sweep,

and coloured lights appear,

> like the moonbeams when they fall
> Through some cathedral window.   (I 52–3, 55–6)

Darwin more than once refers to the 'Eolian Lyre',

> gently swept by Zephyr's vernal wings,

and the soft cadences of its 'love-sick strings'.[19] And Darwin's picture of a church at night, where

> through the colour'd glass the moon beam falls,
>   (*Lov.Pl.* III 23)

may have misled Shelley as well as Scott into thinking that moonlight is strong enough to throw colours visible to the eye. (Or perhaps Shelley was following Scott.)

The rushing sound heralds the arrival of the Fairy Queen:

> Behold the chariot of the Fairy Queen . . .
>> From her celestial car
>> The Fairy Queen descended,
>> And thrice she waved her wand
> Circled with wreaths of amaranth.   (I 59, 105–8)

These might be called the five action-lines in a fifty-five line description beginning in line 59, and they are quite like Darwin's picture in *The Economy of Vegetation* (also beginning in line 59 of Canto I, believe it or not):

> She comes! – the GODDESS! – through the whispering air,
> Bright as the morn, descends her blushing car;
> Each circling wheel a wreath of flowers intwines . . .
> Light from her airy seat the Goddess bounds,
> And steps celestial press the pansied grounds.   (I 59–61, 67–8)

And elsewhere Darwin has an enchantress who 'circles thrice in air her ebon wand' (*Lov.Pl.* II 278).

The soul of Ianthe then arises from her sleeping body, ready to go on a tour of the universe with the Fairy Queen Mab. The 'silver clouds disparted', Shelley tells us, as they enter the 'car of magic'. The Queen shakes the reins and they are off into the night:

> The magic car moved on
> From the celestial hoofs
> The atmosphere in flaming sparkles flew,   (I 212–14)

and the 'burning wheels' created lightning. Compare this with Darwin's

> On wheels of fire, amid a night of clouds,
> Drawn by fierce fiends arose a magic car,
> Received the Queen, and hovering flamed in air.

> (*Lov.Pl.* III 162–4)

Apart from the fierce fiends, nearly all Darwin's words appear.

As the magic car moves on through the universe, Shelley's metaphors soar beyond Darwin's reach. But the destination of the voyagers is quite Darwinian – a temple of Nature:

> Spirit of Nature! here!
> In this interminable wilderness
> Of worlds, at whose immensity
> Even soaring fancy staggers,
> Here is thy fitting temple.   (I 264–8)

By comparison, Darwin's temple is rather prosaic:

> Here, high in air, unconscious of the storm,
> Thy temple, NATURE, rears its mystic form.   (*Tem.Nat.* I 65–6)

This is a reminder that *The Temple of Nature* greatly influenced Shelley. Darwin's poem is 'a work whose assertion of the unity of human and natural spheres left a lasting stamp on Shelley's conceptions', as Stuart Curran remarked.[20] I would go further, and suggest that the very essence of Shelley's nature-poetry is his fusion of the 'human and natural spheres', and that all Darwin's books – from the humanized flowers in *The Loves of the Plants* to the grand evolutionary design of *The Temple of Nature* – celebrate the marriage of humans and nature.

We have now reached the end of Canto I of *Queen Mab*: there are eight more to follow, but I obviously cannot continue to pursue the parallels so minutely. Instead I shall despatch the details to notes.

In Canto II Queen Mab offers Ianthe's spirit a view of the universe, rather like Darwin's in Canto I of *The Economy of Vegetation*, and looks back over the ruins of cities such as Palmyra.[21] Shelley also proclaims Darwin's philosophy of organic happiness in no uncertain terms:

> I tell thee that those viewless beings,
> Whose mansion is the smallest particle
> Of the impassive atmosphere
> Think, feel and live like man.   (II 231–4)

This is in the spirit of *The Loves of the Plants* and also of Darwin's evolutionary belief that 'imperious man'

Arose from rudiments of form and sense,
An embryon point, or microscopic ens.[22]   (*Tem.Nat.* I 313–4

Cantos III – V take us through the evils of the present. Like Darwin
Shelley refers to the monarch's 'gorgeous thrones' and the 'gilded flies
of courtiers who fatten on its corruption.[23] Shelley lashes out agains
'kings, priests and statesmen', war, slavery, supersititions and all the
other evils they bring. 'Nature . . . spread Earth's lap with plenty', but
'Man . . . wantonly heaped ruin, vice and slavery'[24] – the theme is the
same as in Canto IV of *The Temple of Nature*, though Shelley goes fa
beyond Darwin in his social analysis. Even so, many of Darwin's idea
still lurk around, ready to pop out rather incongruously. For example
after deploring that humans are born to bondage, Shelley suddenly tell
us that

The moveless pillar of a mountain's weight
Is active, living spirit;   (IV 142–3

presumably he was impressed by Darwin's piquant idea that 'the tal
mountains'

Are mighty Monuments of past Delight.   (*Tem.Nat.* IV 450

And in Canto V Shelley gives commerce a bad image by transforming it
into Darwin's Upas Tree:

Commerce! beneath whose poison-breathing shade
No Solitary virtue dares to spring.[25]

Cantos VI and VII concentrate on religion, and Shelley's attacks or
religion's 'temples . . . gorgeous and vast' match Darwin's tirade
against Superstition's 'gorgeous fanes'.[26] One of Darwin's anti-wa
couplets,

While mad with foolish fame, or drunk with power,
Ambition slays his thousands in an hour,   (*Tem.Nat.* IV 103–4

seems to have inspired Shelley's lines,

When merciless ambition, or mad zeal,
Has led two hosts of dupes to battlefield,

That, blind, they there may dig each other's graves,
And call the sad work glory.   (VI 178–81)

When Shelley condemns religious wars for

Making the earth a slaughter-house!   (VII 48)

he is hijacking Darwin's summary of the struggle for existence in nature,

Add one great Slaughter-house the warring world!
                                        (*Tem.Nat.* IV 66)

Cantos VIII and IX offer Mab's vision of what the future might be – a golden age of peace and happiness. To begin with, the weather would be completely reformed: the polar frost would melt and 'fragrant zephyrs' would blow gently over a temperate Earth. Darwin believed that the Earth was once temperate – whence the legends of a golden age – and might be so again if we discover the 'golden secret' that 'guides the changing pinions of the winds', and can apply the discovery to ensure that

Autumn and Spring in lively union blend,
And from the skies the Golden Age descend.[27]

In this peaceful world, Shelley tells us,

The lion now forgets to thirst for blood,

which may be a reminiscence of Darwin's amusing couplet,

The Lion-King forgets his savage pride,
And courts with playful paws his tawny bride.

When Shelley tells us 'his claws are sheathed', perhaps he was remembering Darwin's lines about Love guiding with 'ribbon-rein' the indignant Lion', who 'sheaths his retractile claws'.[28] Of course Shelley's picture of a 'happy Earth' would not have been convincing to Darwin, who saw the struggle for existence as central to life, whereas Shelley brings in mild-mannered animals, apparently without realizing that they would each o'erpeople ocean, air and earth', as Darwin put it. Shelley also tells us that

Yon monarch, in his solitary pomp,
Was but the mushroom of a summer day,

thus again echoing Darwin's 'when a Monarch or a mushroom dies',
while ignoring its moral – that each gives rise to the birth of
'unnumbered insects'.[29] These last cantos of *Queen Mab* are not strong
on consistency: they are a vision of the future designed to impress the
soul of Ianthe. At the end of Canto IX her soul returns to her sleeping
body, and she wakes, presumably much wiser after her sleep-learning.

In these early years Shelley's ideas derived more from Godwin than
from Darwin, yet *Queen Mab* shows he was in full sympathy with
Darwin's political and social views. As time went on, and Shelley turned
more towards Nature and philosophical themes, Godwin's influence
waned while the memory of Darwin's poems gathered strength and
added a useful earthy ballast to counter Shelley's high-flying tendencies
towards Platonism.

This chapter would be ridiculously long if I sought out all the
Darwinian echoes, so I shall concentrate on Shelley's best-known
poems. A chronological trek is not necessary, because Shelley had only
eight years of life after *Queen Mab*, and Darwin's influence seems to
have remained fairly constant during that time.

Before leaving *Queen Mab*, however, I should pause for a moment in
tribute to Carl Grabo: his book *A Newton among Poets*, demonstrating
Darwin's influence on Shelley, sparked off my own interest in Darwin;
and several of the parallels I have given were first noted by Grabo.

PROMETHEUS UNBOUND (1818–19)

From *Queen Mab* we may appropriately jump straight to Shelley's
mature statement of his vision of the future, and what is in many ways
his greatest work, the dramatic poem *Prometheus Unbound*, where he
envisages the regeneration of the world through Universal Love. In
Shelley's new world

Love . . . folds over the world its healing wings,

and man's will

Is as a tempest-winged ship, whose helm
Love rules.

Darwin's poems are all celebrations of the power of Love, seen not only in the abstract but also as sexual love, especially in *The Loves of the Plants*. There is a line from *The Economy of Vegetation* that nicely catches his attitude –

> And Love and Beauty rule the willing world.[30]

So we may safely say that 'Love rules' for both Shelley and Darwin.

To usher in his 'new world of man', Shelley brings on his winged 'Spirit of the Earth':

> on its head there burns
> A light, like a green star, [with] emerald beams . . .
> The splendour drops in flakes upon the grass.

This is very like Darwin's winged 'Seraph Sympathy' in *The Temple of Nature*:

> bright o'er earth his beamy forehead bends;
> On Man's cold heart celestial ardor flings,
> And showers affection from his sparkling wings.

Darwin's winged Seraph, he tells us,

> charms the world with universal love,

just as Shelley requires, and the Seraph also

> Lifts the closed latch of pale Misfortune's door,
> Opes the clench'd hand of Avarice to the poor,
> Unbars the prison, liberates the slave . . .

The long speech of Shelley's Spirit of the Earth, in Act III, scene iv, gives a similar picture of a regenerated Earth where 'all things had put their evil nature off'. The Spirit also tells how the people in a town he visited, sensing the great change, suddenly awoke

> and gathered in the streets
> Looking in wonder up to Heaven.

Shelley usually looked askance at anything supernatural descending

from Heaven, so the phraseology is curious. Perhaps he was again
remembering Darwin's Seraph:

> The Seraph, Sympathy, from Heaven descends . . .
> Points with uplifted hand to realms above.[31]

Shelley's Spirit of the Earth is closely linked to Eros or Cupid, because he
dispenses love (though universal rather than individual), as Earl
Wasserman has noted.[32] Cupid flits through *The Loves of the Plants* as
persistently as a moth at a lighted window, so this aspect of Shelley's
Spirit may also owe something to Darwin.

These similarities in theme are matched by many similarities in
scientific imagery. Carl Grabo, in his book *A Newton among Poets*, has
stressed the important role of electricity, particularly atmospheric
electricity, in *Prometheus Unbound*, and pointed out the resemblances to
Darwin's lines on glow-worms, phosphorescence and kindred phenomena in *The Economy of Vegetation*. For example, the 'love-illumined
form' of Darwin's glow-worm,

> Star of the earth, and diamond of the night,
>
> > (*Ec.Veg.* I 196)

is very close to Shelley's star-like Spirit of the Earth, while Shelley's
splendour that 'drops in flakes' is probably an echo of Coleridge's 'elfish
light' that 'fell off in hoary flakes', derived from Darwin's note on
marine phosphorescence, as we have already seen.

As Grabo also remarked,[33] Shelley's Fauns in Act II of *Prometheus
Unbound* are very much like Darwin's Ethereal Powers, which,

> plum'd with flame, in gay battalions spring
> To brighter regions borne on broader wing;
> Where lighter gases, circumfused on high,
> Form the vast concave of exterior sky;
> With airy lens the scatter'd rays assault,
> And bend the twilight round the dusky vault;
> Ride, with broad eye and scintillating hair,
> The rapid Fire-ball through the midnight air.
>
> > (*Ec.Veg.* I 121–8)

The 'lighter gas' here is hydrogen, and Darwin believed that meteors and
fire-balls were produced by the incandescent reaction between hydrogen
and oxygen.[34] Shelley's Fauns discuss the spirits of the wood that fly on

> The bubbles which the enchantment of the sun
> Sucks from the pale faint water-flowers that pave
> The oozy bottom of clear lakes and pools . . .   (*PU* II ii 71–3)

These are bubbles of hydrogen ('inflammable air'), as shown by Darwin's reference in a note to 'the inflammable air, which arises from the mud of rivers and lakes at some seasons, when the atmosphere is light' (*Ec.Veg.*, Add. Notes, p. 79). A subconscious memory of Darwin's verses seems to run through Shelley's further description of the bubbles:

> And when these burst, and the thin fiery air,
> The which they breathed within those lucent domes,
> Ascends to flow like meteors through the night,
> They ride on them, and rein their headlong speed,
> And bow their burning crests, and glide in fire
> Under the waters of the earth again.   (*PU* II ii 77–82)

Shelley's Fauns 'ride on' the 'fiery air' that produces 'meteors through the night', while Darwin's Powers 'ride' the 'Fire-ball through the midnight air'.

A few pages later Shelley introduces the immortal Hours, who seem to be close relatives of Darwin's Ethereal Powers. Shelley's Hours travel in aerial cars:

> I see cars drawn by rainbow-wingèd steeds
> Which trample the dim winds . . .

The Hour that is to preside over the great change in the human condition drives a chariot powered by atmospheric electricity,

> My coursers are fed with the lightning. . . .

Compare this with Darwin's Ethereal Powers, who

>   chase the shooting stars,
> Or yoke the vollied lightnings to your cars.[35]

Much of *Prometheus Unbound* is intensely aerial, like *The Economy of Vegetation*. Shelley is not just trespassing on Darwin's property, however: he is taking it over, lock, stock and barrel. Shelley is the legitimate heir to the inheritance amassed by his literary ancestor, and builds on the legacy with a rush of creative energy. Darwin would, I

think, have applauded the resulting poem, and particularly Shelley's
insistence that social reform would go hand in hand with scientific
advance in the 'new world of man'. Lines like

> The lightning is his slave . . .
> The tempest is his steed, he strides the air . . .   (*PU* IV 418, 421)

parallel Darwin's faith in the future usefulness of electricity and the great
possibilities of air travel.

Shelley's debt to Darwin in *Prometheus Unbound* is deep and
pervasive, but difficult to present concisely. Carl Grabo's pioneering
book of 1930 still stands as the best attempt. It was Grabo who showed
how Darwin's Nymphs of Fire,

> Forms sphered in fire with trembling light array'd,
> Ens without weight, and substance without shade,

and his Gnomes of Earth,

> Orb within orb approach the marshal'd trains,
> And pigmy legions darken all the plains,

help in interpreting Shelley's obscure description of

> A sphere, which is as many thousand spheres,
> Solid as crystal, yet through all its mass
> Flow, as through empty space, music and light:
> Ten thousand orbs involving and involved,
> Purple and azure, white, and green, and golden,
> Sphere within sphere.

Also, in Grabo's view, Shelley's description of the star on the forehead of
the Spirit of the Earth, which emitted beams

> Like swords of azure fire and golden spears,[36]

is intended as the aurora. Since the Earth seen from space often sports an
aurora, like a star on its forehead,[37] this interpretation seems reasonable;
if so, we are back to Darwin's quotation from the Book of Maccabees,
where the aurora is described as a 'shaking of shields and multitudes of
pikes, and drawing of swords, and casting of darts, and glittering of
golden ornaments and harness'.[38]

It is only a short step from electricity to magnetism, and an even shorter step to love. Darwin makes a rather laboured equation between the two,

> The obedient steel with living instinct moves,
> And veers for ever to the pole it loves,

while Shelley slips in the comparison more subtly:

> Like the polar Paradise,
> Magnet-like of lovers' eyes.[39]

This is part of the Earth–Moon dialogue, which shows that, like Coleridge, Shelley was alert to Darwin's suggestion that the Moon's atmosphere might be revived – 'a sufficient quantity of air may in process of time be generated to produce an atmosphere' – and Shelley duly imagines that the Moon's 'solid oceans flow'.[40] Another astronomical image deriving from Darwin is the climactic last line of Act III of *Prometheus Unbound,*

> Pinnacled dim in the intense inane,

which is very similar to Darwin's memorable line,

> Hung with gold-tresses o'er the vast inane.[41]

A few other scenes in *Prometheus Unbound* have the smell of Darwin about them, but Shelley possessed an effective filter en route from his unconscious, so the resemblances are arguable. As an illustration, consider another highly charged scene of *Prometheus Unbound*, expressing the great change when Love began to rule. 'The Nereids', Shelley says, tell of the spirit of love standing in a shell floating on 'the crystal sea' and illumining the 'ocean and the sunless caves' on the day when 'the clear hyaline' was cloven at Love's uprise. This is rather like Darwin's lines about a 'Naiad-Nymph' in her 'crystal cave' braiding 'her hyaline hair'.[42] Shelley's 'good change' brings extreme equality, for love

> makes the reptile equal to the God.

This is Darwin's 'tenderness for all living forms' taken to the limit. Darwin's own phrasing is more restrained, for he merely says that instincts link the reasoning reptile to mankind,[43]

and this is probably closer to what Shelley meant to say.

The unity of the Earth and its creatures is a strong feature of Shelley'
liberation-picture, expressed by 'The Earth' herself in a long speech, o
which I can only give the gist:

> And through my withered, old, and icy frame
> The warmth of an immortal youth shoots down
> Circling. Henceforth . . . all plants,
> And creeping forms, and insects rainbow-winged,
> And birds, and beasts, and fish, and human shapes
> . . . shall take
> And interchange sweet nutriment.[44]

The harmony of the Earth with its plants and creatures is the theme o
both Darwin's poems, and Shelley follows him in his sympathy with th
whole of organic nature.

But Shelley failed to absorb Darwin's most important biological ide.
– his theory of evolution. Shelley specifically says there will be n
bloodshed in his new world: man and beast will live peacefully togethe
and ocean will be 'unstained with blood', which scarcely seems realisti
unless a contraceptive chemical could somehow be added to sea-wate
In contrast to Shelley's pacific ocean we have Darwin's picture of th
web of slaughter in *The Temple of Nature*:

> In ocean's pearly haunts, the waves beneath
> Sits the grim monarch of insatiate Death . . .
> From Hunger's arm the shafts of Death are hurl'd,
> And one great Slaughter-house the warring world!
>
> (IV 55–6, 65–6

Darwin accepts the slaughter as inevitable, yet still manages to b
optimistic, via his philosophy of organic happiness.

Shelley did not altogether ignore Darwin's evolutionary picture. I
Prometheus Unbound there is a long passage about animals now extinc
and former populations of Earth that were 'mortal but not human'. Th
idea of a progression of species is implicit, but Shelley is descriptiv
rather than passionate. Darwin's compelling picture of the struggle fo
existence, in Canto IV of *The Temple of Nature*, seems to have passed hir
by. He learnt much from Darwin but he could have learnt a lot more

Shelley remains a pre-evolutionary poet, to our loss – and to his own, because his worries about the problem of evil could have been stilled.

Why did Shelley reject this part of Darwin's world-picture? He had the vision and intelligence to grasp it, but there were two mental barriers. First, Shelley (correctly) saw Darwin's picture of the struggle for existence as deriving from Malthus's *On Population*, and Malthus's essay was written with the specific aim of refuting Godwin's *Political Justice*, which was Shelley's bible for some years. So Shelley saw Malthus as an implacable enemy and therefore shut his mind to the struggle-for-existence aspects of Darwin. The second barrier was Shelley's Platonic tendency: the idea that life as we now see it was the end-product of messy and chancy slaughter, rather than a reflection of some divine ideal, was distasteful to him.

LYRICS OF NATURE (1819–20)

Darwin and Shelley came closest to each other temperamentally in their empathy with Nature. Both wrote as if they had an innate longing to fly with clouds, swim with fishes or grow with flowers. This resemblance is very striking and, since Darwin was there first, I think it is fair to say that Shelley as a lyricist of Nature lived in the world created by Darwin, though he advanced to a life-style well beyond Darwin's grasp. Darwin's world, as used by Shelley, was basically scientific; but both poets continually enliven the science with myth and legend. Shelley gained much in having a firm scientific base as an anchor for his sometimes too fanciful flights of fancy.

Shelley's *Ode to the West Wind*, perhaps the most famous of his nature-lyrics, has strong Darwinian roots. Shelley tells us his poem 'was conceived and chiefly written in a wood that skirts the Arno, near Florence', when the rising west wind was giving warning of the 'autumnal rains' to follow. He sees the dead leaves being stripped from the trees by the wind to form a mould where the seeds will rise in spring. He celebrates the power of the wind over leaves, clouds and waves, exploiting the natural analogies, first sombrely and then buoyantly –

If Winter comes, can Spring be far behind?

The waking of plants in spring, and the subsequent sexual antics of their stamens and pistils, are the constant theme of *The Botanic Garden*, and there is one scene that is almost a preview of Shelley's own experience in

the mixed lawn and woodland beside the Arno, with the autumn wind
tearing off the leaves:

> When o'er the cultured lawns and dreary wastes
> Retiring Autumn flings her howling blasts,
> Bends in tumultuous waves the struggling woods,
> And showers their leafy honours on the floods,
> In withering heaps collects the flowery spoil,
> And each chill insect sinks beneath the soil. (*Lov.Pl.* I 199–204)

But Shelley's report on his experience, in the opening lines of his *Ode*,
lays emphasis more on the power of the Wind:

> O wild West Wind, thou breath of Autumn's being,
> Thou, from whose unseen presence the leaves dead
> Are driven, like ghosts from an enchanter fleeing,
> Yellow, and black, and pale, and hectic red,
> Pestilence-stricken multitudes: O thou,
> Who chariotest to their dark wintry bed
> The wingèd seeds . . . .   (*West Wind*, 1–7)

Shelley then looks forward to the rebirth of vegetable life in spring,
following Darwin's theme in Canto IV of *The Economy of Vegetation*
(lines 351–628). But the most interesting resemblances to Shelley's
opening lines occur in Canto I. One of these is in the section entitled
'Western Wind unfettered', where Darwin asks the Nymphs to

> Wake with soft touch, with rosy hands unbind
> The struggling pinions of the WESTERN WIND.
>   (*Ec.Veg.* I 429–30)

This might be the subconscious source for Shelley's personification of
the wind and for his alliteration. The other probable echo has its source
in Darwin's lines about 'the flying-chariot' borne on 'wide-waving
wings' through 'the fields of air' (*Ec.Veg.* I 291–2). Shelley had been
much impressed by these lines, and the chariots in nearly all Shelley's
poems (except *The Triumph of Life*) are flying or 'winged' chariots. So
when he says the West Wind 'chariotest' the 'wingèd seeds', he is not
only bringing in quite an unusual verb but also giving it an unusual aerial
bias, to mean 'carry as if on a *flying* chariot'. So a memory of Darwin's
flying-chariot seems very likely.[45]

In his second stanza Shelley looks at the wind's power over clouds:

Loose clouds like earth's decaying leaves are shed,
Shook from the tangled boughs of Heaven and Ocean,
Angels of rain and lightning;

and from these fractostratus clouds Shelley goes on to the 'bright hair' of the cirrus clouds. This is again rather like Darwin's invocation to the Western Wind, particularly when he asks the Nymphs to

wring the rain-drops from his tangled hair. (*Ec.Veg.* I 432)

The *Ode to the West Wind* also resembles *The Economy of Vegetation* in being a deliberate celebration of the four elements. Darwin treats Fire, Earth, Water and Air respectively in his Cantos I–IV, while Shelley devotes his stanzas I–III to Earth, Air and Water respectively, but holds his Fire until the famous image in stanza V,

Scatter, as from an unextinguished hearth
Ashes and sparks, my words among mankind.

The four colours of the leaves in the first stanza have also been linked with the four elements – and with the skin-colours of the far Eastern, African, European and Amerindian races.[46]

All in all, the *Ode to the West Wind* is a fair example of Darwin's influence over Shelley – not immediately obvious because it is so deeply ingrained. This is one of many instances of Shelley's 'large general obligation whch may rather be felt than particularized', as Carl Grabo put it.[47]

The idea that plants feel and that some insight is gained by humanizing them is Darwin's obsessive motif and chief creative achievement in *The Loves of the Plants*: Shelley pursues the same idea just as assiduously in *The Sensitive Plant*. Shelley's take-off point is Darwin's sixteen lines of verse and 300-word note on 'Mimosa. The sensitive plant'. Like Darwin, Shelley sees the mimosa as full of love; he links the plant with the weather; he mentions many of the same flowers as Darwin, and eroticizes them;[48] he even writes in rhyming couplets. So the ambience is similar; but the tone is different. Shelley begins:

A Sensitive Plant in a garden grew,
And the young winds fed it with silver dew,
And it opened its fan-like leaves to the light,
And closed them beneath the kisses of Night.

Darwin is more discursive:

> Weak with nice sense, the chaste MIMOSA stands,
> From each rude touch withdraws her timid hands;
> Oft as light clouds o'erpass the Summer-glade,
> Alarm'd she trembles at the moving shade;
> And feels, alive through all her tender form,
> The whisper'd murmurs of the gathering storm;
> Shuts her sweet eye-lids to approaching night;
> And hails with freshen'd charms the rising light.
>
> (*Lov.Pl.* I 301-8)

Shelley's story of the Sensitive Plant thriving in the well-kept garden, and its downfall as the weeds run riot, plunges into profundities deeper than Darwin cared to discuss in his poems.[49] In tone and philosophical quality Shelley's poem is at some distance from Darwin: however, the similarity in title, subject and technique make it very difficult to deny Darwin's influence.

Darwin is happiest when flying through the air with his Nymphs and Sylphs, and the same applies to Shelley, who was for nearly a century lumbered with the nickname 'Ariel'. In the *Ode to the West Wind* the idea of flying with a cloud was only tentative –

> If I were a swift cloud to fly with thee –

but in *The Cloud* Shelley turns the fantasy into reality, in a brilliant poem that reports on his experience as a cloud. In this scientific monograph, fused with a laughing tale of cloud-adventure, his poetry soars far above the earthbound tramp of Darwin's marching couplets; but there are several resemblances. In Shelley's hackneyed first line,

> I bring fresh showers for the thirsting flowers,

his laughing cloud might be taking a cue from Darwin's good-humoured couplet:

> Through the still air descend the genial showers,
> And pearly rain-drops deck the laughing flowers.
>
> (*Lov.Pl.* I 483-4)

Lines 5-6 of *The Cloud*,

From my wings are shaken the dews that waken
  The sweet buds every one.

are quite like Darwin's shower-scene in Canto III of *The Economy of Vegetation*, where the Goddess of Botany asks the 'sun-illumined shower' to

Feed with dulcet drops my tender broods,
Mellifluous flowers, and aromatic buds.   (*Ec.Veg.* III 511–12)

A less obvious resemblance is Darwin's description of Zeus leading his blushing goddess to the couch imperial in Heaven. He

    rests the crimson cushions upon clouds. –
Earth feels the grateful influence from above,
Sighs the soft Air, and Ocean murmurs love. ·(*Ec.Veg.* III 256–8)

These lines may have contributed to Shelley's picture of the Cloud resting at dusk:

And when Sunset may breathe, from the lit sea beneath,
  Its ardours of rest and of love,
And the crimson pall of eve may fall
  From the depth of Heaven above.   (39–42)

More important than these verbal resemblances is the concept of water circulation from ocean → vapour → clouds → rain → rivers → ocean, which is the theme of Darwin's Canto III and is crucial in Shelley's poem from the first two lines – 'I bring fresh showers . . . From the seas' – to the last. In the concluding verses Shelley's Cloud refers to

The triumphal arch through which I march,

which may hark back to Darwin's aquatic Nymphs, who

       lead with viewless march
The winged vapours up the aerial arch.   (*Ec.Veg.* III 13–14)

Also Shelley's 'genii that move/In the depths of the purple sea' may originate with Darwin's 'Genii presiding over' the operations of Nature. This seems likely, because Darwin calls out the Genii

> From each nice pore of ocean, earth and air,   (*Ec.Veg.* I 85)

a line which probably inspired Shelley's brilliant summary of water
circulation:

> I am the daughter of Earth and Water,
>   And the nursling of the Sky;
> I pass through the pores of the oceans and shores . . .   (73–5)

Darwin the pioneer of meteorology would surely have been delighted at
Shelley's memorable picture of the cycle of water circulation.

Having looked at three of Shelley's strongest lyrics, I conclude with a
weaker one, 'The Indian Girl's Song', once known as 'The Indian
Serenade'. One notorious line in this poem was used by hostile critics in
the 1930s to 'prove' that Shelley was a weakling. The critics made the
elementary mistake of thinking that the 'speaker' of the line was Shelley,
whereas it is really the Indian girl.[50] The line is

> I die! I faint! I fail!

Darwin has three separate dying ladies uttering similar lines in *The Loves
of the Plants*:

> 'I sink, I fall! oh, help me, help !' she cries . . .
> 'I faint, I fall!' – at noon the Beauty cried . . .
> I faint! – I fall! ah me!   (*Lov.Pl.* I 451, II 331, IV 263)

Shelley changed 'fall' to the less euphonious 'fail' because he wanted a
rhyme for 'pale'. Two of Darwin's dying ladies are deadly cold; when the
first one weeps 'tear after tear adown her cheek', the tears turn to 'pearls
of ice'; while the third exclaims, 'I freeze! I freeze!' Shelley's maiden is in a
warm climate but still complains that 'My cheek is cold and white'.
Though Shelley's debt to Darwin is clear, Darwin himself may have been
echoing Wesley's hymn, 'Jesu, Lover of my Soul', which has

> Lo! I sink, I faint, I fall –

as one of its lines.[51] Be that as it may, the Darwin–Shelley link holds,
because Wesley was not one of Shelley's favourite authors.

ADONAIS (1821)

Adonais, an elegy on the death of John Keats, was written in May 1821 and Shelley rightly called it 'the least imperfect of my compositions'. He succeeds in weaving a web of fine verse around various myths of birth and life and death, starting from the Venus – Adonis myth, with Adonis being slain by a boar. This provides an instant cue for lament, but Shelley changes the name to Adonais and widens his character until he becomes almost the spirit of Nature: 'He is made one with Nature'. Shelley also changes Venus to Urania – not the Muse of Astronomy but Aphrodite Urania, goddess of heavenly love (as opposed to Aphrodite Pandemos, the earthly Venus). Shelley's Urania first grieves over the death of Adonais and then, after meditating on the cycle of death and rebirth in Nature, sees him as rising again and transcending death.

For this form of the myth Shelley may draw upon Canto II of *The Temple of Nature*, entitled 'The Reproduction of Life'. Darwin states his theme in two of the early couplets:

> How short the span of LIFE! some hours possess'd,
> Warm but to cool, and active but to rest! . . .
> But REPRODUCTION with ethereal fires
> New Life rekindles, ere the first expires.
>
> (*Tem.Nat.* II 1–2, 13–14)

And again in lines 41–4:

> Organic forms with chemic changes strive,
> Live but to die, and die but to revive!
> Immortal matter braves the transient storm,
> Mounts from the wreck, unchanging but in form.

As a symbol for death and rebirth Darwin introduces Adonis –

> Emblem of Life, to change eternal doom'd,
> The beauteous form of fair ADONIS bloom'd. –
> On Syrian hills the graceful Hunter slain
> Dyed with his gushing blood the shuddering plain.
>
> (*Tem.Nat.* II 47–50)

He amplifies the idea in a footnote:

The hieroglyphic figure of Adonis seems to have signified the spirit of animation or life, which was perpetually wooed or courted by organic matter, and which perished and revived alternately. Afterwards the fable of Adonis seems to have given origin to the first religion promising a resurrection from the dead.

(*Tem.Nat.* II 47 note)

The resurrection is celebrated in a rather appalling couplet:

Soon from the yawning grave the bursting clay
Restor'd the Beauty to delighted day.   (*Tem.Nat.* II 53–4)

'The Beauty' may seem rather an overblown epithet for Adonis; but Shelley calls Adonais 'the loveliest' of Urania's sons, and half-hopes that 'the amorous Deep'

Will yet restore him to the vital air.   (*Adonais*, 25–6)

The verses I have quoted from *The Temple of Nature* are all spoken by the goddess who presides over the whole poem: and she is of course Urania. She is sometimes also called the 'Priestess of Nature' and 'the Hierophant', and her function is to explain the processes of Nature, ostensibly for the benefit of 'the Muse', who feeds Urania with the right questions. After expatiating on reproduction and the joys of love, in plants and aphides and humans, and grieving over the 'countless Dead',

Urania paused, upturn'd her streaming eyes
And her white bosom heaved with silent sighs;
With her the MUSE laments the sum of things,
And hides her sorrows with her meeting wings;
Long o'er the wrecks of lovely Life they weep,
Then pleased reflect, 'to die is but to sleep';
From Nature's coffins to her cradles turn,
Smile with young joy, with new affection burn.

(*Tem.Nat.* II 205–12)

There are many similarities here with Shelley's poem, where Urania first laments her dead favourite, and then finds consolation in the rebirth of Nature in spring:

Oh, weep for Adonais – he is dead! . . .
Most musical of mourners, weep again!

Lament anew, Urania! . . .
And fans him with her moonlight wings, and cries:
'Our love, our hope, our sorrow, is not dead' . . .
Fresh leaves and flowers deck the dead Season's bier . . .
. . . he is not dead, he doth not sleep –
He hath awakened from the dream of life . . .
He is made one with Nature.[52]

Darwin sees sexual love and reproduction as the driving forces of evolution, so it is no surprise to find him praising both:

Behold, he cries, Earth! Ocean! Air above,
And hail the DEITIES OF SEXUAL LOVE!
All forms of Life shall this fond Pair delight,
And sex to sex the willing world unite.   (*Tem.Nat.* II 243–6)

Darwin emphasizes that 'all forms of life' are subject to this happy tyranny, and Shelley happily follows him:

Through wood and stream and field and hill and Ocean
A quickening life from the Earth's heart has burst . . .
All baser things pant with life's sacred thirst;
Diffuse themselves; and spend in love's delight
The beauty and the joy of their renewèd might.
                              (*Adonais* 163–4, 169–71)

Darwin was impressed by the constancy of the product in asexual creatures –

Birth after birth the line unchanging runs,
And fathers live transmitted in their sons   (II 107–8)

– and his keen approval of sexual reproduction sprang from his appreciation that it introduced variety, and hence allowed evolutionary improvement. Shelley missed the evolutionary point, but he expressed the shaping power of the asexual hereditary mould just as cogently as Darwin, and far more poetically:

the one Spirit's plastic stress
Sweeps through the dull dense world, compelling there
All new successions to the forms they wear;
Torturing th' unwilling dross that checks its flight

> To its own likeness, as each mass may bear;
> And bursting in its beauty and its might
> From trees and beasts and men into the Heaven's light.
>
> (*Adonais* 381–7)

The adjective 'plastic' was popular in the eighteenth century for the shaping power of Nature (or God), and Darwin used it in the same sense as Shelley in such lines as

> Hence plastic Nature, as Oblivion whelms
> Her fading forms, repeoples all her realms.   (*Ec.Veg.* IV 59–60)

As Darwin sees it, Reproduction saves the world from Death, and no praise can be too high:

> LOVE with nice touch renews the organic frame,
> Forms a young Ens, another and the same;
> Gives from his rosy lips the vital breath,
> And parries with his hand the shafts of death;
> While BEAUTY broods with angel wings unfurl'd
> O'er nascent life, and saves the sinking world.
>
> (*Tem.Nat.* II 257–62)

Shelley did not commit himself directly to praise of Reproduction, but it is very close to his 'one Spirit's plastic stress' and not far removed from another abstraction in the previous stanza, 'that Power'

> Which wields the world with never-wearied love,
> Sustains it from beneath, and kindles it above.
>
> (*Adonais* 377–8)

Darwin's influence on *Adonais* is demonstrated by his hold over the central theme and the mythical figures, so I shall not go through the peripheral parallels in phrasing. The only one I wish to mention is the famous image of Life as 'a dome of many-coloured glass' staining 'the white radiance of Eternity'. The parallel in Darwin is his explanation of the Portland Vase as a hieroglyph of Eleusinian lore, with the 'shade of MORTAL LIFE', the figure of 'IMMORTAL LIFE' and 'the PRIESTESS' (Urania) who 'Unweaves the many-colour'd veil of Truth'.[53]

Darwin's was of course not the only influence on *Adonais*. Shelley was also much indebted to several other literary models: the elegy for Adonis attributed to Bion; the elegy for Bion attributed to Moschus; Lucretius's *De Rerum Natura*; Spenser's *Astrophel*; Milton's *Lycidas*; and some of Keats's own poems.[54]

WITCH OF ATLAS, EPIPSYCHIDION AND TRIUMPH OF LIFE

Shelley has now had a good share of attention, and I shall not discuss any more of his poems in detail. But I wish to spike the guns of enemies who could say that Darwin influenced only a few of Shelley's long poems. So I shall quote quick examples of echoes in three more of his longer poems.

The Witch of Atlas (1820) is on the surface a carefree fantasy about a playful Witch who flies around in a magic boat dispensing favours or playing tricks on mortals – behaving much like Darwin's Sylphs and Nymphs. The Witch's boat was curiously constructed: it was 'scooped' by Love from 'the long and gourd-like fruit' of a plant grown from 'a strange seed' which Love ('like a horticultural adept') stole from the realm of 'dun Chaos'. This is typical of the poem: the wildly fanciful is mixed with botanical detail 'described with a precision worthy of Erasmus Darwin', as Richard Cronin has remarked.[55] In the prefatory verses Shelley compares his Witch ironically with Wordsworth's Peter Bell, and the Witch's boat is based on Wordsworth's celestial boat, which is itself derived from Darwin.[56] During her travels through the upper atmosphere the Witch would

> Ride singing through the shoreless air . . .
> And laughed to hear the fire-balls roar behind,

just like Darwin's Nymphs, who

> Ride, with broad eye and scintillating hair,
> The rapid Fire-ball through the midnight air.[57]

Not only the Witch but also the pilot of her aircraft – a sexless Hermaphrodite – may owe something to Darwin, who believed that reproduction was initially sexless (see p. 29). The development of sex speeded up evolution and was much to be welcomed for that reason – and others. So Shelley's creative fantasy, perhaps 'the supreme example of myth-making poetry in English',[58] has some resonances from Darwin.

My second choice is Shelley's great love poem, *Epipsychidion* (1821), immortalizing a girl immured in a convent, Emilia Viviani, whom he only met a few times and never alone. The climax of the poem is the imaginary voyage, which begins:

> A ship is floating in the harbour now,
> A wind is hovering o'er the mountain's brow;
> There is a path on the sea's azure floor,
> No keel has ever ploughed that path before;
> The halcyons brood around the foamless isles . . .   (408–12)

This is like one of Darwin's many scenes of love in nature:

> From ozier bowers the brooding Halcyons peep,
> The Swans pursuing cleave the glassy deep,
> On hovering wings the wondering Reed-larks play . . .
>
> (*Lov.Pl.* IV 95–7)

And when Shelley's ship reaches its destination, a dream-island, the air is heavy with the scent of flowers, which

> dart their arrowy odour through the brain.

Darwin refers to the 'arrowy beams' of electricity, which

> dart the red flash through the circling band.

Arrowy is an unusual 'pet word' of his, which he seems to have passed on to Shelley, whose line 'cleaves with arrowy beams the dark-red air' is very close to Darwin's phraseology.[59] The isle's beauty, Shelley says, 'blushes and trembles' as 'veil after veil' is 'drawn aside' by 'Sun or Moon or zephyr'. Perhaps he was half-remembering how, in *The Loves of the Plants*, the saline basil which grows in the Andes

> Mounts the rude cliff, unveils her blushing charms,
> And calls the panting zephyrs to her arms.

Shelley again exploits Darwin's conceit of the wind wooing the mountains when he refers to

> The mossy mountains, where the blue heavens bend
> With lightest winds, to touch their paramour.[60]

So Darwin's obsessive pursuit of sex in The *Loves of the Plants* contributed a little to Shelley's obsessive pursuit of love in *Epipsychidion*.

My final port of call is Shelley's last poem, *The Triumph of Life* (1822), unfinished and enigmatic. The poem as it stands describes the triumphal car of Life and the procession of people who trail in its wake. Shelley's picture derives from Petrarch's *Trionfi*, particularly the first, the Triumph of Love, so the orthodox texts tell us.[61] But I wonder whether Shelley was not inspired more by the Triumph of Despotic Love in Canto II of *The Temple of Nature* (lines 361–410). Darwin imagines Love quelling the war in nature and bringing all the animals into a harmonious procession:

> Despotic LOVE dissolves the bestial war,
> Bends their proud necks, and joins them to his car.   (II 361–2)

Lions, tigers, bulls and horses,

> Chain'd to the car with herds domestic move,
> And swell the triumph of despotic LOVE.   (II 369–70)

Fishes are there, and birds –

> The feather'd nations shed a floating shade.   (II 376)

Insects too rise in dark clouds,

> Sport round the car, and wave their golden wings.   (II 382)

Dryads, Nereids, Tritons, all join in

> And swell the triumph of despotic LOVE.   (II 388)

The repetition here of line 370 is deliberate, to emphasize that this is not just a pretty procession but a recognition that Love alone keeps Life evolving. For Darwin this is the pageant of Life, and all life figures in the procession, even the flowers:

> Delighted Flora, gazing from afar,
> Greets with mute homage the triumphal car.   (II 389–90)

Though Darwin's tone is frivolous, his aim is serious – to focus on Love's vital role in the pageant of Life: it is the Triumph of Life via Love.

Shelley's pageant includes only humans, though he might later have included a wider slice of life, if the poem was to live up to its title. Otherwise his stance is close to Darwin's – a tribute to an abstract Life/Love – and his wording is sometimes reminiscent of Darwin. 'Who are those chained to the car?', Shelley asks in line 208, echoing Darwin's line 369; and again (line 252) Shelley has 'those chained to the triumphal chair' (the *chair* is really the *car*, but he needed a rhyme for *there* and *fair*; the chair is not mentioned again). As in Darwin's line 382, Shelley has his captives sporting round the car in a wild dance, those who lead it being 'fleet as shadows on the green' – probably cloud shadows, but possibly the birds who 'shed a floating shade'? In the last three lines of this, his last and unfinished poem, Shelley refers to 'the car which now had rolled onward' (line 545). The parallels in Darwin are: 'Slow roll the silver wheels' (lines 365 and 397) and 'Slow rolls the car' (line 405).

Shelley certainly knew this section of *The Temple of Nature*, which follows Urania's praise of reproduction (reflected in *Adonais*) and begins with the lines about the Lion-King echoed in *Queen Mab*. And the idea of all Nature cooperating was particularly appealing to him, being an essential feature of the regenerated world he envisaged in *Prometheus Unbound*, when

All things had put their evil nature off.

So the idea that Darwin's pageant may have made a mark on *The Triumph of Life* is not so far-fetched as at first appears.

Shelley's *Laon and Cythna* has many scattered echoes of Darwin, which I shall not attempt to list, while *Alastor* and 'Ozymandias' have resemblances to the lines about 'Thebes, Palmyra, Babylon, Balbec' in *The Temple of Nature*.[62]

A DEFENCE OF POETRY

I have now said more than enough about Shelley's poems; but what of his prose? The obvious crux is the *Defence of Poetry* (1821), his best-known essay. Of course Shelley sides with Wordsworth rather than Darwin in defining the role of poetry: 'A poem is the very image of life expressed in its eternal truth',[63] he says – not mere glittering description. But other aspects of the *Defence of Poetry* can be seen as end-products of a long schooling with Darwin, leading to a matured vision that goes beyond Darwin in two ways: first, Shelley's early faith in science has grown into an integration of science with poetry; second, he sees the perils of rampant technology.

In the *Defence* Shelley seeks to refute the charge that poets should 'resign the civic crown to reasoners and mechanists'. The latter have a valuable place in society, he says, but it is to 'follow the footsteps of poets, and copy the sketches of their creations into the book of common life'. Poetry 'comprehends all science' and is 'that to which all science must be referred'. Poetry 'is as it were the interpenetration of a diviner nature through our own'.[64] As we saw in Chapter 6, Darwin accorded poetry a humbler role, but his easy aeriality and empathy with nature helped to edge Shelley towards this superhuman view.

Shelley also sees beyond Darwin's uncritical faith in technology, and defines the problems that exercise us today. He warns 'the mechanist' and 'the political economist' that unimaginative application of their ideas will 'exasperate at once the extremes of luxury and want', as has happened 'in modern England', where 'the rich have become richer, and the poor have become poorer; and the vessel of the state is driven between the Scylla and Charybdis of anarchy and despotism'.[65]

This sharp social analysis is a digression, and Shelley returns to the main theme in the famous finale to the *Defence*:

> Poets are the hierophants of an unapprehended inspiration, the mirrors of the gigantic shadows which futurity casts upon the present. . . . Poets are the unacknowledged legislators of the World.[66]

That at least is free of Darwin's influence, you may think. But anyone who has read *The Temple of Nature* knows that the poem consists mostly of speeches by 'the Hierophant', alias Urania or 'the Priestess of Nature'. The other speaker is the Muse of Poetry, and between them these two lay down the evolutionary laws by which Nature and society have developed. 'Hierophant' is an unusual word, and Darwin's poetic Hierophant-legislator may have welled up from Shelley's unconscious mind to grace the rhetoric of his peroration.

The really piquant feature of Shelley's finale, however, is that he never could have known how perfectly his specification of the ideal poet fits Darwin. In *The Temple of Nature* Darwin was indeed acting as a mirror for the gigantic shadows of futurity: in the preface he says his aim is to bring 'distinctly to the imagination the beautiful and sublime images of the operations of Nature', and he saw those images in the mirror of evolution – a concept accepted by futurity but rejected by the present (including Shelley). Although his achievement went unacknowledged until after Charles Darwin's work, Erasmus Darwin correctly identified the laws by which life on Earth has developed: he was an unacknowledged legislator of the World. And he wrote in verse.

If Shelley had known that his beau ideal of a poet would turn out to be Darwin, would he have amended his definition? Or, if we could call him back, would he be so impressed by the evidence of his own debts to Darwin that he would let it stand?

GATHERING THE THREADS

It may be useful to itemize Darwin's wide influence over Shelley:

1. Faith in science and technology;
2. Scientific style in nature-poems;
3. The unity of the human and natural spheres;
4. The idea of sentient plants and empathy with nature;
5. Disgust at political tyranny and hope for reform;
6. Hostility to organized religion and a wish for its decay;
7. The idea of universal love as a panacea.

Of course Darwin was not the only force propelling Shelley in these directions: with points 1–4 he was a major force, but with points 5–7 he was only one of several.

To these ideas we may add one that Shelley failed to grasp, that shadow of futurity the theory of biological evolution. And to restore the balance there are two subjects where Shelley outgrew Darwin: in integrating science with poetry, and in appreciating the future perils of technology.

In addition there is the subtler influence generated by Shelley's memory and use of Darwin's words – a prominent feature of this chapter. Like Coleridge, Shelley seems to have remembered nearly all that he read and could distil it from his memory when his brain boiled in poetic creation.

Shelley's devotion to Darwin arose partly from the subconscious storage of memorable phrases and ideas; but there was also a conscious motive. From 1798 onwards Darwin was under frequent attack for his subversive religious and political views. Through Dr Lind, Shelley was well aware that Darwin 'has been assailed with unsparing severity, because his writings have been thought to glow with too ardent a love for freedom, and too keen an indignation against the oppressor',[67] as Dr Stock remarked in his biography of Thomas Beddoes in 1811. Shelley was sure to be biased in favour of anyone who was vilified because he glowed with too ardent a love for freedom. His admiration for Darwin received a further boost.

NOTES

1. T. J. Hogg, *Life of Shelley* i 35.
2. Note on *The Revolt of Islam* in Shelley's *Poetical Works*, p. 157.
3. Shelley, *Letters* i 129.
4. The fullest recent biography of Shelley is R. Holmes, *Shelley: The Pursuit* (1974). For a general review of his work and of 86 recent books on Shelley and his circle, see D. King-Hele, *Shelley: His Thought and Work* (3rd edn, 1984).
5. T. J. Hogg, *Life of Shelley*, i 57.
6. *Ibid.*, i 48.
7. *Ibid.*, i 49–50.
8. *Ibid.*, i 51.
9. *Ibid.*, i 51–2.
10. For the Esdaile Poems, see pp. 79–179 in vol. I of *The Complete Poetical Works of Shelley*, ed. N. Rogers (Clarendon Press, Oxford, 1972).
11. Quotations from *Ec.Veg.* I 252; *Lov.Pl.* II 184; 'Falsehood and Vice', 40, 49.
12. Compare 'Retrospect', line 1 with *Lov.Pl.* II 209–10; lines 7–9 with *Ec.Veg.* II 100, 226–7, 343; IV 66–7; and *Lov.Pl.* II 277; IV 402; line 25 with *Ec.Veg.* IV 65–8; line 61 with *Lov.Pl.* III 103; line 65 with *Tem.Nat.* IV 511, 518–19.
13. See *Complete Poetical Works of Shelley*, vol. I, p. 370.
14. *Ec.Veg.* II 431–98; IV 67; 'Retrospect', 25, 8; *Lov.Pl.* IV 328 note.
15. *Lov.Pl.* III 269–72, 281, 308, 263.
16. 'Henry and Louisa', lines 214–17, 219–20, 233.
17. Shelley, *Letters* i 104.
18. Godwin to Shelley, 10 December 1812, in *ibid.*, i 341.
19. *Lov.Pl.* I 101–4 (see also *Ec.Veg.* IV 245–6).
20. S. Curran, *Shelley's Annus Mirabilis*, p. 15.
21. Compare *QM* II 73–4 with *Ec.Veg.* I 111; *QM* II 109–29 with *Tem.Nat.* III 223–40; *QM* II 110 with *Lov.Pl.* III 197; *QM* II 150 with *Ec.Veg.* II 480.
22. Also compare *QM* I 272 with *Tem.Nat.* IV 427–8; *QM* II 211–15 with *Tem.Nat.* IV 419–24; *QM* II 231–4 with *Tem.Nat.* IV 399–400.
23. Compare *QM* III 134 with *Lov.Pl.* II 211; *QM* III 106–8 with *Lov.Pl.* II 239, *Tem.Nat* IV 377–88 and Pope, *Epistle to Arbuthnot*, 309–12.
24. *QM* IV 89–91, 97–9.
25. *QM* V 44–5; cf. *Lov.Pl.* III 219–54. Shelley refers directly to the poison-tree in *QM* VI 207–8.
26. *QM* VII 97–8; *Lov.Pl.* II 182–3.

27. *QM* VIII 58–69; *Ec.Veg.* IV 307–20.

28. *QM* VIII 124–6; *Tem.Nat.* II 357–8 and *Ec.Veg.* IV 253–8.

29. *QM* IX 31–2; *Tem.Nat.* IV 383–8.

30. The quotations in this paragraph are from *Prom.Unb.* IV 561; *Prom.Unb.* IV 409–10; *Ec.Veg.* IV 62.

31. The quotations in this paragraph are from *PU* III iv 2–5; *Tem.Nat.* III 468–70; 478; 473–5; *PU* III iv 77; 59–60; *Tem.Nat.* III 467, 477.

32. E. R. Wasserman, *Shelley: A Critical Reading*, p. 278.

33. C. Grabo, *A Newton among Poets*, Ch. 8, and pp. 172–4.

34. See *Ec.Veg.*, Add. Note 1. His belief was reasonable, but wrong: the idea that meteors were space debris was too 'way out' for Darwin. But he was right in predicting that hydrogen would be dominant at high altitude: see D. King-Hele, 'A View of Earth and Air', *Philosophical Transactions of the Royal Society*, *A278*, 67–109 (1975).

35. See C. Grabo, *A Newton among Poets*, Ch. VIII, and p. 171. The quotations are from *PU* III iv 130–1, 163 and *Ec.Veg.* I 115–16.

36. Quotations from *Ec.Veg.* I 423–4, II 3–4; *PU* IV 238–43, 271.

37. See R. H. Eather, *Majestic Lights* (American Geophysical Union, Washington, DC, 1980) for magnificent photographs of the aurora, including some from space.

38. *Ec.Veg.*, Add. Note I. Other possible echoes in these lines include Shelley's 'vegetable silver' (*PU* IV 283), probably intended as a fungus and possibly inspired by Darwin's note on *tremella nostoc*, which he compares with 'vegetable mucilage', using the phrase 'silver over' (see *Lov.Pl.* I 427–66). Or it may derive from Darwin's description of 'Diana's trees', as Grabo suggests (*A Newton among Poets*, p. 193).

39. *Ec.Veg.* II 199–200; *PU* IV 465–6.

40. *Ec.Veg.* II 82 note; *PU* IV 356–69.

41. *PU* III iv 204; *Ec.Veg.* I 98. See also *Tem.Nat.* IV 391, 'Waved o'er the vast inane their tresses bright'. The Latin *inane* of Lucretius is a less likely origin. However, Lucretius's *daedala tellus* (*De Rer. Nat.* I 228) and Darwin's 'Daedalean wings' (*Lov.Pl.* II 228) seem to have equal plausibility as the source of Shelley's 'daedal earth' (*Ode to Liberty*, 18) and 'daedal wings'.

42. *PU* II v 20–4, 29–30; *Ec.Veg.* III 29, 31 (cited in *OED* under 'hyaline').

43. PU II v 18, 43; *Tem.Nat.* III 432.

44. *PU* III iii 88–90, 91–3, 95–6.

45. The far-fetched idea that Darwin's 'wide-waving wings' gave rise to the phonetically similar 'wild west wind' is best left buried in a note.

46. For these interpretations, see E. Bass, *Papers on Language and Literature*, vol. 3, pp. 327–38 (1967), and G. M. Matthews, *Shelley: Selected Poems and Prose* (OUP, 1964) P. 199.

47. C. Grabo, *A Newton among Poets*, p. 59.

48. See R. S. Caldwell, *Studies in Romanticism, 15*, 221–52 (1976).

49. See E. R. Wasserman, *Shelley: A Critical Reading*, Ch. 5.

50. See G. M. Matthews, *Shelley: Selected Poems and Prose* (OUP, 1964) p. 30; and *Shelley's Poetry and Prose*, p. 369.

51. John and Charles Wesley, *Hymns and Sacred Poems* (5th edn, 1756) p. 216.

52. *Adonais*, 19, 28–9, 83–4, 158, 343–4, 370.
53. *Adonais* 462–3; *Ec.Veg.* II 326, 331, 335, 339.
54. For details of these influences, see E. B. Silverman, *Poetic Synthesis in Shelley's 'Adonais',* and D. King-Hele, *Shelley: His Thought and Work* (3rd edn) Ch. XIV. The links between *Adonais* and *The Temple of Nature* were pointed out in my *Erasmus Darwin* (1963) pp. 147–8; but I am indebted to Silverman for showing how Shelley profited from Darwin's wider view of Adonis (see pp. 87–8 of his book).
55. R. Cronin, *Shelley's Poetic Thoughts*, p. 68.
56. See Chapter 4; and H. Bloom, *Shelley's Mythmaking,* pp. 173–4.
57. *Witch of Atlas*, 485, 488; *Ec.Veg.* I 127–8.
58. H. Bloom, *Shelley's Mythmaking*, p. 165.
59. Quotations: *Epipsychidion* 451; *Ec.Veg.* I 358, 361; and *Laon and Cythna* I xxi 4. For 'arrowy' in Darwin, see also *Lov.Pl.* II 468 and III 174; and *Ec.Veg.* I 120 and III 67. Ellis's concordance shows that Shelley uses 'arrowy' eight times.
60. Quotations from *Epipsychidion* 472–6; *Lov.Pl.* IV 233–4; *Epipsychidion* 544–5.
61. See I. Roe, *Shelley: The Last Phase* (Hutchinson, 1953), pp. 196–210, and D. King-Hele, *Shelley: His Thought and Work*, p. 356.
62. *Alastor*, 109–14, 'Ozymandias', 2–4, 9–14; *Tem.Nat.* III 223, 231–4.
63. *Shelley's Poetry and Prose*, p. 485.
64. Quotations: *ibid.*, p. 500; p. 501; p. 503; p. 504.
65. *Ibid.*, p. 501.
66. *Ibid.*, p. 508.
67. J. E. Stock, *Life of Beddoes,* p. 50.

REFERENCES

Harold Bloom, *Shelley's Mythmaking* (Yale Univ. Pr., New Haven, 1958).
Richard Cronin, *Shelley's Poetic Thoughts* (Macmillan, 1981).
Stuart Curran, *Shelley's Annus Mirabilis* (Huntington Library, San Marino, California, 1975).
Carl Grabo, *A Newton among Poets* (Univ. of N. Carolina Pr., Chapel Hill, NC, 1930).
T. J. Hogg, *The Life of Percy Bysshe Shelley* (2 vols, 1858) 2 vols (Dent, 1933).
Richard Holmes, *Shelley: The Pursuit* (Weidenfeld and Nicolson, 1974; Quartet Books paperback, 1976).
Desmond King-Hele, *Shelley: His Thought and Work*, 3rd edn (Macmillan, 1984).
P. B. Shelley, *Letters*, ed. F. L. Jones, 2 vols (OUP, 1964).
P. B. Shelley, *Poetical Works*, ed. T. Hutchinson; corrected by G. M. Matthews (OUP, 1970).

Shelley's Poetry and Prose, ed. D. H. Reiman and S. B. Powers (W. W. Norton, New York, 1977).

E. B. Silverman, *Poetic Synthesis in Shelley's 'Adonais'* (Mouton, The Hague, 1972).

Earl R. Wasserman, *Shelley: A Critical Reading* (Johns Hopkins Pr., Baltimore, 1971).

9   Keats

Keats is the best comment on Darwin.
Bernard Blackstone, *The Consecrated Urn*

John Keats (Fig. 13) was born in north London in October 1795. For him there were none of the advantages of wealth and status enjoyed by Shelley. His father, who was a livery-stable manager, died in an accident when John was eight. Subsequent lawsuits divided the family. His mother remarried with unusual rapidity, then separated from her new husband and vanished for three years, returning only to die of consumption when John was fourteen. So his childhood was dogged by death and Chancery proceedings, though the latter eventually yielded some modest financial support for him.

He left school when he was fourteen, in 1810, and for the next five years served an apprenticeship as a surgeon-apothecary with Thomas Hammond of Edmonton. In 1815 he went on to study at Guy's Hospital, under the famous surgeon Astley Cooper, who was a great admirer of Darwin.[1] In July 1816 Keats passed the examination set by the Society of Apothecaries and became a Licentiate of the Society, fully qualified to practise as a surgeon-apothecary. In the autumn of 1816 he resumed his medical studies with a view to becoming a Member of the Royal College of Surgeons. He was acting as dresser at Guy's Hospital, carrying out many minor operations himself. By now he had more years of medical training than Darwin, and was indeed a 'well educated Practitioner', as Robert Gittings has rightly emphasized.[2]

Meanwhile Keats had gradually been discovering himself as a poet, with encouragement from his friend Charles Cowden Clarke. In the autumn of 1816 Clarke introduced him to Leigh Hunt, whose weekly journal *The Examiner* had been eagerly read by Keats for some years. Once immersed in Hunt's literary circle, Keats took a crucial decision. So far he had been a medical practitioner who wrote poems in his spare time, like Darwin. Now he decided to devote himself to poetry. He was just twenty-one: he had spent six years learning to be a doctor; but he was to have less than four years to prove himself as a poet. *Endymion*, his first long poem, occupied him for much of 1817. In 1818 he wrote *Isabella*, went on a walking tour in Scotland, began *Hyperion* and nursed his brother Tom, who died of tuberculosis in December. Keats's great year was 1819, when he wrote *The Eve of St Agnes*, the *Odes*, *Lamia* and *The Fall of Hyperion*. His tuberculosis declared itself fully in 1820: in the autumn he sailed to Italy, on medical advice; and he died at Rome in February 1821, aged twenty-five.

DOCTOR-POETS

The personal resemblances between Darwin and Keats are obvious. Both spent the greater part of their time, and possibly of their intellectual energy, in the medical field; but towards the ends of their lives poetry came to the fore – Darwin wrote about 7000 lines in his last twenty years and Keats about 15,000 lines in his last five years.

Such similarity in externals might of course go with a great disparity in their real interests: but not with Darwin and Keats; they were completely in tune. They shared experience of the horrors of late eighteenth- or early nineteenth-century medicine – the operations without anaesthetics, the perpetual blood-lettings and the general uncontrolled ravages of disease. To endure all this, they had to be tough-minded: Charles Darwin, for example, a few years after Keats, gave up because he was too sensitive. And in both the doctor-poets we can see how tender-heartedness arose to balance the tough-mindedness.[3] Both took great pleasure in the most delicate aspects of the natural world – they loved to 'watch intently Nature's gentle doings'. Both revelled in stories of the classical gods and goddesses, with their 'leaf-fringed legends'. These were two worlds free of bodily defect, free of surgery and debilitating drugs. Both were intensely visual as poets: Darwin thought poetry was painting in words; while Keats often described actual paintings, as Ian Jack has demonstrated.[4] Both Darwin and Keats were innately sceptical of Christianity and indeed all forms of systematic religion: Keats referred to the 'pious frauds of religion' and Darwin included religious credulity in his catalogue of diseases.[5]

They both had faith in beauty: 'Love and Beauty rule the willing world' (Darwin) is just as strong as 'A thing of beauty is a joy for ever' or 'What the imagination seizes as beauty must be truth' (Keats). They seized beauty in quite similar ways too: Darwin's theory of 'ideal beauty' from 'the form of the female bosom' excited much interest and some ridicule; but Darwin's liking for 'the nice curves which swell the female breast' is outdone by Keats

> Cheek-pillowed on my Love's white ripening breast
> To touch for ever its warm sink and swell,[6]

or savouring

> That warm, white, lucent, million-pleasured breast.

From such luxuries it is an easy transition to Keats's sensuous picture of luscious fruits,

> candied apple, quince, and plum, and gourd,
> With jellies soother than the creamy curd,
> And lucent syrops, tinct with cinnamon;
> Manna and dates, in argosy transferr'd
> From Fez; and spicèd dainties . . .   (*Eve of St Agnes*, 265–9)

This would have been just the thing for Darwin's lunch, as Galton's daughter tells us:

> we had on this occasion, as indeed was the custom whenever he came, a luncheon-table set out with hothouse fruits, and West India sweetmeats, clotted cream, Stilton cheese, etc.[7]

It is difficult to think of any subject on which Darwin and Keats would have differed, except analytical science: Keats deplored the analysis of the rainbow, while Darwin gloried in it. Although Keats would not have been much interested in Darwin's mechanical inventions, he would surely have applauded Darwin's efforts to advance medical technology. It was Darwin who first encouraged Beddoes to develop 'pneumatic medicine' in the hope of discovering a cure for consumption, 'this giant-malady', as Darwin called it, which 'destroys whole families, and, like war, cuts off the young in their prime of life. . . . Go on, dear Sir, save the young and fair of the rising generation from premature death; and rescue the science of medicine from its greatest opprobrium.'[8] Unfortunately consumption resisted the pneumatic methods of Beddoes, and Keats was to become one of its most tragic victims.

THE REALM OF FLORA AND OLD PAN

Of all the poets I have discussed, I believe Keats is the closest to Darwin in career, ideas and temperament. Bernard Blackstone, in his book *The Consecrated Urn*, argued that 'Darwin is the best introduction to Keats. Both were doctors, both wrote poetry, both were fascinated by the processes of birth, growth, fruition, decay, death. . . . We find all Keats's fundamental insights in Darwin in what Blake would have called a petrified form' (p. 14). More than 300 pages later Blackstone summarizes his conclusions. Keats's life's work is, he says, 'in one sense a correction of Darwin':

> The beautiful plant figures in Darwin's books . . . meant a lot to Keats. The journey we go from the calixes of 'small buds unfolding' in the early *Sleep and Poetry* to the ultimate *Grecian Urn* is the same journey we go from the opening plates of urn-like seed-cases and flowers in *The Loves of the Plants* to the concluding engravings of the Portland Vase in *The Economy of Vegetation*. The road between traverses, for both poets, the realm of Flora and old Pan. It is adorned with flowers and fruits and corn and branching trees; haunted by spirits of the four elements; it passes over caves bright with crystals and veins of gold and silver ore.   (p. 337)

I find Blackstone's arguments persuasive, and one option for me would be to end this chapter here and now. But Blackstone's parallels between Darwin and Keats, convincing though they may be, do not prove that Darwin really influenced Keats: it could be just that their minds were exceedingly similar.

So I decided to look for verbal resemblances, as with other poets I have discussed. This proves to be a difficult task, because Keats so rarely takes phrases from other poets. As E. C. Pettet remarked, the rarity of direct verbal echoes 'points to some fundamental originality or integrity (or both) that restrained him from taking over images and expressions from other poets, even subconsciously'.[9] Even with poets who are known to have influenced him, such as Spenser, Shakespeare, Milton and Wordsworth, echoes are far from obvious, as the notes to Miriam Allott's edition show. These poets, together with Thomson, Hunt and others, are often mentioned as possible moulders of Keats's vocabulary but Darwin is never mentioned by Keats's editors. Still more daunting is Caroline Spurgeon's study of Keats's own copy of Shakespeare, in hich he underlined many passages: yet even these are only indirectly eflected in his poems. So it is to be expected that any echoes of Darwin ill be few and far between.

In his letters Keats only once mentions Darwin, at the turning-point f his life, in October 1816, when he was about to meet Leigh Hunt and is friends. He told Charles Cowden Clarke that

> It is no mean gratification to become acquainted with Men who in their admiration of Poetry do not jumble together Shakespeare and Darwin.[10]

his can be read in two ways, either as snubbing Darwin, or as half-raising him, implying that there was once a time when Keats himself ated Darwin highly, but now he is wiser. The latter interpretation seems nore likely, because Darwin's reputation had declined greatly by 1816; hus, if Keats had wished merely to contrast Shakespeare with a popular nodern poet, he would have chosen Scott, Moore or Byron for the omparison, not Darwin.

Favourable though his early opinions may have been, Keats reacted adly against Darwin in July 1817. Keats had been eagerly awaiting eigh Hunt's review of his first volume of poems, which was of course ledicated to Hunt. The review eventually came out in three instalments. he first, in *The Examiner* for 1 June, was merely general remarks on inglish poetry. The crucial instalment was the second, published in the ssue of 6 July 1817. Instead of praise, Keats found to his horror that Iunt accused him of having two serious faults, one being 'a tendency to lotice every thing too indiscriminately and without an eye to natural roportion and effect'. A prime example of such writing, Hunt ontinued,

> is afforded in poetry by Darwin, a writer now almost forgotten and deservedly. . . . Darwin would describe a dragon-fly and a lion in the same terms of proportion. . . . His pictures were like the two-penny sheets which the little boys buy.[11]

Keats was appalled. As Robert Gittings says, 'By an irony that he could lot possibly have foreseen, here was Hunt jumbling him together with Darwin'.[12] Keats never really forgave Hunt for his dastardly critique: it lad the good effect of allowing him to escape quickly from Hunt's nfluence; its other effect – bad for me! – was to set Keats squarely against Darwin. So we should expect that echoes of Darwin will be heard unmuffled only in Keats's first volume, the *Poems* published in the spring of 1817.

POEMS PUBLISHED IN 1817

Even in this first volume it is an uphill task to find authentic memories of Darwin. Often Keats uses the same words as Darwin merely because his subject-matter is so similar, and real echoes (if any) are washed away in the stream of chance resemblances. Why not look for unusual words then? That too has its limitations, because Keats is unusually original in devising unusual words. The task is made the more daunting because Keats's editors have already suggested successive debts to Spenser, Mary Tighe,[13] Wieland, Hunt, Wordsworth, Shakespeare, Milton and others; so there seems 'no room at the inn' for Darwin. With these provisos duly registered, I shall begin my uphill journey with tiptoe tread.

Keats was eighteen when in the spring of 1814 he wrote his first poem, the 'Imitation of Spenser'. Its four Spenserian stanzas echo Spenser's 'Bower of Bliss', Fairfax's translation of Tasso, Milton, Thomson and Beattie.[14] With this plethora of parents, do I need to mention Darwin? Yes; because the whole poem is a glittering Darwinian nature-picture of an isle set in a lake, full of Darwin's 'gaudy' colours, with a verdant hill, amber flame, plumage bright, fish of brilliant dye, golden scales, a ruby glow – and even ruddy tears (rose petals). The last line,

> Outvieing all the buds in Flora's diadem,

half hints that Keats wishes to outdo even Darwin in luscious flower-poetry. As Ian Jack remarked, Keats is in this poem 'attempting to paint in words':[15] he has swallowed Darwin's prescription for poetry. He is also, I think, declaring that he will operate as a poet in the visual Darwinian world of flowers, leaves, buds and streams. Here, if anywhere, some unsuppressed echoes of Darwin might be expected.

The poem is not well known, so I shall quote the first stanza in full and then offer some comments:

> Now Morning from her orient chamber came,
> And her first footsteps touched a verdant hill,
> Crowning its lawny crest with amber flame,
> Silvering the untainted gushes of its rill,

4

> Which pure from mossy beds did down distill,
> And after parting beds of simple flowers
> By many streams a little lake did fill,
> Which round its marge reflected woven bowers   8
> And, in its middle space, a sky that never lowers.

The first three lines have many ancestors, including *Comus* and *L'Allegro*, though *orient*, *lawn* and *amber* are in Darwin's habitual vocabulary.[16] Lines 4–6 bring us into the real Darwin country. 'Living silver' and 'liquid silver' are among Darwin's favourite words for flowing water.[17] Keats's curious phrase 'gushes of its rill' might spring from that Darwinian cliché the 'gushing rill': for example Darwin instructs the aquatic Nymphs to cut channels in the peat moss,

> And in new veins the gushing rills direct.[18]

Keats's rill, like Darwin's, flows through moss, and his distinctive line,

> Which pure from mossy beds did down distill,

reminds us that Darwin was very fond of mossy beds: in the first 300 lines of *The Loves of the Plants* he has 'moss', 'mossy beds', a 'mossy couch', 'moss-wove banks and rush-fringed beds' and another 'mossy couch'.[19] Darwin also often ends lines with *distill*, rhymed with rill; the liquid distilled is usually dew, but occasionally tears or drinking water, as these examples show:

> When no soft shower descends, no dew distills . . .
> Bade on your sands no night-born dews distil . . .
> And showers of tears in blended streams distil . . .
> Fresh through a thousand pipes the wave distils.[20]

Keats's phrase 'did down distill' is puzzling. It could be a clumsy rhyming substitute for 'did downwards flow'; but, if so, 'distill' is the wrong word, since it implies (upward) vaporization followed by condensation, as in Darwin's 'dews distill'. So perhaps we should credit Keats with a more precise meaning – namely that, in response to the moisture of the rill, the moss discharges a cloud of spores to give a downy deposit. This interpretation has a precedent in Darwin, who asks the Sylphs to 'clothe with downy hair' the 'myriad Seeds' and refers in his note to seeds that 'are wrapped in down' (*Ec.Veg.* IV 355–7 and note).

Yet another possibility is that Keats originally wrote 'did dews distill', the change from 'dews' to 'down' being either a misprint or an attempt to avoid an obvious echo of Darwin. Of these three possible readings, I prefer the second – the idea of downy spores. That is why I have omitted two commas usually printed in this line. If the 'downy' reading is right, Keats is starting his first poem with the propagation-mechanisms of plants.

Other parallels with Darwin in the 'Imitation of Spenser' are of arguable significance,[21] so I shall pass on to the poem written by Keats in August 1814 after seeing a beautiful woman at Vauxhall, 'the fairest form', he says, 'that e'er my revelling eye beheld'. There is one curiously-worded line, where Keats praises

> The beaminess of those bright eyes.

This may well derive from Darwin's 'glowing Goddess' with 'beamy eye' and 'smile celestial' (*Lov.Pl.* II 382–4), or from his 'Ethereal Virgins' so dazzling that the plants 'brighten in your beamy eyes' (*Ec.Veg.* I 480). *Beamy* is not a common word, but Darwin uses it ten times in *The Botanic Garden*, to express the radiance of a star or of a woman's eyes. So here was a rich store of beaminess for Keats to draw upon.

Beaminess flashes out again in his sonnet 'To Lord Byron' (December 1814), in the form of

> a bright halo, shining beamily,

which might derive from Darwin's line

> The holy halo shoots its arrowy beams.   (*Ec.Veg.* I 358)

Another *beamy* appears in 1815, in 'To Some Ladies', a light poem in the style of Moore, and with echoes of Mary Tighe. Here the context is rather different:

> You list to the nightingale's tender condoling,
>   Responding to sylphs, in the moon-beamy air.   (lines 11–12)

Darwin's many 'moon-beams' provide only trivial parallels; more significant is his picture of darkness, sylphs and nightingales in the last few lines of *The Botanic Garden*. Darwin's 'enraptured Sylphs' hover listening as 'Night approaching near' tells 'his Nightingales' to 'repeat the strain' (*Lov.Pl.* IV 497, 500). 'The strain' to be repeated is the Goddess's story of the 'promiscuous marriage' of the Areoi in Tahiti, where 'the Loves laugh at all but Nature's laws'. This 'punch line' is intentional sauciness, in keeping with the tenor of the whole poem; and Darwin's final fling, in suggesting that *this* is what the nightingales are trying to tell us, is a joke that Keats would have appreciated.

The longest poem in Keats's volume, begun in October 1816, is *Sleep and Poetry*, where he offers a potted history of English poetry and castigates the successors of Pope as 'dismal souled' and 'dead to things ye knew not of', such as 'the dew of summer nights' (lines 187–94). Darwin, being very much alive to such delicate natural phenomena, presumably escapes censure. Indeed he seems to qualify for Keats's praise of poets who write of everything from 'the clear space of ether' to 'new buds unfolding' (168–9), though these lines are apparently intended to describe the Elizabethans. And, as Ian Jack has shown, *Sleep and Poetry* includes word-pictures of several paintings, thus carrying Darwin's theory of word-painting to its ultimate point.

Sleep and Poetry often parallels Darwin in wording. Keats enters 'the realm . . . of Flora and old Pan' and finds there 'white-handed nymphs' with 'shoulders white' (lines 101–7). Darwin enters 'peopled realms of Leaf and Flower' and meets a Nymph 'with snow-white hands' and another with 'white shoulders'.[22] Later, Keats imagines himself flying until the Sun should

> Melt my Dedalian wings and drive me down
> Convuls'd and headlong. (lines 303–4)

Darwin pictures the seeds of the Carline thistle flying on 'Daedalean wings' (*Lov.Pl.* II 22), and he tells us how the balloonist Rosiere was killed in 1785:

> Headlong he rushes through the affrighted air
> With limbs distorted, and dishevel'd hair. (*Ec.Veg.* IV 153–4)

A few lines later Darwin mentions the 'melting wax' of Icarus's 'unfaithful wings'. All the elements of Keats's image are here, and all the active words, if *convulsed* is equated with *distorted*. The melting wax of Icarus's wings is of course in the classical sources, such as Book VIII of Ovid's *Metamorphoses*; but the rushing headlong with limbs distorted is Darwin's own embroidery, so it seems probable that Keats was following Darwin rather than Ovid.

The other long poem in Keats's first book was one of the last to be written, 'I stood tip-toe . . .'. This poem, printed first in the book, is usually (and rightly) said to be influenced in its language by Hunt's *Story of Rimini*. But the scenery owes more to Darwin, because the poem is another pictorial celebration of the most delicate aspects of nature, and some of their phrases are similar: Keats has 'wild briar' and 'woodbine' in successive lines, while Darwin has 'Sweetbriar' followed by 'Woodbine'. Keats has 'the quaint mossiness of aged roots'; 'chequer'd shadows' on the grass; 'sweet-peas, on tip-toe for a flight'. The parallels in Darwin are: 'dwarf Moss that clings' to the bark of 'giant Oaks'; 'soft shadows' that flit over 'the chequer'd landscape'; Nymphs who 'in tiptoe trains . . . join the lone Nightingale' in the woods.[23] The most cogent of these parallels is the word *tiptoe* itself, which is one of Darwin's pet words: he has 'tiptoe friends', 'tiptoe steps', 'tiptoe Graces', 'tiptoe Joys' and 'on soft tiptoe, Night . . .'. Keats can match this with 'tiptoe Night', 'on light tiptoe', 'walk tiptoe', 'she rose tiptoe', 'the tiptoe marquis', 'tiptoe went', and others.[24] Some of the classical legends in Keats's poem also recall Darwin, particularly the love of Cupid and Psyche, where Keats tells us that 'their full lips . . . touch'd', while Darwin says they 'meet with warm lip'.[25] But both descriptions could derive from classical sources, or cameos.

This first book of poems was dedicated to Leigh Hunt with the sonnet 'Glory and loveliness have passed away', written in February 1817. Keats regrets that he sees 'no wreathed incense' upborne,

> No crowd of nymphs soft voic'd and young, and gay,
> > In woven baskets bringing ears of corn,
> > Roses, and pinks, and violets, to adorn,
> The shrine of Flora in her early May.

The Loves of the Plants is one long tribute at the shrine of Flora, and Darwin has many scenes similar to Keats's, for example when the flower-cherubs

> in procession gay
> Adorn with votive wreaths the shrine of May

or the incense-bearing virgins

> With flower-fill'd baskets round the altar throng,
> Or swing their censers, as they wind along.[26]

So, in his first book of poems, Keats chooses to travel in the same country as Darwin, where nature is delicate and bucolic classical legend reigns; and occasionally he echoes Darwin's words. This is as much 'influence' as can be expected with a poet so resistant to the subconscious temptation of verbal copying.

ENDYMION

After Hunt's damaging review in July 1817, Keats presumably resolved to censor all tendencies towards Darwinian phrases: if so, he succeeded, for there are few in *Endymion*, completed in November 1817, despite the similarity in subject matter and verse form (*Endymion* is written in rhyming couplets). However, Darwin and Keats do share several favourite words, and three of them, *vermeil, dewy* and *blushes*, conveniently appear in the first few lines of Keats's roundelay:

> O Sorrow,
> Why dost borrow
> The natural hue of health, from vermeil lips?
> To give maiden blushes
> To the white rose bushes?
> Or is't thy dewy hand the daisy tips?   (*Endymion* IV 146–51)

The same three words appear in Darwin's picture of Lonicera, who

> treads the dewy lawn,
> And decks with brighter blush the vermil dawn,
>   (*Lov.Pl.* I 243–4)

and again (with *hue, lips* and *rose*) when he refers to 'coral lips' and the 'vermil dyes' of 'modest Rubia', whose 'beauty glows'

> As blushes in a mist the dewy rose,

while four 'favoured youths'

> deck the pale-eyed nymph in roseate hues.
>   (*Lov.Pl.* I 374–8, 382)

Vermeil and *dewy* are 'poetic' words, and it could be argued that these similarities are mere coincidence. But Keats's use of blush is so excessive that it has provoked a book – *Keats and Embarrassment*, by Christopher Ricks. Darwin's Nymphs and Goddesses are continually blushing (or tittering): in the very first paragraph of *The Loves of the Plants* we have the Rose admiring 'the warm blushes of his bashful bride' and there are ten more blushings in Canto I alone, such as

> So shines the Nymph in beauty's blushing pride.   (I 339)

Keats has 41 blushes or blushings in some 15,000 lines of verse, but Darwin has 39 in the 4384 lines of *The Botanic Garden*: so Darwin emerges as the blushing winner. By a curious irony, Ricks in his book draws heavily on Charles Darwin's *Expression of the Emotions in Man and Animals* but never mentions Erasmus: the grandson studied the subject more scientifically, but it was the grandfather who probably led Keats into blushing.

Many verbal parallels arise in the long lengths of *Endymion* and *The Botanic Garden*, because nature and classical legend form the basis of both poems. The first is 'flowery band' in line 7 of *Endymion* (and *Lov.Pl.* IV 170). I shall not detail the parallels, however, because I doubt their significance. Instead I shall quote one of Darwin's word-paintings, which in its day was deemed fine and memorable,[27] followed by a similar picture from *Endymion*. Here is Darwin telling us how Venus rose from the sea:

> With rosy fingers, as uncurled they hung
> Round her fair brow, her golden locks she wrung . . .
> The bright drops, rolling from her lifted arms,
> In slow meanders wander o'er her charms,
> Seek round her snowy neck their lucid track,
> Pearl her white shoulders, gem her ivory back,
> Round her fine waist and swelling bosom swim,
> And star with glittering brine each crystal limb.
>
> (*Ec.Veg.* II 55–6, 59–64)

Perhaps Keats was remembering these lines when he described Arethusa:

> O that her shining hair was in the sun,
> And I distilling from it thence to run
> In amorous rillets down her shrinking form!

To linger on her lilly shoulders, warm
Between her kissing breasts, and every charm
Touch raptur'd!   (*Endymion* II 943–8)

Endymion was savagely criticized in *Blackwood's* by Lockhart. After referring to the 'settled, imperturbable drivelling idiocy' of the poem, Lockhart told Keats:

It is a better and a wiser thing to be a starved apothecary than a starved poet; so back to the shop Mr John, back to 'plasters, pills, and ointment boxes'.[28]

So by another strange mischance Keats was reminded again, most painfully, of the profession he shared with Darwin: presumably the effect was to alienate him still further from Darwin.

THE EVE OF ST AGNES

This richly tapestried tale from 'ages long ago', of Porphyro visiting his beloved Madeline on St Agnes's Eve, is one of the finest of Keats's poems. Robert Gittings sums it up as 'tangible, physical and above all, highly coloured and pictorial . . . like some jewelled fresco from a church wall'.[29] This amounts to saying that the poem is deeply Darwinian, for Darwin's trade mark was brightly coloured pictures set in jewelled, glittering couplets. Darwin himself called *The Loves of the Plants* 'diverse little pictures . . . which . . . may amuse thee by the beauty of their persons . . . or the brilliancy of their dress' (Proem). This was what Wordsworth called 'the dazzling manner of Darwin' and his 'gaudiness'.

As well as being highly pictorial, *The Eve of St Agnes* reflects the rich diversity of Keats's reading, with touches of *Romeo and Juliet*, Boccaccio, Wieland's *Oberon*, French romances, Coleridge, Mrs Radcliffe, Beattie and Mary Tighe, as well as the medieval fresco 'The Triumph of Death'.[30] Darwin needs to be added to this list, not only for helping with the pictorial qualities but also for some verbal echoes.

Darwin has a chilling picture of a church by night in *The Loves of the Plants*:

Hoarse on their hinge the ponderous portals jar;
As through the colour'd glass the moon beam falls,

> Huge shapeless spectres quiver on the walls;
> Low murmurs creep along the hollow ground,
> And to each step the pealing ailes resound;
> By glimmering lamps, protecting saints among,
> The shrines all trembling as they pass along . . .
>
> (*Lov.Pl.* III 22–8)

Two possible reminiscences of these lines in *The Eve of St Agnes* are
when the Beadsman walks

> Along the chapel aisle by slow degrees:
> The sculptur'd dead, on each side, seem to freeze;   (13–14)

and again when Porphyro stands

> beside the portal doors,
> Buttress'd from moonlight.   (76–7)

A third and more convincing parallel occurs when Keats comes to the
'casement high and triple-arched' which

> With many coloured glass fronted the moon,

as Keats wrote in his first draft.[31] The moonbeams shone through the
glass

> And threw warm gules on Madeline's fair breast.   (218)

Keats's first-draft line resembles Darwin's second line, and the 'warm
gules' shows that Keats, like Shelley, was misled into thinking that
moonlight could throw colours. This mistake might have arisen from
misreading Darwin or, as Pettet suggested,[32] from Scott's picture in the
Lay of the Last Minstrel, which may itself have derived from Darwin.
Another scene from *The Loves of the Plants* that might be relevant is:

> Froze by enchantment on the velvet ground
> Fair youths and beauteous ladies glitter round . . .
> By each cold nymph her marble lover lies.   (II 273–4, 289)

This is similar in spirit to the Beadsman's view of the sculptured dead –
'Knights, ladies' – who 'seem to freeze' and 'ache in icy hoods and mails'
(18). Though the similar subject matter seems to point towards some

reminiscence here, the verbal parallels are only in rather common words
– portal, coloured, moon, aisle, freeze, ladies.

There are three other verbal parallels involving less common words.
When Keats brings in 'many a tiptoe, amorous cavalier', he could be
fusing Darwin's 'tiptoe Joys' and 'amorous . . . Suitor-train' in *The
Loves of the Plants*.[33] Second, Keats's picture of Madeline,

> And on her hair a glory, like a saint,

scarcely differs from Darwin's picture of Tropaeo,

> A saint-like glory trembles round her head.[34]

The third parallel is between Madeline asleep,

> Blinded alike from sunshine and from rain,
> As though a rose should shut, and be a bud again,

and Darwin's larval silk-worm,

> Web within web involves his larva form,
> Alike secured from sunshine and from storm.[35]

These parallels bring into sharp focus the difficulty of judging
Darwin's influence. It is (just) possible to argue that all these verbal
resemblances are mere chance. On the other hand, you can argue that the
whole poem is much indebted to Darwin, not only for its vividly pictorial
qualities, but also for its theatrical presentation of lovers meeting. In *The
Botanic Garden* Darwin often digresses to tell us about lovers brought
together in dramatic circumstances. For example, there is 'the beauteous
Aegle', who catches the Plague and is forced by her family to live in the
garden. Her lover, like Porphyro, defies danger to join her and, like
Porphyro, takes advantage of the situation. Aegle, says Darwin,

> Braves the chill night, caressing and caress'd,
> And folds her Hero-lover to her breast.   (*Ec.Veg.* IV 113–14)

She recovers, he is uninfected, and they live happy ever after. There are
several other such episodes in *The Loves of the Plants*, often with touches
of bathos when you pause to reflect that the lovers are supposed to be
vegetables.

From the examples I have given, I think it is fair to suggest that

memories of Darwin did creep into *The Eve of St Agnes* from time to
time, mixed with many other reminiscences. But the point cannot be
conclusively proved.

THE ODES

Most of the poems by Keats that I have not yet mentioned have
occasional parallels with Darwin; but they are (with one exception) so
infrequent that they could well be chance resemblances rather than real
echoes. So I shall confine my discussion to the three major Odes written
in April–May 1819, plus the September poem often linked with them,
To Autumn. The Odes are, in a sense, the most Darwinian of all Keats's
poems, being entirely set in a summer world of nature, full of loving
natural detail and rich in classical legend. In another sense, they are the
most Keatsian of his poems, original in language and form, with only
occasional and oblique reflections of his wide reading. When Milton,
Spenser, Shakespeare and Wordsworth fail to make a strong impression,
we should not expect too much of Darwin.

The exception I mentioned is the *Ode to Psyche*. Among the amorous
plants of *The Botanic Garden* Cupid might almost be called the leading
'character', if we dismiss the Goddesses, Nymphs, Sylphs and Gnomes
as characterless: the frontispiece of *The Loves of the Plants* shows 'Flora
at play with Cupid' – a caption that sums up the poem's theme. Though
less important than Cupid, Psyche has a place too:

> Fair Psyche, kneeling at the ethereal throne,
> Won with coy smiles the admiring court of Jove,
> And warm'd the bosom of unconquer'd Love.

(In this instance 'Love' is a rhyming alias for Cupid.)

> Beneath a moving shade of fruits and flowers
> Onward they march to Hymen's sacred bowers.

> (*Ec.Veg.* IV 48–52)

Hymen, with his golden chain,

> Joins the fond pair, indulgent to their vows,
> And hides with mystic veil their blushing brows.

Round their fair forms their mingling arms they fling,
Meet with warm lip, and clasp with rustling wing.

(Ec.Veg IV 55–8)

The procession to Hymen's bowers, Darwin tells us, is

> described from an antient gem on a fine onyx in possession of the Duke of Marlborough, of which there is a beautiful print in Bryant's Mythol. Vol. II p.392.

The last couplet derives

> from another antient gem of Cupid and Psyche embracing, of which there is a print in Spence's Polymetis, p. 82.

These two prints are reproduced as Fig. 16. An allied but rather different description appears in *The Temple of Nature*:

> Now on broad pinions from the realms above
> Descending Cupid seeks the Cyprian grove;
> To his wide arms enamour'd Psyche springs,
> And clasps her lover with aurelian wings.   (*Tem.Nat.* II 221–4)

An aurelia is a butterfly, or, strictly, a chrysalis. Darwin notes: 'A butterfly was the ancient emblem of the soul after death as rising from the tomb of its former state, and becoming a winged inhabitant of air from an insect creeping upon earth.'

Keats's *Ode to Psyche* is like Darwin's first picture in its scenario, though closer to the second verbally. He tells us how, while walking in a forest,

> In deepest grass, beneath the whispering roof
> Of leaves and trembled blossoms . . .
> 'Mid hush'd, cool-rooted flowers,

he saw Cupid and 'the winged Psyche' lying 'calm-breathing',

> Their arms embraced, and their pinions too;
> Their lips touch'd not, but had not bade adieu.

This is almost as close as Keats ever comes to copying anyone, in his mature poems, and it seems that Darwin's floral setting of delicate and sensuous legend was appealing enough to store in his memory; his attention may have been drawn to Darwin's picture by an article on Cupid and Psyche in *The Champion* for 29 January 1815, which ends by reprinting the full twelve lines from Darwin and his note on the gems.

If we accept that the *Ode to Psyche* is linked with Darwin, there are several other possible echoes. For example, Darwin has Cupid in a car climbing the 'green slopes' of Mount Ida, and trailing a procession led by Zephyr, who flings

> Soft showers of roses from aurelian wings.
> Delighted Fawns, in wreaths of flowers array'd,
> With tiptoe Wood-boys beat the chequer'd glade . . .
> Each to her oak the bashful Dryads shrink,
> And azure eyes are seen through every chink.
> (*Ec.Veg.* III 228–30, 233–4)

This is deeply Keatsian, recalling many similar scenes,[36] including the 'rosy sanctuary' that Keats prepares for Psyche, where 'zephyrs' lull the 'moss-lain Dryads'. Also there might possibly be a link between the *aurelian wings* of Cupid and Psyche in Darwin and their *aurorean love* in Keats (the *Oxford English Dictionary* records Darwin's *aurelian* and Keats's *aurorean* as the first uses of these adjectives).

Keats may also have remembered how

> the bright star, which leads the morning sky,
> Hangs o'er the blushing east his diamond eye,   (*Lov.Pl.* IV 43–4)

because Darwin's next line introduces Tropaeo, whose 'saint-like glory' we have already met. This is the plant seen flashing at evening twilight –

> So shines the glow-fly, when the sun retires,
> And gems the night-air with phosphoric fires.   (*Lov.Pl.* IV 51–2)

Darwin's 'star which leads the morning sky' – it is of course the same as the evening star (Vesper) – his many amorous swains and his evening glow-fly could have been fused into Keats's vision of Psyche, fairer than

> Vesper, amorous glow-worm of the sky.

Finally, Darwin's 'trains of virgins' with 'flower-fill'd baskets' who throng 'round the altar' of the temple of nature and 'swing their censers'[37] provide a parallel with Keats's lines regretting that Psyche has no 'temple',

> Nor altar heap'd with flowers,
> Nor virgin-choir,

and 'no incense sweet'

> From chain-swung censer teeming.

Some of these echoes may be illusory, but cumulatively they seem to confirm that Darwin had some influence on the *Ode to Psyche*. Of course there were other influences too, including Milton, Mary Tighe's *Psyche* and the story in Apuleius;[38] but Darwin's contribution probably equals any of these – or so it seems to me.

The *Ode on a Grecian Urn* was written only a few weeks after the *Ode to Psyche*, and there is some continuity between them. The poem might be a response to Darwin's plea,

> bid Mortality rejoice and mourn
> O'er the fine forms on Portland's mystic urn.
> > (*Ec.Veg.* II 319–20)

And Keats might have had Darwin's description of the Portland Vase in mind when he asked

> What leaf-fringed legend haunts about thy shape
> Of deities or mortals, or of both,

because fringing leaves are prominent in Blake's engravings, and one panel of the Vase represents 'Mortal Life' and the other 'Immortal Life', in Darwin's interpretation.[39] The youth on the second panel is beckoned forward to immortal life by the Cupid-like figure of 'Love Divine' as Darwin calls him. And 'Love Divine' leads Darwin to the all-embracing line which rounds off his cameo of Cupid and Psyche:

> And Love and Beauty rule the willing world.   (*Ec.Veg.* IV 62)

This sentiment might have contributed something to the famous finale of Keats's ode:

'Beauty is truth, truth beauty' – that is all
Ye know on earth, and all ye need to know.

The other parallels in the poem are arguable. The 'green altar' and the heifer 'with garlands drest' coming to the sacrifice might seem to resemble Darwin's 'turf-built altar' twined with 'fresh garlands' (*Ec.Veg.* IV 610–1), even if he has no heifer or sacrifice. However, this parallel seems to be spurious, because the scene probably derived from Haydon's article in *The Examiner* for 2 May 1819, 'On the cartoon of the sacrifice at Lystra', abetted perhaps by Mary Tighe's lines about the 'royal sacrifice' and 'the milk-white bull' which 'they to the altar led'.[40] Keats's third stanza celebrating 'happy, happy love' is similar in spirit to Darwin's many passages in praise of love, and Keats's striking characterization of love as 'for ever panting' might possibly be linked with Darwin's 'panting lover' (*Lov.Pl.* IV 394). But these are almost microscopic parallels, and it is safe to say that Keats is very much less indebted to Darwin in the *Ode on a Grecian Urn* than in the *Ode to Psyche*.

The nightingale, or 'night's sweet bird', is among Darwin's stock images; but I have found only two parallels with Darwin in Keats's *Ode to a Nightingale*. The first is between Keats wishing to fly

on the viewless wings of Poesy,

and Darwin calling up the shapes

That shrined in air on viewless wings aspire.   (*Lov.Pl.* II 295)

The second concerns Keats's line,

The coming musk-rose, full of dewy wine,

which is quite like Darwin's aquatic Nymphs,

Musk'd in the rose's lap fresh dews they shed.   (*Ec.Veg.* I 79)

Musk roses also appear in *A Midsummer Night's Dream* (II ii 52) and *Lycidas* (line 146), but Darwin's wording is closer to that of Keats.

Darwin's musk-perfumed Nymphs wait on the Goddess of Botany in company with 'gay Sylphs', who

> beat the fragrant air
> On winnowing wings, and waft her golden hair.

> (*Ec.Veg.* 175–6)

Keats's picture of Autumn sitting on a granary floor,

> Thy hair soft-lifted by the winnowing wind,

may include a mixed remembrance of Darwin's line, with his excessive *w*-alliteration muted by altering *waft* to *soft*. In his first draft Keats had 'winnowing wing',[41] which is even closer to Darwin. I have found no other likely echoes in *To Autumn*.

So it seems that the *Ode on a Grecian Urn*, the *Ode to a Nightingale* and *To Autumn* are very little indebted to Darwin, verbally. However, all the *Odes* are deeply imbued with an outlook on nature that is identical to Darwin's: like him, Keats draws in classical myth whenever the chance arises, and seeks out the delicate and lively doings of small-scale nature. Keats certainly moved in a Darwinian world; yet it should also be said that this choice could have been spontaneous, or derived from classical models such as Ovid's *Metamorphoses*. The *Ode to Psyche* offers the only secure example among the odes of a debt to Darwin.

WORD BY WORD

I agree with Bernard Blackstone that the world of nature as defined by Darwin was the realm in which Keats passed his life as a poet. But because Keats had such an unusual talent for not copying anyone, even his favourite authors, the verbal parallels I have presented are not likely to convince everyone. So I shall now try a different approach.

If Keats was indebted to Darwin, the debt should be detectable in the complete record of his verbal usage. An obvious test is to look at Darwin's favourite words, to see how many are also in favour with Keats. So I have picked out sixteen of Darwin's favourite words, common and uncommon, my choice being random and impromptu, apart from a bias towards words having the intial letters *b* and *c*. Table 1 shows how often each of the words was used, per 10,000 lines, by Shakespeare and Milton (who are known to have influenced Keats), by Darwin in *The Botanic Garden*, and by Keats, Shelley and Byron. I have included Byron as a 'control' – a contemporary of Keats whose vocabulary was remote from Darwin's. To compile the Table, I counted the number of uses of each word by each poet from the standard concordances for Shakespeare, Milton, Keats, Shelley and Byron, and then divided by 11, 1.8, 1.5, 3.6 and 10 respectively to obtain the frequency per 10,000 lines. The numbers of uses by Darwin in *The Botanic Garden* were divided by 0.4384 (as the poem has 4384 lines). Frequencies greater than 2.0 are given to the nearest integer; frequencies less than 2.0 are given to one decimal place.

Table 1   Frequency of use of selected words, per 10,000 lines, by six poets

Word	Poet Shakespeare	Milton	Darwin	Keats	Shelley	Byron
azure	0.3	2	46	4	20	3
beamy	0	0	23	2	0.8	0
beauty	25	14	146	53	21	25
blush	9	1.1	89	27	5	9
bosom	14	8	109	21	30	20
bright	9	59	246	99	82	27
car	1.4	2	48	7	9	1.4
charm	7	21	121	30	14	15
crystal	1.8	12	71	24	10	1.3
dew	5	16	91	45	48	6
glittering	0.8	4	57	2	6	4
lustre	1.4	4	57	5	7	1.8
moss	0.5	3	43	24	10	0.6
pant	1.5	0	41	14	10	3
tiptoe	0.2	0	14	7	0	0.7
verm(e)il	0	1.1	16	4	0.6	0

NOTES: *Beamy* includes *beamily, beaminess*; *blush* includes *blushes, blushing*, etc.; *bright* includes *brighter, brightest, brightly, brighten, brightness*; *charm* covers nouns and all forms of the verb; *crystal* includes *crystalline*; *dew* includes *dewy, dewdrops*; *lustre* includes *lustrous*; *moss* includes *mossy, enmossed*; *pant* includes *panting, panted*.

The most striking feature of the Table is that Darwin uses all the sixteen words far more often than any other of the poets. This is a measure of his consciously 'poetic' diction, and also confirms that the words chosen are genuine favourites of his. He is particularly fond of *beauty*, *blush*, *bosom*, *bright* and *charm*, thus incidentally revealing the persistent sexuality of *The Botanic Garden*. The heightened language and the sexual awareness were two of the ingredients that contributed to the poem's success.

But the object of the Table is not to analyse Darwin: it is to see whether some of Darwin's favourite words appealed to Keats. Clearly they did. Although he only once rises to more than half Darwin's frequency, Keats is at least twice as keen as any other of the poets on *beauty*, *blush*, *crystal*, *moss*, *tiptoe* and *vermeil*, so these can be set down as favourite words of Keats as well as of Darwin. Also Keats shares with Shelley a strong liking for *bright*, *dew* and *pant*, while Shelley (but not Keats) is fond of *azure*.

Three other features of the Table deserve a mention. First, Byron was apparently quite immune to infection by Darwinian language: his frequencies are all less than 20 per cent of Darwin's. Second, none of the three later poets takes much notice of Darwin over *beamy*, *car*, *glittering* or *lustre*: all have frequencies less than 20 per cent of Darwin's. Third, the 'Shakespeare' and 'Milton' columns are of little significance, except as independent standards: if the vocabulary of Shakespeare or Milton influenced Keats, it was not via the words chosen here.

Returning to Keats, we may summarize the Table as follows:

(a) The sixteen words in the Table are genuine favourites of Darwin, because they are used far more often by him than by any of the other five poets;

(b) Six of the sixteen words are used much more often by Keats than by any of the four remaining poets;

(c) This total of six increases to nine if we add in three words that Keats *and* Shelley use much more often than the other three poets.

So the Table shows that Keats's stock of favourite words included more than half of the favourite words of Darwin selected here. Indeed Keats's total of nine handsomely exceeds Shelley's total of four – and Darwin's influence on Shelley is well established. So I think it is fair to say that the Table confirms statistically the verbal links between Darwin and Keats.

A thorough sceptic could find one escape route, however. Keats was considerably indebted to William Sotheby's translation of Wieland's *Oberon*[42] and to Mary Tighe's *Psyche*. And both these poems were strongly influenced by Darwin, as we have seen in Chapter 7. So perhaps Keats's Darwinian vocabulary came partly via Sotheby or Tighe rather than directly from *The Botanic Garden*? There is some force in this argument; yet the link between Darwin and Keats is not much weakened if there was an intermediary. Often it is difficult to decide the most likely source. For example, Keats twice uses the word *pillowy*, coined by Darwin and copied by Sotheby. Keats may have hit upon the word himself or he may have absorbed it either from Darwin or from Sotheby – more probably from Darwin, because *pillowy* also appears in the last lines of *The Loves of the Plants*, already mentioned as a possible source for Keats's 'To Some Ladies'.

Keats's debt to Darwin is revealed, fairly convincingly in my view, by the parallels with Darwin in the early poems, in *The Eve of St Agnes* and in the *Ode to Psyche*; and the idea of a link between Darwin and Keats is strongly confirmed by the Table of favourite words. The conventional list of contemporary authors who influenced Keats starts with Wordsworth, Hunt, Sotheby and Tighe. But it could be argued that he owed as much to Darwin as to any of these; and it is certainly wrong that Darwin should not even be mentioned in the annotated editions of Keats.

NOTES

1. See D. King-Hele, *Doctor of Revolution*, p. 301.
2. R. Gittings, *John Keats*, Ch. 5.
3. See R. A. Sharp, *Keats, Skepticism and the Religion of Beauty*.
4. I. Jack, *Keats and the Mirror of Art*. For percentages of visual, tactual images, etc., see R. H. Fogle, *The Imagery of Keats and Shelley*.
5. Keats, *Letters* ii 80. Darwin, *Zoonomia* ii 408–11.
6. First version of the sonnet 'Bright star . . .'
7. *Life of Mary Anne SchimmelPenninck*, ed. C. C. Hankin (Longman, 1858) i 152.
8. Letter to T. Beddoes, 17 January 1793, *Letters of Erasmus Darwin*, pp. 228, 230.
9. E. C. Pettet, *On the Poetry of Keats*, p. 7.
10. Keats, *Letters* i 113.
11. *The Examiner*, 6 July 1817, p. 429.
12. R. Gittings, *John Keats*, p. 214.
13. See E. V. Weller, *Keats and Mary Tighe* for details of more than 300 parallels between Keats and Tighe: most are of dubious significance, but a fair number appear to be real echoes.
14. See R. Gittings, *John Keats*, pp. 69–70, and M. Allott, *Poems of Keats*, pp. 3–4.
15. I. Jack, *Keats and the Mirror of Art*, p. 21.
16. Number of uses in *The Botanic Garden*: 'orient', 6; 'lawn', 13; 'amber', 3.
17. See *Ec.Veg.* II 406 and III 265, and *Lov.Pl.* I 460.
18. *Ec.Veg.* III 466. The next three lines have three words in common with Keats

(*silver, flowers* and *amber*), but the context is different. For other 'gushing rills', see *Lov.Pl.* I 418.

19. *Lov.Pl.* I 8, 27, 209, 231, 265.
20. *Lov.Pl.* I 363; *Ec.Veg.* II 459, II 468, I 273. See also *Ec.Veg.* III 47.
21. The unusual 'bowers/lowers' rhyme occurs in *Lov.Pl.* I 469–70; 'Afric's ebony' (line 17) parallels 'Afric's sable sons' (*Lov.Pl.* IV 326); 'cerulean sky' (line 27) parallels 'cerulean lustres' (*Ec.Veg.* I 339).
22. *Ec.Veg* III 521, III 283 and II 62.
23. 'I Stood Tip-toe . . .', lines 35–6, 40, 68, 57. *Ec.Veg.* IV 497–9; *Lov.Pl.* I 7–8; *Ec.Veg.* II 618, 620.
24. *Ec.Veg.* III 406; *Tem.Nat.* I 95, 148; *Lov.Pl.* II 318, IV 497. *Endymion* I 831, II 261, 358; *Lamia* I 287; *Cap and Bells* 150, 262.
25. 'Tip-toe', lines 143–4; *Ec.Veg.* IV 58.
26. *Lov.Pl.* IV 157–8; *Tem.Nat.* I 161–2.
27. Anna Seward calls it 'the most beautiful portrait of Venus . . . given by any Bard, ancient or modern' (*Memoirs of the Life of Dr Darwin*, pp. 211–2).
28. *Blackwood's*, 3, 524 (August 1818).
29. R. Gittings, *John Keats*, p. 410.
30. See *ibid.*, Ch. 19, M. R. Ridley, *Keats's Craftsmanship*, Ch. IV, and W. W. Beyer, *Keats and the Daemon King*, Ch. IV.
31. *The Poems of John Keats*, p. 466.
32. E. C. Pettet, *On the Poetry of Keats*, p. 19.
33. *St Agnes*, 60; *Lov.Pl.* II 318 and III 82.
34. *St Agnes*, 222; *Lov.Pl.* IV 46.
35. *St Agnes*, 242–3; *Tem.Nat.* II 299–300. Noted by Hassler, *Comedian as the letter D*, p. 79.
36. E.g. 'I Stood Tip-toe . . .', 140–56; *Endymion* I 6–7.
37. *Tem.Nat.* I 159–62 (quoted in part on p. 236).
38. For Milton and Apuleius, see Miriam Allott's notes to *The Poems of John Keats*, pp. 514–21; for Tighe, see E. V. Weller, *Keats and Mary Tighe*, p. 325; for a general commentary, see W. J. Bate, *John Keats*, pp. 487–98.
39. *Ec.Veg.* II 321–40 and Add. Note XXII.
40. See *Examiner*, 2 May 1819, pp. 285–7; and Mary Tighe, *Psyche* I 33 lines 1–2.
41. See M. R. Ridley, *Keats's Craftsmanship*, p. 285.
42. See W. W. Beyer, *Keats and the Daemon King*.

REFERENCES

Miriam Allott (ed.), *The Poems of John Keats* (Longman, 1970).
Walter Jackson Bate, *John Keats* (Harvard Univ. Pr., Cambridge, Mass., 1963).
W. W. Beyer, *Keats and the Daemon King* (OUP, New York, 1947).
Bernard Blackstone, *The Consecrated Urn* (Longman, 1959).
Richard Harter Fogle, *The Imagery of Keats and Shelley* (Univ. of N. Carolina Pr., Chapel Hill, NC, 1949).
Robert Gittings, *John Keats* (1968) (Penguin Books, 1971).
Ian Jack, *Keats and the Mirror of Art* (Clarendon Press, Oxford, 1967).
John Keats, *Poetical Works*, ed. H. W. Garrod (OUP, 1956).

The Letters of John Keats, ed. H. E. Rollins, 2 vols (Harvard Univ. Pr., Cambridge, Mass., 1958).

E. C. Pettet, *On the Poetry of Keats* (CUP, 1957).

Christopher Ricks, *Keats and Embarrassment* (Clarendon Press, Oxford, 1974).

M. R. Ridley, *Keats's Craftsmanship* (1933) (Methuen, 1963).

R. A. Sharp, *Keats, Skepticism and the Religion of Beauty* (Univ. of Georgia Pr., Athens, Ga., 1979).

Caroline F. E. Spurgeon, *Keats's Shakespeare* (OUP, 1928).

10   The Younger Generation

Thou art not for the fashion of these times.

W. Shakespeare, *As You Like It*.

Two poets of the younger generation, Shelley and Keats, have qualified for separate chapters, but Byron does not, because he took little notice of Darwin. So Byron is just one of seven writers born after 1780 who are treated individually in this chapter. The others are Mary Shelley, Leigh Hunt, T. L. Peacock, T. L. Beddoes, John Clare and Eleanor Porden.

BYRON (Fig. 14)

Darwin and Lord Byron (1788–1824) are involved in a curious web of personal and family links. Until the age of ten, Byron lived with his mother in Aberdeen. In 1798, on the death of 'the wicked Lord Byron' of Newstead Abbey, he inherited the title and came with his mother to Nottinghamshire. After living in lodgings at Nottingham, and elsewhere, Mrs Byron finally settled in 1803 at Southwell, six miles west of Newark and rich in ecclesiastical history. Her immediate neighbours and friends were the Pigot family: Mrs Margaret Pigot, who was a widow; her son John, three years older than Byron; and her daughter Elizabeth, who was six years older than Byron.

Although Byron did not usually stay long at Southwell, he spent a crucial twelve months there on coming home from Cambridge in the summer of 1806, aged eighteen. 'The Pigot house had become his adopted home', as Leslie Marchand says,[1] and it was Elizabeth Pigot who encouraged him to publish his juvenile poems. His first book, *Fugitive Pieces*, was printed at Newark in August, 'merely for the perusal of a few friends'. Copies went to John and Elizabeth Pigot and to their uncle, the Revd John Becher, who thought some of the erotic poems were too warm. So the would-be poet obediently withdrew the book and published at Newark in January 1807 a 'miraculously chaste' version, *Poems on Various Occasions* (the second edition was retitled *Hours of*

253

Idleness). The interesting point is that the poems suppressed were mostly in the comic-erotic vein that eventually emerged again in *Beppo* and, above all, *Don Juan*, and proved to be Byron's forte. There is every indication that Elizabeth Pigot approved of the original publication: how was it that an apparently conventional young lady (with a clergyman guardian-uncle) should have come to terms so easily with the true Byron? Was she already conditioned by the comic-erotic *Loves of the Plants*?

The answer seems very likely to be 'yes', because Elizabeth's father, Dr John Pigot (1756–94) was a close colleague of Darwin. Dr Pigot had married in 1781 and probably came to Derby in 1782, the year Darwin began practice there. John Pigot was a member of St John's College, Cambridge, and it seems likely that he was invited by Darwin as a junior partner in his practice, who could deputize when Darwin was away on his frequent journeys to rich and distant patients. When Darwin set up the Derby Philosophical Society in 1783, Pigot was a founder-member, and he also helped Darwin with the Derby Dispensary. As a child, Elizabeth Pigot was a close friend of the Darwins' eldest daughter Violetta: they were of the same age and probably both went to the Miss Parkers' school at Ashbourne. If so, Byron's early literary mentor was brought up *à la* Darwin.[2]

Southwell is only five miles from Elston, and, when Mrs Byron came to Southwell, Erasmus's brother Robert still lived at Elston, where his brother John was rector. Since Southwell is the seat of the bishopric, the Revd John Darwin must have been acquainted with the Revd John Becher, Byron's friend and censor.

The other links come through Darwin's wife Elizabeth. The story begins with the wealthy Juliana, widow of the third Duke of Leeds. He died in 1731 and within a year she was snapped up in marriage by the elegant but penurious Earl of Portmore (1700–1785), though she continued to style herself the Dowager Duchess of Leeds. Darwin's wife Elizabeth (1747–1832) was the daughter of Lord Portmore and the Duchess's governess, Elizabeth Collier. So Elizabeth Darwin had the Duchess of Leeds as 'step-mother'. The marital affairs of the Dukedom of Leeds suffered another perturbation in 1778 when Amelia, wife of the (future) fifth Duke of Leeds, eloped with an adventurer – Captain Byron, the poet's father. They married, and Augusta Leigh was their daughter. So Byron's step-mother would have been Duchess of Leeds. As the final link in the chain, Elizabeth Darwin's son by her first marriage, Sacheverel Pole, had a daughter Elizabeth, who was married in 1816 to George Byron. And he succeeded to the title on the poet's death in 1824. So Elizabeth lived to see one of her grand-daughters become Lady Byron; and Erasmus, even if he failed to influence the sixth Lord Byron, was definitely step-grandfather-in-law to the seventh Lord.[3]

Many of the titled families in Derbyshire and Nottinghamshire, such as the Duke and Duchess of Devonshire, came to Darwin for medical advice. Newstead is nearer than Chatsworth to Derby, and well within Darwin's sphere of influence as a doctor; so perhaps the 'wicked Lord' was a patient? However, I have found no reference to any Byron in Darwin's letters and papers. So Darwin probably did not treat either the wicked Lord or the poet's deformed foot. He did tread on Byron's toes posthumously, however, when Byron's wife Annabella tried to apply the principles of *Zoonomia* in 1815. On their honeymoon, Byron's anger about his foot, she says,

> impressed me with some doubts of his Sanity. At least I supposed it *might* amount to one of the hallucinations which are described by Darwin in his chapter on Diseased Volition . . . I thought it desirable to break through the morbid reserve which . . . prevented him from ever naming it directly.[4]

Byron, it seems, did not relish his wife's scientific approach, which was one of the pretexts for his separation in 1816 from 'the princess of parallelograms', as he called her.

These family links may be a welcome change from the pursuit of verbal parallels, but they are almost irrelevant in discussing Darwin's possible influence on Byron's poetry.

Byron sprang to fame with the publication of *Childe Harold* in 1812, but his much-quoted libel on Darwin as 'that mighty master of unmeaning rhyme' appeared earlier, in his *English Bards and Scotch Reviewers* (1809), written in anger at the treatment of *Hours of Idleness*.

Byron's alliterative quip is often cited by those who want to put Darwin down. Yet 'mighty master' is decidedly flattering by comparison with the offhand dismissal of 'vulgar Wordsworth' and his 'childish prattle' a few lines later. The libellous word is *unmeaning*, because Darwin's verse is tight-packed with information, whatever its other defects.[5] That leaves us with 'mighty master of . . . rhyme', and the wording comes to seem decidedly complimentary.

The full quotation is not so favourable, however. Just before dealing with Darwin, Byron launches into apparently sincere but probably sarcastic praise of such writers as Martin Shee, who can 'pour the easy rhyme's harmonious flow', Waller Wright, whose *Horae Ionicae* was inspired by 'no common Muse', and translators like Bland and Merivale. 'Let these', he says, 'restore the muse's violated laws';

> But not in flimsy Darwin's pompous chime,
> That mighty master of unmeaning rhyme,
> Whose gilded cymbals, more adorn'd than clear,
> The eye delighted, but fatigued the ear;
> In show the simple lyre could once surpass,
> But now, worn down, appear in native brass;
> While all his train of hovering sylphs around
> Evaporate in similes and sound:
> Him let them shun, with him let tinsel die:
> False glare attracts, but more offends the eye.
>
> (*English Bards*, lines 893–902)

A footnote states: 'The neglect of the *Botanic Garden* is some proof of returning taste. The scenery is its sole recommendation.' Byron continues:

> Yet let them not to vulgar Wordsworth stoop,
> The meanest object of the lowly group,
> Whose verse, of all but childish prattle void,
> Seems blessed harmony to Lamb and Lloyd.   (lines 903–6)

Another footnote identifies Lamb and Lloyd as 'the most ignoble followers of Southey and Co.' Byron then advises Scott to

>   resign to minstrels rude
> The wilder slogan of a border feud.   (lines 911–12)

And so it goes on:

> Let simple Wordsworth chime his childish verse,
> And brother Coleridge lull the babe at nurse . . .
> Let Hayley hobble on, Montgomery rave.   (lines 917–18, 923)

Let them all 'scrawl on', he says, 'till death release us from the strain'.
   So Byron subjects most of the established poets to what is little better than vulgar abuse, while Darwin has the privilege of a reasonably argued

critique. *English Bards and Scotch Reviewers* is a monumentally perverse poem and Byron was ashamed of it. He called it 'this foolish lampoon' and told Coleridge in 1815, 'I have long done all in my power to suppress the circulation'.[6] Still, his comments on Darwin do seem to be sincere, and he probably had read *The Botanic Garden*, either spontaneously or at the suggestion of Elizabeth Pigot.

When we come to look for links between Darwin and Byron as poets, however, there is not much to find. Nearly all Byron's poems are about real people, whereas Darwin writes mainly about scenes of nature populated by figures who are either quite unreal (Sylphs, Nymphs, etc.) or rather wooden. Byron's style at its best is supple and conversational, Darwin's just the opposite. Darwin's vocabulary is poles apart from Byron's too, as shown by Table 1 at the end of the previous chapter. The only resemblance is that both liked rhyming couplets, and some of Byron's most popular poems, such as *The Corsair* (which sold 10,000 on the day of publication), were in rhyming pentameters.

Darwin and Byron resembled each other much more closely as men than as poets. John Jump has characterized Byron as 'disillusioned and sceptical; impatient of cant; robust, high-spirited and humane'.[7] The same adjectives can be applied to Darwin, except that he remained optimistic rather than 'disillusioned' until he was over sixty. But he was as sceptical of human nature as Byron: 'extreme was his scepticism of human truth', Anna Seward tells us, and he was 'impatient of the sallies of egotism and vanity'.[8] Anna credits Darwin with 'a very peculiar species . . . of satiric wit', and that is why, like Byron, he was such a fine and lively letter-writer. Another similarity is that both were keen on sex, in a relaxed and teasing manner, and hated war (though Byron came to be involved in one). Both were basically sceptical, and slightly frivolous, in their approach to religion, although Byron never quite threw off his early indoctrination in Calvinism, while Darwin had no such inhibitions. Darwin was reported as saying that 'God, the existence of a soul, or a world to come . . . are only the bugbears by which men of sense govern fools.'[9] Byron would have been uneasy at saying anything so specific, though he poked fun at religious observances.

For both, frivolity was an essential part of their verse technique. Byron is at his best in *Don Juan*, skipping lightly from topic to topic, never really committing himself. Darwin skips just as disconcertingly between subjects in his *Botanic Garden*. His treatment is basically comic,[10] and he never commits himself to the myths he sometimes brings in to explain the mechanisms of nature. As Donald Hassler remarks in his provocative article on 'Byron and Erasmus Darwin':

> Darwin chooses the infinite variety of real things over the unity of
> some belief, and the result is a rich melange that holds the potential
> for a high comic tone of the acceptance of limitation – the Byronic
> purpose of socializing man in an infinitely complex world.[11]

As Hassler sees it, both Darwin and the Byron of *Don Juan* were
encyclopedic, sceptical and essentially comic in their world-view, and he
suggests that Byron learnt much from Darwin's example, Byron's
failure to acknowledge Darwin being merely another example of the
tendency to hide our deepest influences from view.

I have reread Byron's poems without finding enough parallels with
Darwin to indicate any such debt. There are resemblances between the
comic tones of *Don Juan* and *The Botanic Garden*; but in view of Byron's
critique in *English Bards*, I wonder if he ever appreciated Darwin's comic
intention.

Verbal parallels between Byron and Darwin are few, and probably
chance likenesses. I shall mention three. First, Byron's picture of the
carnage at Waterloo – 'the earth is cover'd thick . . . in one red burial
blent' – is rather reminiscent of the fate of the army of Cambyses in *The
Economy of Vegetation* – 'one great earthy Ocean covers all'.[12] Second is
the unByronic episode at the beginning of *The Giaour*, featuring a
personified Rose,

> Sultana of the Nightingale,
> The maid for whom his melody,
> His thousand songs are heard on high,
> Blooms blushing to her lover's tale:
> His queen, the garden queen, his Rose.   (*Giaour*, 22–6)

This recalls the scene in *The Loves of the Plants* where the Nightingale
with his melody woos the blushing 'Queen of flowers':

> So, when the Nightingale in eastern bowers
> On quivering pinion woos the Queen of flowers;
> Inhales her fragrance, as he hangs in air,
> And melts with melody the blushing fair.   (*Lov.Pl.* IV 309–12)

The third parallel is from *The Corsair*. Byron's couplet,

Flash'd the dipt oars, and sparkling with the stroke,
Around the waves' phosphoric brightness broke,

(Corsair, I 571–2)

resembles Darwin's lines about gilding 'the surge with insect sparks' that
flash 'round the bright oar' (quoted in Chapter 5) and his glow-fly which

gems the night-air with phosphoric fires.   *(Lov.Pl.* IV 52)

If these seem dubious, other parallels are even more so.[13]

Apart from these crumbs, I have drawn a blank with Byron, though
his best-known link with Darwin – over the origin of *Frankenstein* – has
still to be mentioned in the next section. I hope my defeat by Byron will
at least show that when there is no visible link with Darwin, I do not seek
to create one.

MARY SHELLEY (Fig. 15)

Darwin stands as the 'onlie begetter' of *Frankenstein*, the seminal work
of science fiction, for Mary Shelley's original preface begins:

The event on which this fiction is founded has been supposed, by Dr
Darwin, and some of the physiological writers of Germany, as not
of impossible occurrence.

The book was conceived during the course of conversations between
Shelley and Byron in Switzerland in the summer of 1816 (when Mary
was eighteen), and in the preface to the 1831 edition of *Frankenstein* she
gives a longer account of its origins:

Many and long were the conversations between Lord Byron and
Shelley, to which I was a devout but nearly silent listener.

On one occasion they discussed 'the nature of the principle of life':

They talked of the experiments of Dr Darwin (I speak not of what
the Doctor really did, or said that he did, but, as more to my
purpose, of what was then spoken of as having been done by him),
who preserved a piece of vermicelli in a glass case till by some
extraordinary means it began to move with voluntary motion.

The clumsy sentence in brackets suggests that Mary searched for an account of this experiment in Darwin's books, but failed to find anything. I can confirm that, to the best of my knowledge, Darwin does not describe any such experiment.

The most likely source for the Shelley–Byron conversation is the eleven-page note on 'Spontaneous vitality of microscopic animals' in *The Temple of Nature*. However, Darwin specifically states that spontaneous vitality is 'only to be looked for in the simplest organic beings, as in the smallest microscopic animalcules' and not in 'the larger or more complicated animals'.[14] This rules out the vermicelli – and indeed Frankenstein's monster too. A few pages later, Darwin refers to a vegetable mould observed by Priestley 'and called by him conferva fontinalis', which 'is believed to be propagated and enlarged in so short a time by solitary generation as to become visible to the naked eye'.[14] This is about the nearest Darwin comes to vermicelli, and S. H. Vasbinder[15] has made an ingenious phonetic comparison between *conferva fontinalis* and *vermicelli*, suggesting that Mary misheard the former as the latter. This is just possible; or perhaps Shelley misremembered Darwin's note and spoke misleadingly. Another possibility is that he was thinking of Darwin's description of Edgeworth's wooden automaton, which crept across the room in response to changes in atmospheric humidity (*Lov.Pl.* III 131, note). Whatever the truth may be, *Frankenstein* was the memorable result.

Mary Shelley was a prose writer, not a poet, so I shall not discuss her work further. I had to mention *Frankenstein* because it is the most explicit and probably the best-known example of Darwin's influence on Romantic literature. Ironically, it can also be said to be something of a fraud, or, to put it more kindly, a monstrous mutant of Shelley's interest in Darwin. Looking at the episode more positively, however, we can say that Darwin captured Shelley's attention with his discussion of spontaneous vitality, and that without Darwin there would probably have been no *Frankenstein*.

LEIGH HUNT

James Henry Leigh Hunt (1784–1859) was a central figure among the Romantic poets of the younger generation. With his brother John he founded *The Examiner* in 1808. It soon became the leading radical weekly, and, after a strong article about the Prince Regent in 1812, the Hunts were sent to prison for two years. While Hunt was imprisoned, Byron and Shelley visited him; and Keats wrote a poem to celebrate his release. In the autumn of 1816, at a critical time for both Keats and Shelley, it was Hunt who befriended them and helped them on their literary careers with his famous article on 'Young Poets' in *The Examiner* for 1 December 1816: he hailed Shelley as 'a very striking and original thinker' and said that Keats's manuscripts 'fairly surprised us with the truth of their ambition, and ardent grappling with Nature'. Hunt was a prolific essayist and wrote a fine *Autobiography*; but his poems are now little known, apart from a few anthology-pieces like 'Abou Ben Adhem', 'Jenny Kissed Me' and the sonnet on 'The Nile'. However, in his own time, *The Story of Rimini* (1816) was much admired, by Keats among others; and Shelley's *The Cloud* was inspired by Hunt's 'The Nymphs' (1818), which still retains a sprightly charm.

In 1822, Hunt went to Italy to edit *The Liberal*, with Shelley and Byron as intended contributors: Shelley sailed to Leghorn to meet Hunt, but was drowned on the return trip. The hopes for *The Liberal* sank with him.

In his *Autobiography* Hunt looks back to his childhood when 'in the world of literature . . . the most prominent poets were Hayley and Darwin'.[16] So he was aware of Darwin at an early age. Hunt's first book of verse, *Juvenilia*, was published in 1801 when he was sixteen, and it runs to 236 pages. Many of the poems are derivative, and Darwin figures with Thomson and Spenser among Hunt's models. For example, the 'Lines to Miss S—— H——, on her Marriage' begin with Venus rising from the sea as in *The Economy of Vegetation* (I 59–63), and we are regaled with female 'charms' three times in the first twelve lines; thus Hunt outdoes even Darwin's overfondness for 'charms'. The *Juvenilia* are thickly sprinkled with Darwinian words like *glittering* and *gaudy*, and when Hunt praises Britain's 'naval bulwarks' for withstanding 'the iron tempests' of the fierce French, perhaps he is remembering Darwin's description of a harpooned whale as bearing 'the iron tempest' on his back.[17] The best poem in Hunt's book is 'The Palace of Pleasure', full of worldly wisdom about the pursuit of pleasure and its perils. The poem is in 130 Spenserian stanzas and the diction is deliberately archaic, in the manner of Spenser. But the theme resembles Darwin's poem on the pursuit of pleasure by personified plants, and the language is also often Darwinian: indeed I wonder whether Hunt was intending a parody of Darwin in lines such as

> Enraptur'd breezes bore the charm around,
> And in one chain of joy all Nature's works were wound,

and

> Not gaudy, gay, or glittering in the air.[18]

Though Hunt himself was scornful of his *Juvenilia*, 'The Palace of Pleasure' is a great credit to a sixteen-year-old; and some of Hunt's readers think it as good as any of his later poems.

Why am I lingering over the *Juvenilia* of a minor poet? Because Hunt's subsequent poems offer no evidence that I can find of any debt to Darwin. Even the 'Songs and Chorus of the Flowers' has no obvious link. As with Tom Moore, I have drawn a blank, and I shall go no more a hunting in Moore or Hunt in search of echoes of Darwin.

Hunt's rejection of Darwin is not surprising. At the time when Darwin's reputation declined, Hunt was in his teens and would have been likely to fixate on current valuations. Hunt was nineteen in 1803–4, when the reviewers were savaging *The Temple of Nature*.

Hunt makes two oblique comments on Darwin in *The Feast of the Poets* (1814). This is an imaginary get-together of living poets, and the arrival of Crabbe provokes the rebuke that 'where he would strike out a line particularly grand or melodious, he has evidently no other notion of one than what Pope or Darwin has given him'.[19] The other comment is in a wordy note about Pope:

> The late Dr Darwin, whose notion of poetical music . . . was of the school of Pope, . . . was perhaps the first who, by carrying it to its extreme pitch of sameness, and ringing it affectedly in one's ears, gave the public at large a suspicion that there was something wrong in its nature.[20]

In 1817 came the derogatory remarks about Darwin in Hunt's review of Keats's *Poems*, already quoted in Chapter 9. Hunt's occasional later references to Darwin are usually antagonistic. In *Imagination and Fancy* (1844), Hunt says that 'Darwin absurdly pronounced nothing to be poetry which could not be painted'.[21] In *Men, Women and Books* (1847) he dismisses Darwin's Ode on May as 'not worth quoting'.[22] For me it is not worth quoting more from Hunt: in his mature work he aligned himself with the anti-Darwin orthodoxy.

PEACOCK

Thomas Love Peacock (1785–1866), a close friend of Shelley, is now famous as a novelist for his witty conversation-pieces like *Nightmare Abbey*; but for the first ten years of his literary career he was a poet not a novelist.[23] His first long poem was *Palmyra* (1806), reflections on the ruins of the ancient city. Though Peacock was writing some years after *Lyrical Ballads*, he rejected their style and called Wordsworth 'a morbid dreamer'. Instead Peacock returned to the eighteenth century for his technique. Anyone going back to eighteenth-century styles in 1806 was in danger of writing like Darwin; but Peacock avoids this fate by using tetrameters rather than Darwin's rhyming pentameters, and his poem is probably more indebted to Gray's Pindaric odes than to Darwin.

However, *Palmyra* does lean towards Darwin at times. Darwin's picture of 'the desolation of Palmyra' amid its 'wasted plains' and 'mouldering tombs' (*Lov.Pl.* III 197–202) was well known,[24] and Peacock's references to its 'wasting domes, and mouldering tombs' (*Palmyra* XI 4–5) are in a similar vein; but both pictures may stem from Volney's *Travels*. A more convincing parallel occurs when Peacock describes a destructive sandstorm –

> The whelming weight of ruin falls.

The sense and the *w*-alliteration are suspiciously like Darwin's sandstorm that overwhelms the army of Cambyses –

> Wheeling in air the winged islands fall.

The suspicion is confirmed by a very close resemblance: within Peacock's 'desert-whirlwind',

> The eddying sands in mountain-columns rise;

within Darwin's 'whizzing whirlwind' over the 'live desert',

>   vast columns rise
> Of eddying sands,

and 'mountains mountains urge'.[25] Peacock also follows Darwin in *Palmyra* by adding factual footnotes which are longer than the poem.

The *Palmyra* volume includes a shorter poem, *Fiolfar, King of*

Norway, which often seems redolent of Darwin in language and scenery and Peacock's fine picture of the aurora (in section II) is better than Darwin's. Peacock's next long poem, *The Genius of the Thames* (1810) has no signs of any link with Darwin: even the footnotes are much less intrusive. Peacock's unfinished *Ahrimanes* (1814?) has one stanza in Darwinian vein, with 'dewy flowers' on which 'every drop' beams 'like a diamond', so that

> All nature glitters like an orient bride.[26]

Peacock's best poem is *Rhododaphne* (1817), which much influenced Shelley. The all-pervading theme is Love, not of the plants but of the youth Anthemion and the nymph Rhododaphne. In the opening scene 'fairest youths and maids' move in procession to the altar of the Temple of Love; and Love, 'the first-born of Night and Chaos', is said to 'burst in due season' from the egg of Night. This is very like the first canto of *The Temple of Nature*, where 'trains of virgins' move 'in bright procession' to the altar of the temple of 'Immortal Love', who 'hung sublime' over 'Chaos' and 'warmed into life the bursting egg of Night'.[27] There are also a few verbal parallels with *The Botanic Garden*. For example, Rhododaphne emerging from the sea, her hair

> Unringleted, and glittering bright
> With briny drops of diamond light,

is very like Darwin's Venus rising from the sea, with her locks 'uncurled' and gemmed with 'bright drops' of 'glittering brine'.[28]

Such parallels are rare, however, and it seems fair to summarize by saying that Peacock was mildly indebted to Darwin's poetic diction, shared Darwin's keen interest in classical mythology, and occasionally remembered his phrases. But Peacock outgrew Darwin, and the remnants of his regard are scattered raggedly among his poems.

Peacock devotes a long chapter of *Melincourt* (1817) to arguing that the orang outang – and Sir Oran Haut-Ton in particular – is of our species; but he bases his argument on Lord Monboddo's *Origin and Progress of Language*, and never mentions Darwin's theory of evolution.

BEDDOES

Thomas Lovell Beddoes (1803–1849) was a doctor as well as a poet, and this is the first of several strong personal links with Darwin. No one was more closely asociated with Darwin in the 1790s, medically and politically, than the poet's father Dr Thomas Beddoes; and his mother Anna was the daughter of Richard Lovell Edgeworth, Darwin's friend and champion. So T. L. Beddoes had every chance of coming under Darwin's influence.

But Beddoes as a poet moves in the dark areas of Romanticism. His own death resulted from attempts at suicide, and in his poems he often welcomed death like a lover:

> Death hath his dimples everywhere;
> Love only on the cheek.[29]

Where Darwin saw the triumph of Love over Death, Beddoes is obsessed by the triumph of Death. Beddoes may have been influenced – or so H. W. Donner suggests[30] – by his father's poem *Alexander's Expedition*, written in deliberate imitation of Darwin; and he was strongly addicted to Shelley. But, to my surprise, I have not found any apparent echoes of Darwin in the poems of T. L. Beddoes.

CLARE

John Clare (1793–1864) wrote in a direct and earthy style far removed from the poetic diction of Darwin. But many of Clare's poems celebrate the world of nature in accurate detail, so some affinity between them might be expected.

This expectation is immediately fulfilled, in Clare's first poem, 'The Morning Walk', probably written in 1806 when he was thirteen, though revised later. He lists the flowers he sees, and brings in Darwin by name:

> There the unheeded daisy grows;
> There the golden kingcup blows;
> There the stinking bryony weaves
> Round the hazel her scallopt leaves.
> Here the woodbine and the rose
> All their blushing sweets disclose.
> Ah, lovely Lucy, to describe
> The different flowrets tribe by tribe
> Would be too much for me or you
> Or any shepherd lad to do.

Nay, had I Darwin's prying thought,
Or all the learning Ray has taught,
How soon description would exhaust
And in sweet Flora's lap be lost.[31]

That Clare had read Darwin can scarcely be disputed, and there are
some verbal parallels to confirm it. In *A System of Vegetables* Darwin
took great pains to choose or coin adjectives to describe the shape of
leaves, and *scallop'd* is one of them; so Clare's 'scallopt leaves' may
derive from Darwin, and possibly also 'flowret', because Darwin coined
and popularized the word *floret*. Two of Clare's lines,

Here the woodbine and the rose
All their blushing sweets disclose,

seem to be a toned-down version of two overdone couplets in the
opening paragraph of *The Loves of the Plants* (I 17–20), when Darwin
threatens to tell us

How the young Rose in beauty's damask pride
Drinks the warm blushes of his bashful bride;
With honey'd lips enamour'd Woodbines meet,
Clasp with fond arms, and mix their kisses sweet.

'Woodbine . . . rose . . . blush . . . sweet' are all here, and 'disclose' is
not far away, for Darwin liked to disclose charms:

Loose wave her locks, disclosing, as they break,
The rising bosom and averted cheek.   (*Lov.Pl.* IV 339–40)

So Clare's debt to Darwin is announced more clearly, and earlier, than
with any other of the poets I have discussed.

After such a promising start, I expected more parallels with Darwin in
Clare's later poems, In fact I have found none that can be regarded as
more than chance resemblances resulting from their often similar subject
matter.[32] It seems that Clare's naturalistic style and distinctive
vocabulary were so nearly at the opposite pole to Darwin's that the
original link between them was soon stretched beyond breaking point.
Clare, like Hunt and Peacock, outgrew his early inclination towards
Darwin.

However, Clare's general liking for Darwin remained alive and well.
He acquired a copy of Darwin's poems after 1824 – it was the 1825

edition of *The Botanic Garden* bound with the 1824 edition of *The Temple of Nature*.[33] In 1829, when H. F. Cary gave him a copy of Hayley's poems, Clare wrote, 'I do not like him near so well as Darwin but perhaps the subjects are the cause.'[34] The subjects surely were the cause; just as the poles-apart styles were the cause of Clare distancing himself from Darwin as a poet. *The Shepherd's Calendar* and *The Loves of the Plants* offer two diametrically opposed ways of looking at nature – the completely naturalistic and the consciously contrived.

ELEANOR PORDEN

Eleanor Anne Porden (1795–1825) is not well known today, but in her own time she won more acclaim than Shelley or Keats. Her extraordinary poem *The Veils*, published in 1815, was 'crowned by the Institut de France',[35] and at a time when France and Britain were at war. The poem, 5141 lines in rhyming couplets or triplets, purports to tell us how a knight and maiden overcome the forces of evil; but Miss Porden uses the story as a peg on which to hang much of the knowledge she acquired by attending the scientific lectures at the Royal Institution by Sir Humphry Davy and others. The persons of the poem comprise eight mortals, including the hero Henry and heroine Maria; fifty-three gnomes (the villain Albruno and fifty-two others, all named after minerals); thirteen sylphs of air; thirty-two pyridae, or spirits of fire; and eleven hydidae, or nymphs of water. The resemblances to Darwin are obvious, and are made explicit in the preface, where Miss Porden states that 'the machinery is founded on the Rosicrucian doctrine . . . used by Darwin in the Botanic Garden'. Not only the machinery, but also the rhyming couplets and the language, seem to derive from Darwin – the poem is rich in lustres, charms, glittering gems and other brilliants. Since the author states her allegiance so clearly, there seems no need to detail the resemblances.[36]

The best feature of *The Veils* is its up-to-date science. Having absorbed the Royal Institution lectures, Miss Porden was very well informed, for example on the implications of fossils:

> The fragments here in mouldering ruin hurl'd,
> Of many a race that fill'd the early world,
> Where watery relics earthborn tribes surround,
> And tropic fruits in polar climes are found . . .

> (*The Veils*, III 277–80)

But the scientific logic jostles with wildly imaginative fictions, as when the fiery pyridae attack the mineral-Gnomes: the battle rages for hundreds of lines and gives rise to such bizarre couplets as

> There young Asbestos lay, depriv'd of breath,
> Tho' pale and cold, yet lovely e'en in death.   (II 821–2)

The success of *The Veils* induced Miss Porden to publish *The Arctic Expeditions* (1818), again in Darwinian vein but only 201 lines long. In 1822 she produced another amazing poem, *Coeur de Lion*, the story of the third Crusade. This epic of adventure, romance and blood-bestrewn combat runs to nearly 15,000 lines – almost 50 per cent longer than *Paradise Lost* – but Miss Porden turns out the couplets with unflagging energy. Her poem on the Arctic expeditions led to her meeting John Franklin the explorer, and she married him in 1823: she died of consumption in 1825, five days after Franklin had set off on another Arctic trek.

OUT OF TUNE WITH DARWIN

To round off this chapter I should mention those poets born after 1780 who apparently ignored Darwin.

Thomas Hood (1799–1845) sang to quite a different tune: a link between the authors of *The Song of the Shirt* and *The Loves of the Plants* seems unlikely. And so it proves.

George Darley (1795–1846) appears more promising. His *Nepenthe* (1839) is alive with delicate nature-painting, helped on by some of Darwin's favourite words, like *glittering* and *lustre*. But I have not found any specific parallels. Darley never came closer to Darwin than in his surname.

Henry Kirke White (1785–1806) was born at Nottingham and earned himself a place at St John's College, Cambridge – indeed he was still there at the time of his early death from consumption.[37] Kirke White wrote poems to mark the death of Cowper (1800) and Thomas Dermody (1802), and his failure to do the same for Darwin (1802) suggests lack of interest. In his poems Kirke White twice refers to 'vollied lightnings', and he has some of Darwin's words (italicized) in his picture of *graceful* skating by *moonlight* on waters *congealed* by frost.[38] These seem to be chance resemblances, however, and the only road along which Kirke White truly followed Darwin was that from Nottinghamshire to St John's, Cambridge.

I have read – or at least skipped through – many other poets to see whether they had any leanings towards Darwin. I found nothing of consequence in the poems of Ebenezer Elliott (1781–1849), Allan Cunningham (1784–1842), Bernard Barton (1784–1849), Felicia Hemans (1793–1835), T. B. Macaulay (1800–1859), William Barnes (1801–1886), Letitia Landon (1802–1838) or W. M. Praed (1802–1839). There may be further poets who took Darwin as a model; but if so, I have missed them. Some of the eight listed above might be regarded more as Victorians than as Romantics: we need not quibble about definitions, however, as none of them followed Darwin.

I have to draw a line somewhere, and I have chosen to treat Tennyson (1809–1892), and his coevals and successors, as beyond my time limit. Also I have kept to poets writing in English, thereby excluding Alexander Pushkin (1799–1837), who was marginally indebted to Darwin.[39]

CONCLUSION

This chapter has shown how several poets of the younger generation were indebted to Darwin in their earliest work – Clare, Hunt, Peacock and most of all Eleanor Porden. Also Darwin had a crucial influence on *Frankenstein*, by Mary Shelley's own account. But the poets named above all grew away from Darwin in their later writings; and for the others – T. L. Beddoes, Darley, Hood, Kirke White and many more – Darwin seems to have been quite out of fashion.

Byron had much in common with Darwin besides their family connections and intermarriages. Both were sceptical, impatient of cant, strong-minded and humane. Byron's best poems, like Darwin's, are essentially comic, with disconcerting jumps from topic to topic, as in real life. Byron was well aware of Darwin's work but not appreciably beholden to him, despite these resemblances.

So this chapter, unlike all the others, proves to be largely negative in outcome. Darwin had much more effect on the poets writing in the 1790s – the years when he was most famous – than on the subsequent generation. Of the younger poets, those most indebted to him were Shelley and Keats.

NOTES

1. L. Marchand, *Byron: A Portrait*, p. 42. See W. W. Pratt, *Byron at Southwell* for a fuller account of his debt to the Pigots.

2. For J. H. Pigot, see R. F. Scott, *Admissions to the College of St John*, Part IV (Deighton Bell, Cambridge, 1903) p. 427.
3. See under 'Leeds, Duke of' in the *Complete Peerage*, and the family trees in K. Pearson, *Life of Galton* (CUP, 1914) and M. Elwin, *Lord Byron's Wife*.
4. M. Elwin, *Lord Byron's Wife*, p. 270.
5. See G. Tillotson, *Augustan Poetic Diction* (Univ. of London Pr., 1964) pp. 93–4.
6. Byron, *Letters* iv 285–6; v 220, 269.
7. J. D. Jump, *Byron*, p. 150.
8. A. Seward, *Memoirs of the Life of Dr Darwin*, p. 3.
9. *Life of Mary Anne SchimmelPenninck*, i 242.
10. See D. M. Hassler, *The Comedian as the Letter D: Erasmus Darwin's Comic Materialism*.
11. D. M. Hassler, *Ball State University Forum*, 20, 77 (1979).
12. *Childe Harold* III xxvii, *Ec.Veg.* II 488–98. Cf. also Pope's 'universal darkness buries all' (*Dunciad* IV 656).
13. For example, *Lara* I xi 11–15 is rather like *Lov.Pl.* III 23–8; there are a number of vague resemblances in Act II, scene i of *Cain*, set in 'the abyss of space'; and Byron's early poem *To Mary* (which upset the Revd Becher) may have drawn on some of the erotic descriptions in *Lov.Pl.*
14. *Tem.Nat.*, Add. Note I.
15. S. H. Vasbinder, 'A Possible Source of the Term "Vermicelli" in Mary Shelley's *Frankenstein*', *Wordsworth Circle*, 12, 116–17 (1981).
16. Leigh Hunt, *Autobiography* (Cresset Press, 1949) p. 47.
17. L. Hunt, *Juvenilia* (2nd ed, 1801) p. 26: *Ec.Veg.* I 456.
18. L. Hunt, *Juvenilia*, pp. 206, 221.
19. L. Hunt, *Feast of the Poets* (1814) p. 47.
20. *Ibid.*, p. 27.
21. L. Hunt, *Imagination and Fancy* (Smith, Elder, 1891) p. 91.
22. *Lov.Pl.* II 309–24; *Men, Women and Books* (Smith, Elder, 1891) p. 115.
23. See C. Dawson, *His Fine Wit*, pp. 3–70, for discussion of Peacock's poems.
24. See, for example, *Edinburgh Magazine*, 2, 314 (1818).
25. *Palmyra* XVII; *Ec.Veg.* II 493, 473–6, 488.
26. *Ahrimanes*, canto II, stanza 12 (Peacock, *Works* vii 281). Cf. *Ec.Veg.* III 509–14.
27. *Rhododaphne*, I 1–40; *Tem.Nat.* I 15–18, 159–60.
28. *Rhododaphne*, VI 46–55; *Ec.Veg.* II 55–64.
29. *The Works of Thomas Lovell Beddoes*, ed. H. W. Donner (OUP, 1935) p. 105.
30. H. W. Donner, *Thomas Lovell Beddoes* (Blackwell, Oxford, 1935) p. 39.
31. J .W. and Anne Tibble, *John Clare* (Cobden Sanderson, 1932) pp. 39–40, with small changes in punctuation.
32. An example of a non-significant parallel is Darwin's 'her flush'd cheek with brighter blushes burns' (*Ec.Veg.* II 176) and Clare's 'their cheeks with blushes burn' (*Shepherd's Calendar*, July, line 38).
33. See M. Grainger (ed.), *The Natural History Prose Writings of John Clare* (OUP, 1983) p. 359.
34. *Letters of John Clare*, ed. J. W. and Anne Tibble (Routledge, 1951) p. 224.
35. E. M. Gell, *John Franklin's Bride* (Murray, 1930) p. xii.

36. For details, see the review of *The Veils* in *Quarterly Review*, *16*, 387–96 (1817).
37. For Kirke White, see R. D. McGhee, *Henry Kirke White* (Twayne, Boston, 1981).
38. *Ec.Veg.* I 116, Kirke White, *Poems* (Aldine edn, 1860) pp. 3 and 140; *Ec.Veg.* III 561–70, Kirke White, *Poems*, p. 106.
39. See R. F. Gustafson, 'The Upas Tree: Pushkin and Erasmus Darwin', *Pub. Mod. Lang. Ass.*, *75*, 101–9 (1960).

REFERENCES

Lord Byron, *Letters and Journals*, ed. L. A. Marchand, 11 vols (Murray, 1973–81).
Carl Dawson, *His Fine Wit: A Study of T. L. Peacock* (Routledge, 1970).
Malcolm Elwin, *Lord Byron's Wife* (Macdonald, 1962).
J. H. Leigh Hunt, *Juvenilia*, 2nd edn (London, 1801).
John D. Jump, *Byron* (Routledge, 1972).
Leslie Marchand, *Byron: A Portrait* (Murray, 1971).
Thomas Love Peacock, *Works*, 10 vols (Constable, 1924–34).
Eleanor Anne Porden, *The Veils* (Murray, 1815).
Willis W. Pratt, *Byron at Southwell* (1948) (Haskell House, New York, 1973).
J. W. and Anne Tibble, *John Clare* (Cobden Sanderson, 1932; Joseph, 1972).

11 Retrospect

Darwin's verse deserves a somewhat closer scrutiny than it has received up to now from the historian of ideas . . . It made its mark on Blake, Byron, Wordsworth, Coleridge, Shelley and Keats.

B. Blackstone, *The Consecrated Urn*

Poets draw on a limited stock of words familiar and unfamiliar – Shakespeare's stock was about 15,000 words. If we could anatomize the poet's memories, we might find these words stored in various guises, some singly, some linked in phrases subconsciously recorded from previous reading or listening, all awaiting a trigger from an external source to propel them into a poem. In one sense, poets are often 'original': a poem is often provoked by an event, and events are often original, so rich is human and natural life. In another sense, poets are nearly always doomed to be unoriginal, merely rearranging existing words to express ideas that are rarely new. Yet a truly creative rearrangement is possible and can generate a new world-view, or at least a fresh perspective.

There is here a contrast between science and literature, and a likeness too. The contrast is that scientists can find something really 'original' – for example, Herschel's discovery of a new planet. The likeness is that, in science as in literature, the major achievements are the creative insights, as when Newton saw how the Moon was bound to the Earth by a universal law of gravitation.

The interplay of imitation and originality in literature leads into deep waters. The processes are too subtle, fluid and evanescent to be pinned down in words. But I do need at least to skim over the surface of these unfathomable waters to see what others have said, before summing up my exploration of Darwin's influence on the Romantic poets.

IMITATION AND ORIGINALITY

The 'problem of originality' is almost as old as literature. W. J. Bate, in his book about the burden of the past, quotes an Egyptian scribe of 2000 BC who asked in effect, 'What is there left to do?' Many centuries later, Aristotle called man the imitative animal: our long years of learning tend to brainwash us into becoming compulsive imitators. Montaigne produced a fable: 'The bee rifles the flowers here and there, but she afterwards makes honey of what she has gathered, which is all her own'; similarly the poet 'transforms and blends' things borrowed from others, 'so as to make a work all his own'. Samuel Johnson remarked that 'in books which best deserve the name of originals, there is little new beyond the disposition of materials already provided'. Mary Shelley was often asked how she could have imagined such a story as *Frankenstein*; and she gave her answer in the 1831 preface: 'invention, it must be humbly admitted, does not consist in creating out of void, but out of chaos. . . . Everything must have a beginning.' She then goes on to say how Darwin supplied *her* beginning. In Robert Frost's view, poets 'let what will stick to them like burrs where they walk in the fields'. T. S. Eliot, in his essay on 'Tradition and the Individual Talent', says of the poet that often

> not only the best, but the most individual parts of his work may be those in which the dead poets, his ancestors, assert their immortality most vigorously. And I do not mean the impressionable period of adolescence, but the period of full maturity.

A further comment by Eliot is particularly relevant to Darwin's influence:

> The poet must be very conscious of the main current, which does not at all flow invariably through the most distinguished reputations.[1]

John Beer has neatly summarized the theme of this paragraph: 'The good poet takes from his predecessors things which are recognizably theirs, yet grafts them so successfully on to his own work that they can never be reclaimed.'[2]

More often in recent centuries, as Beer remarks, poets have come to see the writings of the past not as a store to be raided, 'but as a completed citadel which they are powerless to enter; or they experience the past in the form of an overwhelming seizure by some powerful predecessor'.[2] He gives various examples, such as Coleridge reporting himself seized by Kant 'as with giant's hand'; and a somewhat similar seizure by Darwin is implied by Coleridge's praise of Darwin as the first literary character in Europe. This 'anxiety of influence', discussed in Harold Bloom's book of that title and W. J. Bate's *The Burden of the Past and the English Poet*, is only tangentially relevant in my comparisons (except possibly for Coleridge).

For my purposes I need to return to the simpler concept of the poet subconsciously and creatively stealing from his predecessors. The greater part of a poet's material is, as M. R. Ridley remarked,

> in a kind of superior rag-bag of the artist's mind, in which the scraps are not docketed with their provenance, as though they were in a card-catalogue; so that he cannot tell to what kind of garment, owned by whom, this bit of flannel, or that piece of gingham, or that other attractive bit of silk originally belonged.[3]

Pure plagiarism is of course always possible, and difficult to disprove: 'nor can the nicest judgment always distinguish accidental similitude from artful imitation', as Johnson said. However, plagiarism is not of any importance in this book and I shall say no more about it.

As I indicated in Chapter 1, the book has been an exercise in probability. Except on the rare occasions when an author admits a debt, it cannot be 'proved' that a close parallel implies a subconscious borrowing. However, the power of parallels is cumulative, as Ridley stressed:

> If we have reason to suspect that a given work is a source, every additional verbal parallel, or parallel in situation, greatly increases the probability that our conjecture is a sound one.[3]

Being a mathematician, I have at times been tempted to evaluate numerically the significance of parallels – only to abandon the idea because the probability depends so crucially upon the reader's perception of the 'unusualness' of the phrase. If two poets use the phrase 'bright eyes', the parallel is of no signficance; if they both use 'susurrant silicules', we should suspect one was echoing the other, or both were following an earlier source. But the real examples are nearly always in the arguable area between these extremes. Because the judgments are so subjective, I have in this book often given what may seem to be too many possible parallels. My problem is that different readers will see significance in different parallels, depending on their culture and memories. My best hope is that half the parallels I have selected may be judged significant by a majority vote.

Although the probability of a single parallel cannot be mathematically assessed, the effect of multiple parallels can be – if you make your own subjective assessment of each. Suppose you have four rather unconvincing parallels, each of which you assess as having a 20 per cent probability of significance. The probability of real influence for all four together is 59 per cent. If you have six instead of four, the probability of influence for all six together rises to 74 per cent.[4] This is the numerical justification for Ridley's remarks on the importance of multiplicity, and for my practice of quoting several parallels when the first is not fully convincing.

This result applies either to a single poem or to an author's complete works, though it would be more impressive to find four parallels bunched in one sonnet than in, say, a poem of 14,000 lines – unless the parallels in the long poem are all close together, or unless the sonnet is the only one by that author to reveal any parallels. So, while the importance of multiplicity cannot be denied, the final judgment remains subjective, because the individual parallels are subjectively assessed.

DARWIN'S INFLUENCE

From the parallels in this book I would conclude that Darwin exercised quite an important influence over Blake, Wordsworth, Coleridge, Shelley and Keats, and many lesser poets, such as Campbell, Anna Seward and Mary Tighe. Others who were indebted to Darwin at some stage in their careers include Crabbe and Goethe in the older generation, and Clare, Leigh Hunt, Peacock and Mary Shelley in the younger.

If I am right, why is Darwin's influence not mentioned in the standard histories of literature? The answer seems to be: because of a numbing side-effect of the nomenclature 'Augustan' and 'Romantic' – useful though these terms are as simplistic labels for distinctive styles. The nerve channels that ran from the Augustans to the Romantics were part of the experience of a poet living then; but these links have been accidentally amputated by historians who have tacitly credited the myth that there is a high wall about the year 1797, dangerous to jump over. The idea of such a wall is absurd, and no one defends it: yet many critics behave as if it exists – to the detriment of Darwin, who is sometimes called the last (and by implication the worst) of the Augustans, best kept hidden behind the wall. His stature has been concealed and his contemporary reputation has been falsely stated by many historians of literature.

We need to keep on remembering that in the 1790s Darwin was regarded as a great poet. This has been shown by numerous quotations scattered through earlier chapters, but I will add three more witnesses, for the benefit of first-and-last-chapter-only readers. Coleridge told Godwin in 1801:

> I have myself met with persons who professed themselves idolatrous admirers of Milton, and yet declared it to be their opinion that Dr Darwin was as great a poet.[5]

The second witness is the anonymous author of the satiric poem *The Gentleman* (1818), who also offers a more gentlemanly spelling of Darwin's name: 'When Dr Darwyn's Loves of the Plants first appeared, I heard many young men extol it above Pope and Milton.'[6] The third witness is Charles Darwin, writing in 1879, when Erasmus's reputation as a poet had sunk very low: 'I have myself met with old men who spoke with a degree of enthusiasm about his poetry, quite incomprehensible at the present day.'[7]

It should not be necessary for me to have to give such examples; but historians of literature tend either to ignore Darwin,[8] or to smear him with snide remarks,[9] implying that his high reputation in the 1790s was a mere fad, and that only the young and gullible were taken in. But the most influential of Darwin's champions, such as Horace Walpole, Cowper and Hayley, were not at all young – in 1795 they were 78, 64 and 50 respectively. Possibly Wordsworth and Coleridge were 'young and gullible', but if so their gullibility enriched their poetry.

Nor was the glow of so high a reputation snuffed out completely by parodies and religious denunciations. In an essay 'On the Darwinian School of Poetry' in the *Edinburgh Magazine* in 1818, the writer is critical of Darwin for 'never touching the heart' and for overloading everything with ornament, but also says:

> No poet in our language – not even Dryden excepted – has given such an extent of modulation to the heroic couplet – or rung, upon the same specified quantity of syllables, such a variety of changes.[10]

Darwin's reputation survived well into Victorian times. For example G. L. Craik, in his popular *History of English Literature* (published in 1861 with a fourth edition in 1869), criticizes Darwin's verse quite severely: it 'has no divine soul . . . its very life is galvanic and artificial'. Yet he admits that the style is imposing, 'with its sonorous march and glare of decoration', and says that 'no writer has surpassed him in the luminous representation of visible objects in verse'.[11] The space that Craik allots to various poets is also revealing: he gives Byron three pages, Keats four, Shelley six, Shakespeare nine, Milton twelve, and Darwin eighteen. When Darwin was rated so highly in his own day, and by some critics for so long afterwards, we need not be surprised that he had wide influence.

An unexpected feature of his influence is that he had more effect on the greater poets than on the lesser. Blake, Wordsworth and Coleridge took much more from Darwin than did Scott, Southey or Landor. In the younger generation Shelley and Keats were more indebted than Beddoes or Leigh Hunt. The reason may possibly be that Darwin was, in Eliot's phrase, 'main current', even though not (after 1800) of the highest reputation. He would qualify as 'main current' because he took the whole world of nature and man as his realm, and because his world-view appealed strongly to Wordsworth, Shelley and Keats. A possible objection to this explanation is that it places Byron, who was almost immune to Darwin, 'outside the main current': the term is too vague to quarrel about, however, and can merely be regarded as another way of saying that Byron's tone, vocabulary and attitude to Nature differ from those of Wordsworth, Coleridge, Shelley and Keats.

Are the Romantic poets less original than they are cracked up to be, in view of their debts to Darwin? The answer depends on your preconceptions. If you believe that *Lyrical Ballads* sprang unparented into the world, influenced only by the old ballads, you may perhaps be disconcerted at the suggestions that the underlying theory was a direct reaction against Darwin and that many of the poems have Darwinian overtones. However, if you believe rather that poets draw heavily on their store of remembered reading, you will not be too surprised at Darwin's influence on any single poet. But you may still be surprised, as I am, that all but one of the six leading poets of the time (or seven if we add in Crabbe) are so much indebted to him. Presumably the explanation is that *The Botanic Garden* was very memorable – 'it arrests the attention too often', as Coleridge said – and so at times had an almost mesmeric effect.

Did the Romantic poets themselves realize the extent of their debts to Darwin? Many a poet, when questioned, has nothing to declare in the way of influence, and is taken aback when a keen analyst produces a source. So it is, I suspect, with the Romantic poets: very few of them knew how much they owed to Darwin. The exceptions are Crabbe and possibly Coleridge, who was all too aware of the problems of subconscious borrowing:

it is scarcely practicable for a man to write in the ornamented style
on any subject without finding his poem, against his will and
without his previous consciousness, a cento of lines that had pre-
existed in other works.[12]

And he gave this as his reason for abandoning poetry. At the other
extreme is Keats, whose amazing talent for integrating without copying
may imply that he was unaware of any debt to Darwin.

Having tried to trace some of the sources of so many poems, I should
end with a word about the origin of this book – or risk being hoisted with
my own petard. I believe the spark came about twenty-five years ago
when I first read Bernard Blackstone's *The Consecrated Urn*, and in it
the unproved statement that stands as a motto to this chapter. My book
has in effect been an examination of that statement, which emerges from
the challenge with five of its six colours still flying.

CONCLUSIONS

As my comments on the various poets are scattered through the book, I
shall now run round and gather them up as best I can in two pages. Let
me preface this finale by stressing again that, although I pursue only the
poets' links with Darwin and ignore their links with other writers, that
does *not* mean that I deny or denigrate the other links.

I begin the round-up with Blake, who responded to *The Loves of the
Plants* within a few months, in *The Book of Thel*, which depends visually
and verbally on Darwin's poem. With *The Economy of Vegetation*, Blake
responded before publication, because he engraved five of the nine
plates, and there are parallels with Darwin's words or imagery in *The
French Revolution*, *America*, the *Visions*, the books of *Urizen*, *Ahania*
and *Los* and (more arguably) in *The Four Zoas* and *Milton*. Blake also
seems to have drawn on Darwin in several of the *Songs of Experience*,
including 'The Tyger' and 'A Poison Tree'.

Wordsworth admitted being 'under an injurious influence from the
dazzling manner of Darwin' in the early 1790s, as is evident in
Descriptive Sketches and the 'Salisbury Plain' poems. Wordsworth drew
confidence from Darwin's great success with a poem about nature and
adopted Darwin's idea that plants feel. The plain style of *Lyrical Ballads*
was a direct reaction against Darwin's 'gaudiness', but many poems in
Lyrical Ballads have links with either *The Botanic Garden* or *Zoonomia*,
including 'The Thorn', 'Goody Blake', 'Lines Written in Early Spring'

and *Tintern Abbey* – which, like the *Immortality* ode, was much influenced by *Zoonomia*. In *The Prelude* and later poems there are only a few echoes.

The young Coleridge was greatly impressed by Darwin, especially after that traumatic talk with Darwin in 1796 about his philosophy of life. Coleridge called Darwin 'the first *literary* character in Europe' and tried to emulate him as a poet of profound and wide-ranging knowledge. Coleridge, it seems, had much of *The Botanic Garden* stored in his memory with instant access, and echoes of it can be heard in most of his poems of the 1790s, including *Religious Musings*, 'The Eolian Harp', *The Destiny of Nations*, the *Ancient Mariner* and *Kubla Khan*. And the *Ancient Mariner* also enshrines Darwin's philosophy of universal sympathy. Coleridge the critic was deeply indebted to *Zoonomia*, particularly for the theory of dramatic illusion (or 'theatric reverie' as Darwin calls it); and Darwin's theory of biological evolution was for Coleridge an irritant that he spent much effort in combating, particularly in his *Theory of Life*.

Most other poets of the older generation (born before 1780) responded to Darwin favourably. Cowper and Hayley praised Darwin excessively; but their major poems predated his. Crabbe was very close to Darwin, with his rhyming couplets, 'verbal photography' and love of botany: each influenced the other. Goethe admitted a debt to Darwin: both were Nature-philosophers and Orphic poets. Thomas Campbell drew heavily on Darwin in his *Pleasures of Hope*, and so did many lesser poets who were Darwin's literary disciples – Anna Seward, William Sotheby, Mary Tighe, Brooke Boothby and others. Several poets well known at the time, including Scott, Southey, Moore and Landor, were touched only lightly by Darwin, or not at all.

Darwin exercised a wide-ranging influence over Shelley, helping to inspire him with faith in science and technology, and lead him towards his scientific style of nature-poetry. Shelley's ideas of the unity of the human and natural spheres probably came via Darwin, as did his empathy with Nature, expressed in the *Sensitive Plant* for example. Many verbal echoes can be found in most of Shelley's major poems – in *Queen Mab*, *Prometheus Unbound*, *Adonais*, the *Ode to the West Wind*, *The Cloud* and others.

Keats was probably the closest of the poets to Darwin in experience, personality and interests: both revelled in 'Nature's gentle doings' and the 'leaf-fringed' classical legends, probably as a reaction against grim medical realities. Keats had a marvellous capability for concealing his borrowings, but there are a number of parallels with Darwin in his early poems, in *The Eve of St Agnes* and in the *Ode to Psyche*. A numerical comparison shows that a large proportion of Darwin's favourite words were also overused by Keats – examples are *beauty, blush, crystal, moss, tiptoe* and *vermeil*.

The other poets of the younger generation (born after 1780) took much less notice of Darwin: some of the early poems of Clare, Peacock and Leigh Hunt, and Mary Shelley's *Frankenstein*, reveal debts to Darwin; but no one else seems to have heeded him much, apart from the precocious Eleanor Porden. Darwin and Byron were rather similar in temperament, and Byron's best poems are like Darwin's in being sceptical-frivolous and in skipping from topic to topic. Despite these and other links, including family intermarriage, parallels between Darwin and Byron are few.

From the evidence in this book, it can be argued that Darwin wielded a greater influence than any other eighteenth-century author on Blake, Wordsworth, Coleridge, Shelley, Keats and other poets I have mentioned, taken *in toto*. He broke through the invisible barrier between the Augustans and the Romantics. Darwin was not the greatest of eighteenth-century poets in achievement, but he was the greatest in long-range influence, because the matter and manner of Wordsworth, Coleridge, Shelley and Keats came to dominate English poetry for the next century.

NOTES

1. For the origins of the quotations in this paragraph, see W. J. Bate, *The Burden of the Past and the English Poet* (Chatto & Windus, 1971) p. 3; W. W. Beyer, *The Enchanted Forest*, p. viii; R. P. Knight, *The Landscape* (1795) p. x; Mary Shelley, *Frankenstein*, 1831 Preface; C. Day Lewis, *The Poet's Task* (Clarendon Press, Oxford, 1951) p. 12; T. S. Eliot, *Selected Essays* (Faber, 1932) pp. 14, 16.
2. J. Beer, in *Interpreting Blake*, ed. M. Phillips (CUP 1978) pp. 197–8.
3. M. R. Ridley, *Keats's Craftsmanship*, pp. 102–3.
4. The overall probability of influence with n parallels, each of probability p, is $\{1 - (1-p)^n\}$. Thus if $p = 0.2$ (i.e. 20 per cent) and $n = 6$, the overall probability is $1 - 0.8^6 = 0.74$.
5. S. T. Coleridge, *Letters* ii 738 (1801).
6. *The Gentleman: A Satire* (Baldwin, 1818) p. 97.
7. C. Darwin, *Life of Erasmus Darwin* (Murray, 1879) p. 92.
8. E.g. M. E. Novak, *Eighteenth-Century English Literature* (Macmillan, 1983).
9. E.g. G. Saintsbury, *A Short History of English Literature* (Macmillan, 1907) p. 597.

10. *Edinburgh Magazine*, 2, 315 (April 1818).
11. G. L. Craik, *History of English Literature* (4th edn, 1869) ii 383, 384, 387.
12. S. T. Coleridge, *Letters* iii 469 (1814).

ACKNOWLEDGMENTS

I am most grateful to the following for permission to reproduce illustrations:

> Fig. 1: Mr George Darwin and the Master and Fellows of Darwin College, Cambridge.
> Figs 2, 4, 12–14: The National Portrait Gallery, London.
> Fig. 3: Board of Cornell University Library, Ithaca, New York.
> Figs 5, 6, 8, 10 and 16: Syndics of the Cambridge University Library.
> Fig. 11: Detroit Institute of Arts.
> Fig. 15: Bodleian Library, Oxford.

I also wish to express my appreciation of the unrivalled facilities of Cambridge University Library, without which this book would have taken about five years longer to write.

Index

Figures in *italics* indicate the leading references on a subject. Books and poems are indexed under the author's name, except for Erasmus Darwin's, which are indexed under their titles. The notes are not indexed.